The Pilgrim's Progress

CRITICAL AND HISTORICAL VIEWS

LIVERPOOL ENGLISH TEXTS AND STUDIES

General editor: PHILIP EDWARDS

The Pilgrim's Progress

CRITICAL AND HISTORICAL VIEWS

Edited by
VINCENT NEWEY

LIVERPOOL UNIVERSITY PRESS

Published by
LIVERPOOL UNIVERSITY PRESS
Press Building, Grove Street, Liverpool L7 7AF

Copyright © 1980 by
Liverpool University Press

ISBN 0 85323 194 X

First published 1980

British Library Cataloguing in Publication Data

'The pilgrim's progress', critical and historical views
Liverpool English texts and studies
1. Bunyan, John, Pilgrim's progress
I. Newey, Vincent   II. Series
823'.4   PR3330.A9
ISBN 0–85323–194–X

Text set in 11/12 pt VIP Bembo, printed and bound
in Great Britain at The Pitman Press, Bath

Preface

The aim of this book is to provide a fresh, detailed, and varied consideration of *The Pilgrim's Progress*, and to promote further reassessment of the work's qualities and significance. Although Bunyan has been fortunate over the years in attracting the interest of such scholars as F. R. Leavis, Roger Sharrock and Henri Talon, and, in America, Stanley Fish and U. M. Kaufmann, Roger Sharrock himself rightly points out that the amount of recent critical attention even to *The Pilgrim's Progress* is 'far out of proportion to the importance of his masterpiece'.[1] It was in a firm sense both of the importance and the relative neglect that the present volume originated.

Some of the following essays offer general interpretations of the book, focusing on questions like the unity of the two Parts, the tension between allegory and naturalism, the modernity of Bunyan's vision, and the literary-historical status of his distinctive handling of the language and values of the people; some examine specific aspects of style and content, from dialogue and the use of 'place' to the major theological tenets; and some approach *The Pilgrim's Progress* through relevant comparison and through its antecedents, especially popular romance. Collectively, we are concerned above all with seeing *The Pilgrim's Progress*, not just as an ideological document or social statement, but as a complex, diverse, and salient literary and cultural text.

This study of Bunyan has been very much a corporate enterprise. As its editor I would like to thank my fellow contributors for their patient and ready co-operation, and express my particular indebtedness to Professor Philip Edwards for his frequent practical advice, and to Dr Gordon Campbell whose immense good judgement ensured a most fruitful interplay between the preparation of this volume and

1. Introduction to *The Pilgrim's Progress: A Casebook* (London, 1976), p. 22.

the conference at Liverpool celebrating the three-hundredth anniversary of *The Pilgrim's Progress*, of which he was organizer. We are grateful to Mr J. G. O'Kane and Rosalind Meek, of the Liverpool University Press, from whom we have received valuable professional guidance; and to Professor Michael Bourn, for his helpful and friendly comments. Without the truly expert and always cheerful assistance of our secretaries, Cathy Rees and Joan Welford, we should still be floundering in a morass of untyped, sometimes barely decipherable pages. Finally, thanks are due to Mr Keith Durham who did the chronological table at short notice.

V.N.

Department of English
Liverpool

NOTE

References to *The Pilgrim's Progress* are taken throughout from the Penguin English Texts edition, ed. Roger Sharrock (Harmondsworth, 1965). Unless otherwise specified in footnotes, references to other works by Bunyan are to George Offor (ed.), *The Works of John Bunyan,* 3 vols (Glasgow, Edinburgh, and London, 1862).

Contents

Chronology

1628	Petition of Right.	John Bunyan born at Elstow, Beds, the first child of Thomas Bunyan ('a repairer of pans and kettles') and his second wife Margaret. B.'s baptism recorded on 30 November.
1631	Donne d. Dryden b.	
1633	Donne, *Poems* (posthumously). Herbert d.	B. educated for a short time at Elstow, or at Bedford Grammar School.
1639	Fuller, *A History of the Holy War*.	On leaving school he joins his father's trade.
1642	Outbreak of Civil War. Fuller, *The Holy State and The Profane State*.	
1643	Browne, *Religio Medici*.	
1644	Milton, *Areopagitica*.	Death of mother; father remarries within two months of her demise. B., unsettled by these events, joins Parliamentary army (to 1647), and is stationed at Newport Pagnell.
1645	Milton, *Poems*.	
1646	Vaughan, *Poems*. Crashaw, *Steps to the Temple*.	

1649	Execution of Charles I.	First marriage (possibly 1648). (Four children by this marriage.) His wife introduces him to the Christian religion, chiefly through two books: probably Arthur Dent's *The Plaine Man's Pathway to Heaven* and Lewis Bayly's *The Practice of Piety*.
1650	J. Taylor, *The Rule and Exercise of Holy Living*.	Years of spiritual conflict involved in conversion to Christianity (1649–53). (Later to be described in *Grace Abounding*.)
1651	Hobbes, *Leviathan*.	
1652	Herbert, *A Priest to the Temple*. H. More, *An Antidote against Atheism*.	
1653	Cromwell made Protector.	B. joins Bedford Nonconformists.
1655	Marvell, *The First Anniversary of the Government under O.C.*	Moves to Bedford and begins preaching after nearly fatal illness. Continues in his father's trade.
1656		*Some Gospel Truths Opened* (his first publication).
1657		Formal recognition as preacher.
1658	Death of Cromwell.	Death of wife. Indicted at local assizes for preaching. Publishes *A Few Sighs From Hell, or the Groans of a Damned Soul*.

1659		Marries second wife, Elizabeth. (Two children by this marriage.)
1660	Restoration of Charles II. Revival of Acts against Nonconformism. Closure of Meeting Houses. Regular (orthodox) church attendance made compulsory. Preaching by non-episcopal members forbidden.	B. arrested near Bedford while conducting a private service. His refusal to guarantee an end to his preaching leads to imprisonment in County Jail, Bedford, initially for a term of three months.
1661		B.'s wife travels to London with petition for his release. House of Peers rejects petition. B. still attending Nonconformist meetings in Bedford through the unofficial aid of a sympathetic jailer. This activity stopped by the end of 1661.
1662	Butler, *Hudibras I*.	Second Petition for B.'s release; same outcome.
1663	Butler, *Hudibras II*.	
1665	The Great Plague.	B. making and selling bootlaces in prison in an attempt to support his wife and family. Early prison writings include *Profitable Meditations, Christian Behaviour, The Holy City*, and (in 1666) *Grace Abounding to the Chief of Sinners*.

1666	Fire of London.	B. released from prison, but rearrested in a few weeks.
1667	Milton, *Paradise Lost.*	Less prolific output of publications during second phase of imprisonment— probably working on *The Pilgrim's Progress.*
1668	Cowley, *Essays in Verse and Prose.*	
1671	Milton, *Paradise Regained* and *Samson Agonistes.*	
1672	Repeal of Acts against Nonconformists.	Released from prison. Given licence to preach. Begins preaching all over the country and occasionally abroad.
1673	Test Act (forbade any- one to hold Church office who did not attend Anglican Communion at least once a year).	
1674	Death of Milton.	
1675	Revival of former Acts against Nonconformism.	Brief imprisonment for con- travention of Acts.
1676		Death of father.
1678	Marvell d.	*The Pilgrim's Progress I* (2nd edition, 1679; 3rd edition, 1680).
1680	Butler d.	*The Life and Death of Mr Badman.*
1682	Dryden, *Religio Laici.* 'T.S.', *The Second Part of The Pilgrim's Progress*	

1684		*The Second Part of The Pilgrim's Progress.*
1685	Charles II d. Accession of James II.	*The Pharisee and the Publican.* Makes out deed endowing all his worldly goods to his wife. (Fear of further legal persecution.)
1687	Dryden, *The Hind and the Panther.*	B. turns down offer of administrative post in Bedford under the government of James II.
1688	Pope b.	Contracts fever on journey from Reading to London on horseback in heavy rain. Dies on 31 August at house of friend, John Strudwell, of Holborn Bridge. Buried in Bunhill Fields, Finsbury.

Christiana's Key:
The Unity of *The Pilgrim's Progress*

N. H. KEEBLE

When Coleridge made his celebrated claim that in Bunyan's 'admirable Allegory . . . his piety was baffled by his genius' he was careful to specify that the 'admirable Allegory' he had in mind was 'the first Part of Pilgrim's Progress'.[1] This bias in favour of Part I was to be characteristic of subsequent nineteenth-century comment on *The Pilgrim's Progress*. The superiority of Part I was taken for granted by J. A. Froude in his biography of Bunyan published in the English Men of Letters series in 1880. The principal of St Andrews, John Tulloch, held that the second part 'must yield to the first in the freshness and life of its scenes and incidents'; for the Revd Dr John Brown, pastor of Bunyan Meeting for the last forty years of the nineteenth century, Part II was 'undoubtedly inferior' to Part I; and even though Sir Charles Firth shared Macaulay's particular appreciation of Great-heart as the type of a Parliamentarian officer, the second part remained for him too 'inferior . . . on the whole to the first'. As late as 1929 the historian of the novel E. A. Baker could still dismiss Part II as falling far short of the power of Part I and fit only for children.[2]

This view may still be met with—in a recent article Elizabeth Adeney finds 'the thoughts and the prose . . . slacker' in Part II than in Part I[3]—but twentieth-century comment has more usually taken another tack. Developing the insights of Southey and Scott,[4] commentators have come to see Part II not as inferior to Part I but as different from it. And there is, further, general agreement on the nature of the distinction to be made. When E. M. W. Tillyard described Part I as 'epic' and Part II as 'emblematical' and 'exemplary' he was capturing essentially the difference Henri Talon had cast in terms of a contrast between Part I as 'a novel of character or action' and Part II as 'a novel of manners'.[5] In

Talon's view, 'To the swift and tense spiritual drama of the first part' there succeeds 'a bourgeois novel' which, celebrating 'with a new spirit of serenity' the joys of companionship and admitting with a new sympathy the weak and the scrupulous, quite lacks the 'passionate urgency' of Part I. Hence, 'The two books are different and can be appreciated for totally different reasons'.[6] To similar effect Roger Sharrock quotes with approval Monsignor Knox's aphorism 'Christian goes on a pilgrimage, Christiana goes on a walking tour'[7] and in his study of Bunyan he develops the argument that Part II is separated by a 'gulf' from Part I which the frequent references to the earlier work serve only to emphasize. In place of the lonely heroism of the first part we have in Part II 'a bustling, and on the whole a cheerful picture, of the life of a separatist church': 'We enter a more humdrum world, but a gracious and good-humoured one' which differs from that portrayed in Part I particularly in its admission of the part to be played by women and the home in the Christian life.[8] Critics now also agree that in its sympathetic treatment of a wider variety of experiences and human character than Part I, Part II insists less on strict Calvinist orthodoxy and renders its fictional world in a manner which is, as F. R. Leavis put it, 'more novel-like' than that of the earlier work.[9] Firth's recognition long ago that the allegory in Part II tends often either to be strained or to lapse altogether and that Bunyan is in constant danger of forgoing the allegorical mode for the realistic has become critical orthodoxy.[10] These changes of tone, manner, and emphasis are cogently linked to Bunyan's own greater domestic and spiritual ease when he came to write Part II, and to the greater experience of the practical difficulties of the corporate Christian life which his ministry had brought him since the writing of Part I.[11]

These distinctions are well made and are a proper corrective to the older view of the inferiority of Part II. Recognition that, as Rosemary Freeman says, the 'sternness' of Part I yields to 'compassion' in Part II[12] enables us to appreciate the peculiar qualities of the second part. Nevertheless, we are in some danger of so stressing these differences that we no longer see the two parts of The Pilgrim's Progress as constituting a single work at all. Rather than pursue parallels between the two parts, critics prefer to underline the distinctness of the parts by associating each of them with other of Bunyan's works. In Part I we find allegorized 'the personal drama of Calvinism': Bunyan has but recast the material he had handled autobiographically in Grace Abounding. In Part II, on the other hand, with the focus no longer on the individual, we find a social realism which is akin to the manner of Mr Badman and portends Defoe. [13] The implication is clearly that each of the parts of The Pilgrim's Progress has more in common with these works than either has with the other. The notion that, together, they might constitute a more satisfying work than either alone, that The Pilgrim's Progress depends upon their relationship as the two parts of a single work for its full effect, is thus discountenanced. Rather than that it is mutually enriching, their association appears as a mere circumstance, an accident of biography. They are so unlike in concern and execution that the relationship between them is but formal, consisting in the title, the fact that Christiana is Christian's wife, and the incidental topographical details of the journey.

Hence, Part I is seen as 'a complete and self-sufficient narrative' in no need of a sequel. [14] Cross-references from Part II are of an artificial kind which Part I does not need for its exposition any more than the success of Part II depends upon reminders of Part I. Even for R. M. Frye, who sees the individualism of Part I and the communalism of Part II as constituting, together, a 'stereoscopic view' of the complete Christian life, the parts remain distinct wholes, juxtaposed and complementary narratives, but 'each complete in itself'. [15] The logic of this view of The Pilgrim's Progress has, indeed, resulted, in the most recent full-length study of Bunyan, in a thesis which depends entirely upon the distinctness of the parts. Monica Furlong, noting again that Part II is 'distinctly different' from, and 'more cheerful' than, its predecessor, sees the second part as the culmination of Bunyan's progress from fear, anxiety, and repression to a 'new serenity, a new tenderness, a new forgiveness of himself and others', such as he has, indeed, 'ceased to be a Puritan', at least as she understands the term. [16]

Bunyan, we may surmise, would not have been much

impressed to learn that in Part II he had ceased to be a Puritan. In fact, from the title-page of Part II on, he is almost tiresomely anxious that his reader should associate Part II with Part I. Surely, whatever differences of tone or emphasis may emerge, our initial impression as we take up the second part is one of familiarity? Indeed, we often could make little headway with Part II without knowledge of Part I. The topographical details of the journey remain the same, with the various localities and incidents frequently identified merely by reference to Christian's story. The pilgrims in Part II 'went on until they were come to the place that Simple, and Sloth and Presumption lay and slept in, when Christian went by on pilgrimage' (p. 262); Christiana loses her bottle of spirits where 'Christian lost his roll'; the Shepherds of the Delectable Mountains welcome these pilgrims 'as they had done Christian before'. In the same way, characters are often identified by their relationship to figures in Part I. Mrs Timorous is the daughter of the Timorous who met Christian on the Hill Difficulty; the man who 'tumbled the hills about with words' is the son of 'Great-grace, of whom you read in the first part of the records of the *Pilgrim's Progress*' (p. 343). Indeed, so reliant is Bunyan upon Part I, that when the pilgrims in Part II 'come to the place where Christian's burthen fell off his back, and tumbled into a sepulchre' (p. 257) he does not bother to remark that there is a cross there. Although it had been the first feature noted when Christian came to the spot it is now but mentioned incidentally later by Great-heart (p. 261). Clearly, Bunyan is taking for granted his readers' awareness of this crucial detail. Similarly, he does not in Part II introduce Prudence, Patience, and Charity: the names appear in passing, as though prior introductions had been given, some time after Great-heart and his party have arrived at the House Beautiful. There can be no doubt that, whatever the effect, Bunyan's intention was not that Part II should be a new tale but a remaking of the old one, with which it should be closely associated by the reader.

These repeated echoes of, and references to, the first part may alert us to the fact that Part II is not so much unlike its predecessor in conception and emphasis as we are sometimes led to believe. It is not quite accurate to give the impression

that all the epic heroism lies with Christian and all the
realistic domesticity with Christiana. It may well be that the
fine emblem in the Interpreter's House of the 'venturous
man' who quietly says 'Set down my name, Sir' and then
cuts his way through to the palace (pp. 64–5, 81) captures for
us the dominant tone of Part I. We recall that in the House
Beautiful they talk after supper of the 'great warrior' Christ.
But it is in Part II that the famous hymn 'Who would true
valour see' occurs; that we meet Valiant-for-Truth, 'a true
man' with his 'right Jerusalem blade', and the epic image (so
much admired by C. S. Lewis)[17] of him fighting until his
sword was bound to his arm with blood (pp. 348–9). It is in
Part II that Great-heart, who 'loved one greatly that he found
to be a man of his hands', takes his 'sword, and helmet and
shield' and valorously defends the pilgrims against the giants
Grim, Maul, Slaygood, and the monster of Vanity Fair. It is
Great-heart who so takes to old Honest as 'a cock of the right
kind' when he learns of his courage. Conversely, it is in Part I
that Hopeful reminds us that *'Two are better than one'*; that we
see the strength of Christian friendship in the relationships
of Faithful and Hopeful with Christian and the joys of
Christian fellowship in the House Beautiful. It is in Part I that
the supposedly valiant Christian weeps for the loss of his
family and has to be encouraged by Hopeful in Doubting
Castle to 'pluck up the heart of a man'. Above all, it is in Part
I that we hear the story of Little-faith. When Hopeful
wonders at Little-faith's lack of courage it is Christian who
defends him, saying 'all the King's subjects are not his
champions; nor can they, when tried, do such feats of war as
he' (p. 169). Clearly, the ethos of Part I is not merely heroic;
nor is that of the second part without heroism.

Bunyan, then, deliberately associates Part II with Part I,
and there is considerable thematic continuity between the
two parts. However, to say that Part II is linked to Part I by
technical details and the reiteration of certain ideas may
appear merely to suggest a certain repetitiveness, even a lack
of invention on Bunyan's part. While we may allow that such
reiteration teaches the universality of Christian's experience,
we must yet admit that simply to underline that a former
work is generally applicable is a poor motive for a new work.

To add that, as is certainly the case, Part II often glosses and elucidates the incidents of Part I—the long discourse on the imputation of Christ's righteousness, for example, is introduced directly to explicate further Christian's loss of his burden (pp. 258–62)—is still not to offer a very compelling defence of the second part's integral relationship to the first. It may be that Bunyan intended no more than this: to reinforce and comment upon Part I. We could draw this sense from Bunyan's promise in the preface to Part II that

> Besides, what my first pilgrim left concealed,
> Thou my brave second pilgrim hast revealed;
> What Christian left locked up and went his way,
> Sweet Christiana opens with her key.   (p. 215)

And we recall the disconcerting fact that at the end of Part II Bunyan foresees the possibility of a *third* part. Was it never going to end? If Bunyan thought he could go on explicating indefinitely then it would seem that questions of artistic completeness were certainly not in the forefront of his mind. Nor, as a Puritan, would he have thought it proper they should be. 'I write', declared his contemporary Richard Baxter, 'not to win thy praise of an artificial comely Structure; but to help souls to Holiness and Heaven.'[18] Bunyan would have agreed.

This supposition that Bunyan was not interested in artistic unity may draw some support from what can be gathered about the history of the composition of Part I. Apologetic prefaces decrying the merits of the following book, often claiming that it was written in haste, not intended for publication, and only now printed at the instigation of friends, were standard form for works of popular divinity in the seventeenth century, but in the famous prefatory lines to Part I Bunyan seems to have been genuinely surprised by his own creation. To suppose the work was not the unpremeditated result of sudden inspiration is to imply that the circumstantial details here adduced amount to a deception which ill accords with everything we know of Bunyan's character. It is true we should be wary before assuming that any writer is the natural genius he may appear, but, as C. S. Lewis has remarked,[19] the succinct directness of the line 'Still as I pulled

it came' (p. 31) captures the ease of inspired writing with a
naive plainness which has the stamp of authenticity. Further,
the episodic structure of Part I bears out the claim that,
falling 'suddenly into an allegory', ideas multiplied 'Like
sparks that from the coals of fire do fly'. But if Bunyan was
not, like Spenser, writing his allegory to a preconceived plan,
then his curious postulation at the end of Part I of the
possibility of a second part cannot be seen as the expression
of a clearly formulated artistic purpose:[20]

> What of my dross thou findest there, be bold
> To throw away, but yet preserve the gold.
> What if my gold be wrapped up in ore?
> None throws away the apple for the core:
> But if thou shalt cast all away as vain,
> I know not but 'twill make me dream again.   (p. 207)

The possibility is conditional. What Bunyan is saying—and
again, it is a Puritan writer's commonplace—is that if he fails
to persuade the reader of his message with this work he will
try again. It is the preachers', not the artists', motive he
expresses.

However, if this suggests that Part I took Bunyan by
surprise and that Part II was no part of any original plan,
Bunyan's subsequent literary career works rather against the
prevalent view of the distinctness of the parts. He went on
next to Mr Badman (1680), which he presented to the reader
as a companion piece to The Pilgrim's Progress: finding the
progress of his pilgrim to glory had met with general
acceptance 'it came again into my mind to write, as then, of
him that was going to heaven, so now, of the life and death of
the ungodly and of their travel from this world to hell'.[21]
This, then, was a premeditated work: its theme is determined
by the prior existence of The Pilgrim's Progress. In The Holy
War, which followed in 1682, Bunyan yet more clearly writes
with self-possession. Roger Sharrock has pointed out that in
the two years which had elapsed since Mr Badman Bunyan
had, unusually, published nothing.[22] The hypothesis that he
was devoting all his time to the new book is borne out by its
structure, for a multi-level allegory of the complexity of The

Holy War would need careful planning. This work, then, was begun with its end in view: and it was published immediately, with none of the misgivings and hesitancy which had left *The Pilgrim's Progress* in manuscript for some years.[23] Indeed, the prefatory lines alone bespeak, when compared to those prefaced to Part I of *The Pilgrim's Progress*, a new confidence, a new grandeur of conception and design.

When, then, Bunyan comes to Part II of *The Pilgrim's Progress* he is in a situation very different from that in which, 'to divert my self' and with no thoughts of publication, he had written Part I. He now enjoys acclaim and is assured of his public: the preface to Part II delights to point out that Part I had broken both social and geographical boundaries (pp. 213–14). Indeed, the publication of spurious continuations, than which there can be few greater compliments to a writer, was instrumental in provoking Part II, and Bunyan can now confidently point to his own literary style as proof of the authenticity of this work. If Part I was the result of inspired meditation upon his own experience, initially for his own edification, Part II is consciously undertaken for the benefit of an assured public and to discredit impostors. It is, in fact, quite the opposite situation to the one envisaged at the end of Part I. Bunyan, the assured artist, knows what he is about: he has chosen to return to *The Pilgrim's Progress*.

Having made this choice it was, as we have seen, no part of Bunyan's purpose to disguise the fact. He clearly intended the reader of the sequel to have Part I in mind, and so must have felt that Part I could shed light on Part II. More significantly, in returning to the matter of the earlier book he must also have felt that the image of the pilgrimage could yield more than had been realized, and hence, that Part II might shed light on Part I. Such, indeed, is a more satisfactory interpretation of those lines in the preface—'further to reveal' what his first pilgrim 'had left concealed'—than the reading which holds they promise mere commentary on Part I. To gloss a point is not to reveal anything concealed but to expound what has been revealed.[24] And, if this is so, then in making his choice Bunyan, now the experienced writer and pastor, has come to see the revelation of Part I as but a partial revelation. And, following this train of thought further for a moment, if Part II were both to make clear and supply this deficiency, then it would become no mere adjunct to Part I but essential to a true understandihg of it.

As soon as we come to test this speculation against the text, we meet a stumbling-block. Surely, as a narrative, Part I *is* complete? Christian dies, having achieved his quest. Whatever else may be said, must we not admit a new start at the beginning of Part II, and, to that extent, the autonomy of Part I and the separateness of the two parts? A possible line of defence here might be that *The Pilgrim's Progress* is not merely a fictional narrative. The fiction (as Bunyan's prefaces are at pains to point out) is but an expository device, a means to an end. That end Bunyan shared with all Puritan writers in whatever genre: to present and expound a model of the Christian life that the reader may the better evaluate his own experience and determine his future conduct. Hence, that the story has finished tells us nothing about the completeness of the creation of which the story is but a part: the question remains, how complete, or satisfactory, is the presentation of the Christian life in Part I? Unhappily, this line cannot be held, for it errs the other way: it treats *The Pilgrim's Progress* as merely a moral treatise, which it is not, anymore than it is merely a fiction. To ignore the crucial structural role of the fiction and the inescapable impression of finality which its completion gives to Part I is to argue as though Bunyan, like most of his forbears, had but illustrated his teaching with *exempla*. As we know, he went one better. Only if Part II amplifies the meaning of Part I through a fiction which is itself bound up with that of Part I will it cease to be a separate work and become artistically, as well as morally, relevant.

Let us look to the beginnings. At the opening of Part I we meet a man near the end of his tether, trapped and haunted by his oppressive consciousness of sin and the fear of imminent damnation. He turns to his family for relief, but they, supposing that he is the victim of a 'frenzy distemper', lose patience when rest fails to 'settle his brains' and take to chiding and mocking his obsession (pp. 39–40). He withdraws into himself, until finally, the Word and its preachers having convinced him his only hope of relief from his anguish lies in the Christian way, he forsakes his family, refusing their pleas when they 'cry after him to return': he 'put his fingers in his ears, and ran on crying, "Life, life, eternal life"' (p. 41). The point is clear: Christian prefers the claims of Christ to those of natural affection. The margin refers us to Luke 14: 26: 'If any man come to me, and hate not his father, and mother, and wife, and children, and brethren, yea, and his own life also, he cannot be my disciple.'

Several commentators have seen something selfish, almost repulsive, in this forsaking of his family, this abandonment of them to destruction.[25] The point is pertinent to the extent that, when Part I is read in isolation, there is conflict here between the moral truth 'No servant can serve two masters' and the affecting fiction in which it is embodied: if we are appalled by the extremity of Christian's predicament, how much more dire and affecting is that of those he deserts? On this matter of desertion more will be said in a moment: here, we may note that it is not easily done. Christian's wife is 'dear' to him; his children are 'sweet babes' (p. 39). Part of Christian's dilemma is precisely that his inescapable guilt and fear prevent him from caring for them as the loving father and husband he once was (p. 48). Wordly Wiseman's arguments sway him, at least in part, by holding out the prospect of a home in the village of Morality to which Christian may bring his family (p. 50). And at the House Beautiful Christian weeps for the loss of them (p. 84). This opening does not deny human affection: on the contrary, we miss the real measure of Christian's anguish and the true quality of his commitment if we miss this tension.

Part II begins in a different key. Here is a new, a gentler, start. Christiana does not suffer the depths of Christian's anguish: she has neither his sense of sin, nor his uncertainty as to the remedy, nor his doubts as to salvation. And, in setting out, she takes with her those dear to her. But why, if she has not Christian's burden, does Christiana go on pilgrimage? Bunyan is in no doubt that it is natural affection for her husband, self-recrimination at her treatment of him and the encouragement of his example which prompts her (pp. 222–3). The implication of this is clear: had Christian *not* abandoned his family in an apparently selfish desire to gain his own salvation, Christiana never would have set out. In other words, Christian has quite literally saved his family by abandoning it: in preferring Christ before the creature he has made possible the salvation of the creature. Thus, without in any way retracting or qualifying its stark presentation of moral opposites, the opening of Part II does yet give a new perspective to the opening of Part I. Not only do we find that God works through means other than the Word and its preachers, but, more significantly, that what may have seemed culpable in the man and cruelly arbitrary in his God (why Christian and not Christiana?) is in fact neither. Both fiction and moral—the single-mindedness of the hero and the mercy of his God—are the more persuasive now that we better appreciate the implications of the incident. Only by reading the opening of Part II can we appreciate truly what happens at the opening of Part I.

With this clue we can detect that the entire fictional and thematic conception of Part II is bound up with Part I. Like Christian Bunyan had a wife and four children when he had the opportunity of release from prison if he would but give over preaching: in the unforgettable passage in *Grace Abounding* in which he faces the choice before Christian at the opening of Part I he is tormented by the suffering and hardship he will inflict upon his family if he refuses the chance to remain with them, especially by the thought of what will become of his blind child. Yet he does refuse the pull of affection and resolves to forsake them. In so doing, he had the encouragement of promises in Jeremiah (49: 11, 15: 11), and 'this consideration, that if I should now venture all for God, I engaged God to take care of my concernments'.[26] Bunyan leaves his family under divine protection. That is the secret: God does not forsake those who forsake all for him. Here, at the beginning of Part II, Christian himself is the agent of divine grace. Part II begins in the realization that 'no man is an island'; that, despite the apparently lonely individualism of Part I, no man acts in isolation. Actions do have consequences for others, and right actions, however seemingly cruel, do have beneficial consequences. In short, this is *still* Christian's story. The apparent narrative completeness of Part I, we realize, was as illusory as Christian's seeming isolation.

Lest we have missed the point, Christiana underlines for us

the crucial role played by Christian in the inception of her own tale. Mercy grieves for her relations left behind, and Christiana replies:

> Bowels becometh pilgrims. And thou dost for thy friends as my good Christian did for me when he left me; he mourned for that I would not heed nor regard him, but his Lord and ours did gather up his tears and put them into his bottle, and now both I, and thou, and these my sweet babes, are reaping the fruit and benefit of them.   (pp. 232–3)

This is why we are so constantly reminded of Christian in Part II and why Christiana and her companions have an easier pilgrimage. It is not that Bunyan's inspiration is flagging, but that Christian's prayers and example are a constant encouragement to these pilgrims. Part I had prepared us for this: Faithful and Hopeful are both drawn to pilgrimage by Christian's example (pp. 101, 135, 176–7). The vast library of Puritan biography was written precisely because the example of the saints could encourage and sustain those who followed. Had there been no Part II, or were the pilgrimage of Part II not easier, the operation of God's grace would have been severely circumscribed. As it is, coming to the scene of Faithful's martyrdom, the pilgrims of Part II 'thanked him that had enabled him to bear his cross so well, and the rather, because they now found that they had a benefit by such a manly suffering as his was' (p. 336). No wonder Bunyan could complacently envisage a Part III: human lives end, but this story does not end. Standfast dies asking Great-heart to tell the wife and children he had left of his own, Christian's, and Christiana's examples, and praying that they may set out in their turn (p. 371).

That claim 'Bowels becometh pilgrims' has been taken by Professor Sharrock as representative of the changed tenor of Part II,[27] and so it is. However, we err if we suppose that Part II offers a new, more positive view of human nature and affection than Part I. Certainly, this defence of sentiment is, as we have seen, part of the genesis of the second pilgrimage. Part II begins by finding that human affection can be utilized to God's purpose, and, in its subsequent attention to the child-parent relationship, friendship, women, and marriage, it does develop this insight. But if we can only appreciate the full import of Christian's pilgrimage in Part II, equally we can only rightly read this defence of natural affection in the light of Part I. The fellowship of Part II is made possible only because Christian in Part I had not over-valued the creature. Had he done so, he and his family would be squabbling yet in the City of Destruction. Taking the two parts together we find there is no contradiction between Christian's rejection of his family and Christiana's care for her children but that 'all the charities' of family life are released when human affection is subordinated to the one commitment. I paraphrase Milton: at the supreme moment in Book IX of *Paradise Lost* Milton gives to Adam, as he refuses to desert Eve, sublime expression of human love. Adam is never nobler than here, even as he is never more misguided. What appears noble, his refusal to desert his loved one, is, in truth, ignoble, as the desertion at the opening of Part I which appeared ignoble is, in truth, noble. Milton and Bunyan share the Puritan perception that absolute devotion to any human being leads not to blissful freedom but to servitude. What is less often stressed, and what the dignity of Adam's lines, (as, too, the wedding hymn of Book IV) and Part II of *The Pilgrim's Progress* bear out, is that they also share the Puritan joy and delight in human love rightly directed.

This leads to a final point about the opening of Part I. It sets what for many seems to be the key-note and crucial failing of the book: that Christian succeeds by avoiding and rejecting the world. Robert Bridges gave eloquent expression to the view that Part I fails as a moral treatise because Christian actually does very little.[28] Bunyan was neither mystic nor antinomian: he did make it clear in Part I that Christian joined himself to a church and reminded us that 'The soul of religion is the practic part' (p. 115). Nevertheless, it is true that Christian's church membership and moral life have nothing like the imaginative force of his spiritual struggles. The attempt to trust solely in Christ's righteousness is all: Apollyon speaks home when he picks on Christian's proneness to despondency and vainglorious desires as his twin failings (p. 92). Once again, Part II does not make a new start but draws out what was partially concealed by the emphasis of Part I. Both complacency and pride, and despair still meet us, but, handling now a group of pilgrims, Bunyan is able to give fuller weight to our bearing towards others. The predominantly passive Christian is replaced by Great-heart, who takes on all giants, including Despair. Christian's severe plain-dealing to the misguided yields to compassion-ate counsel to the weak. Above all, in Part II there is the conception of Mercy. 'And now abideth', wrote St Paul, 'faith, hope and charity, these three; but the greatest of these is charity' (1 Corinthians 23: 13). If Part I had handled faith and hope, Part II turns to charity. But it is the same text: Christian's faith resulted in charity; Mercy's charity is the result of her faith. A writer cannot, with equal force, say everything at once: the stress does fall differently in Part II, but there is neither contradiction, rejection, nor retraction; there is completion of the portrait of the saint.

It is, of course, in the composition of the pilgrim group in Part II that we notice this change of emphasis and tone most clearly. Bunyan has gone out of his way to make it up of women, children, the old, the infirm, those plagued by scruples and haunted by despondency, timidity, and fear—characters as unlike those 'lion-like men' Christian and Faithful as we could imagine. And to all of them he shows a tender concern: the Shepherds of the Delectable Mountains greet them with the words:

> you are welcome to us, for we have for the feeble, as for the strong; our Prince has an eye to what is done to the least of these. Therefore infirmity must not be a block to our entertainment.   (p. 342)

With these sentiments Great-heart wholly agrees. Although Christian came, incidentally, to Little-faith's defence in Part I, is it not a very different thing to have Little-faith's kin carrying the day in Part II?

I suggested earlier that the correspondence of details between Part I and Part II underlined the universality of Christian's experience. Puritan divines were in no doubt that in essentials the operation of divine grace conformed to a pattern which could be drawn from the New Testament.

Thus, they could outline the process of regeneration, tabulating and analysing its stages, as did, for example, the Presbyterian Isaac Ambrose in four stages which correspond to the main movements in Christian's experience.[29] Bunyan himself produced a broadsheet plan of the routes to heaven and hell,[30] and his own *Grace Abounding*, though remarkable for its detail, yet follows the pattern established in innumerable treatises from William Perkins's *A Case of Conscience* (1592) on.[31] Hopeful's autobiography in Part I again runs true to type. Alternatively, divines could list the characteristic marks of the converted saint, as did Arthur Dent in his eight 'signes of saluation'.[32] As Richard Baxter succinctly put it, 'God's dealings are much what the same with all his servants in the main'.[33]

Yet this is not the whole truth, any more than that Part I, which outlines this typical experience of grace, is the whole of *The Pilgrim's Progress*. In his early years Richard Baxter was greatly troubled because he 'could not distinctly trace the workings of the Spirit upon my heart in that method which Mr Bolton, Mr Hooker, Mr Rogers and other divines describe; nor knew the time of my conversion, being wrought on by degrees'. This personal experience led him to the realization that 'God breaketh not all men's hearts alike'.[34] This apparent contradiction of 'God's dealing are much what the same with all his servants in the main' is entirely typical both of Baxter[35] and of Puritanism generally. As pastors passionately determined to preach what they firmly believed was a practical religion Puritan divines were deeply suspicious of merely speculative metaphysics and theology. Having to hand the press by which to fulfil this commission to expound and apply the Christian revelation to all conditions of men, they became the first significant body of writers to address themselves seriously to the actual everyday experiences of their fellow men. These divines were thus, as L. B. Wright has remarked, 'realists':[36] Baxter's defence of the minute discriminations of his theological works on the grounds that 'the real differences of particular cases is so great as maketh it *necessary*, unless we will deceive men'[37] typifies this determination to face facts. The practical bias of the body of Bunyan's own work is entirely representative. But they were not only realists: the Puritans inhabited a world divinely sustained and directed, that is, a world of divine significance which enabled, nay, necessitated, the interpretation of experience, the seeking out of the typical. Behind the confusing appearances to which they addressed themselves lay constant truth. Their writing is thus disconcertingly ambivalent, both representative or typical ('God's dealings are much what the same') and realistic ('God breaketh not all men's hearts alike')—medieval and modern, we might say. If the finely poised ambivalence of Marvell's 'Horatian Ode' is the most perfect artistic consequence of this ability to look both at and beyond reality, the oxymoron we all use, 'realistic allegory', testifies no less to this quality in Bunyan's vision. An apparent contradiction in terms, yet this is undoubtedly what Bunyan has given us.[38] But we can only appreciate the justice done by Bunyan to both the immutability of God's purpose and the diversity of the human experience of grace if we take *The Pilgrim's Progress* as a whole. Part II follows the key stages in the journey from the Wicket Gate to the Celestial City mapped out in Part I; these are constant. But in its treatment of them, it allows various responses to and experiences of these stages. Thus, as we have seen, the occasion of Christiana's pilgrimage differs from Christian's, but she still receives assurance of election; similarly, the Shepherds of the Delectable Mountains welcome the new pilgrims 'as they had Christian before', but they also 'had them to some new places' (pp. 341–3). Examples could be multiplied, but above all, the pilgrims now travelling the same route are an unlikely and unheroic band, yet they achieve the quest as surely as Christian.

This is not to say Bunyan is forsaking those 'lion-like men' of Part I. On the contrary, it is in Part II that Mr Holy-man reminds us that 'There are two things that they have need to be possessed with that go on pilgrimage, courage and an unspotted life' (p. 333), and, as we noted earlier, throughout Part II the heroism of Part I remains an inspiration. What is happening is that Bunyan is both placing that heroism in a new perspective and enlarging the scope of his conception of it. Retrospectively, the experiences of Christian appear in a new light: he was valorous, certainly, but was he quite the almost legendary figure he has become in Part II? To himself he seemed weak, vacillating, prone to despair. This is not the Christian remembered by the pilgrims of Part II who view the scene of his struggle with Apollyon as Great-heart recalls 'Verily Christian did here play the man, and showed himself as stout, as could, had he been here, even Hercules himself' (p. 292). That allusion, so unusual for Bunyan, shows the kind of imaginative company Christian now keeps. It is not that the pilgrims of Part II have a false notion of Christian: rather, the dross of circumstance has slipped away and the pure example remains. We could almost say that it is only in Part II that Christian assumes the hero.

If Bunyan can thus encourage us that even our imperfect victories can inspire others, yet more important he finds heroism in Part II in less likely places than in Part I. Great-heart tells the story of that 'most troublesome' of pilgrims, Mr Fearing, whom 'Every thing frightened . . . that he heard any body speak of, that had the least appearance of opposition in it' (p. 302). No hero, this. Yet the apparently chicken-hearted Mr Fearing nimbly ascended Hill Difficulty, had no fear of the lions before House Beautiful, and descended into the Valley of Humiliation without a stumble. Great-heart feared a riot when they passed through Vanity Fair, for it seemed that Mr Fearing 'would have fought with all the men in the Fair' (p. 306). For him the Valley of the Shadow of Death was quieter and the River of Death shallower than ever Great-heart had known them. Clearly, beset with fears as to his election, Mr Fearing is yet 'a choice spirit', one with the heart of the matter in him. He is, in fact, Christian.

This recognition of the heroism of the weak and common man, this finding of the great medieval exemplars of the knight and the saint in ordinary people, was the real genius of Puritanism. This marks its modernity. Yet it is a suggestive fact that, while the historians find the movement's revolutionary highspot in the 1640s, the literary masterpieces come after the final collapse of its political ambitions and millenarian hopes in 1660. No longer diverted by the possibility of political reformation it is as if it returns to its true pastoral concern for personal reformation. Just so, in the poem to

Book IX of *Paradise Lost*, Milton, the disappointed survivor of Cromwell's era, redefines the heroic concept in terms of a personal dedication 'Not less but more heroic' than that military prowess upon which (as Marvell realized) Cromwell had too much depended and which, in older epic and romance, had righted wrongs and restored harmony in the commonwealth. Adam comes to learn, in terms entirely consonant with the whole of *The Pilgrim's Progress*, that, in obedient submission to the will of God, the true believer finds him

> Merciful over all his works, with good
> Still overcoming evil, and by small
> Accomplishing great things, by things deemed weak
> Subverting wordly strong, and wordly wise,
> By simply meek; that suffering for truth's sake
> Is fortitude to highest victory,
> And to the faithful death the gate of life.

So does the epic become a challenge to each individual to achieve that 'paradise within' which is 'happier far' than that lost by Adam and Eve or any that wordly power might establish.[39] Its achievement is, certainly, an heroic quest: but neither for Milton nor Bunyan reserved for the old heroes. He 'Who would true valour see' had best read the whole of *The Pilgrim's Progress*.

NOTES

1. Roberta Florence Brinkley (ed.), *Coleridge on the Seventeenth Century* (New York, 1968), p. 475.

2. J. A. Froude, *John Bunyan* (1880), pp. 171–2; John Tulloch, *English Puritanism and its Leaders* (1861), p. 472 (Tulloch did allow that the portraits in Part II 'show, if possible, a freer and easier mastery of hand' than those in Part I); John Brown, *John Bunyan*, rev. F. M. Harrison (tercentenary edn, 1928), p. 265; Macaulay's review of Robert Southey's edition originally published in the *Edinburgh Review* of 1830 and Charles Firth's introduction to the Methuen edition of 1898, both reprinted in Roger Sharrock (ed.), *The Pilgrim's Progress: A Casebook* (1976), pp. 75, 99–100 (hereafter *Casebook*); E. A. Baker, *The History of the English Novel*, 10 vols (New York, 1924–39), iii. 61–2 (but cf. ibid., preface, p. 6).

3. Elizabeth Adeney, 'Bunyan: a unified vision?', *The Critical Review*, xvii (1974), p. 109.

4. Robert Southey (ed.), *The Pilgrim's Progress: with a Life of John Bunyan* (1830), pp. xcvi–xcvii; Scott's *Quarterly Review* (1830) review of this edition, reprinted in Sharrock (ed.), *Casebook*, pp. 60–61.

5. E. M. W. Tillyard, *The English Epic and its Background* (1954), p. 393; Henri Talon, *John Bunyan*, trans. Barbara Wall (1951), p. 219.

6. Talon, *John Bunyan*, pp. 158n., 57, 159, 164–5.

7. Roger Sharrock, 'Spiritual autobiography in *The Pilgrim's Progress*', *Review of English Studies*, xxiv (1948), pp. 107–8.

8. Roger Sharrock, *John Bunyan* (paperback edn, 1968), pp. 138, 141.

9. In Sharrock (ed.), *Casebook*, p. 216.

10. Ibid., p. 102. The incident of Matthew's gripes is a favourite example for this line of argument; see, for example, Sharrock, *John Bunyan*, pp. 145–6 and Dorothy Van Ghent, *The English Novel* (paperback edn, New York, 1961), pp. 22–3. Talon, *John Bunyan*, pp. 161–2, implicitly allows the point when he defends the incident against the charge of bad taste on the grounds that it is, if allegorically crude, realistically accurate.

11. E.g. Sharrock, *John Bunyan*, pp. 138–41 and Monica Furlong, *Puritan's Progress* (1975), pp. 114–15.

12. Rosemary Freeman, *English Emblem Books* (1948), p. 208.

13. E.g. Sharrock (ed.), *Casebook*, pp. 13–14; Talon, *John Bunyan*, pp. 140, 164; F. R. Leavis in Sharrock (ed.), *Casebook*, pp. 216–19; Tillyard, *English Epic*, pp. 394, 396. The link between Part I and *Grace Abounding* is established *passim* in the notes to the Oxford English Texts edition of *The Pilgrim's Progress*, ed. J. B. Wharey, rev. Roger Sharrock (2nd edn, Oxford, 1960) (hereafter referred to as OET edition in these notes).

14. Sharrock, *John Bunyan*, pp. 73–4.

15. In Sharrock (ed.), *Casebook*, p. 145; cf. Robert Shenk's argument (which questions the lonely individualism of Part I and anticipates my paper at some points) that the pilgrimage is a 'collective adventure' in 'John Bunyan: Puritan or Pilgrim?', *Cithara*, xiv (1974), pp. 77–93.

16. Monica Furlong, *Puritan's Progress*, *passim*.

17. In Sharrock (ed.), *Casebook*, p. 200.

18. Richard Baxter, *The Life of Faith* (enlarged edn, 1670), preface, f. a2.

19. In Sharrock (ed.), *Casebook*, p. 196.

20. For a contrary view, see OET edn, p. 338, n. to p. 164.

21. John Bunyan, *Grace Abounding and the Life and Death of Mr Badman* (Everyman edn, 1928), preface to *Mr Badman*, p. 139.

22. Sharrock, *John Bunyan*, p. 118.

23. For the dating of the composition of Part I, see Sharrock's argument in OET edn, pp. xxi–xxxv.

24. OET's note on these lines, p. 339, holds that 'The promise here held out that allegories concealed in the First Part will be revealed by the Second is not fulfilled'; the thrust of this paper is that the entire Second Part is such a revelation.

25. Notably Robert Bridges, in Sharrock (ed.), *Casebook*, pp. 107–8, 112. Monica Furlong finds the parallel circumstance in Bunyan's own life similarly culpable, *Puritan's Progress*, pp. 161, 175–6, and cf. pp. 193–4.

26. Bunyan, *Grace Abounding and . . . Mr Badman*, §§ 324–31, pp. 96–9.

27. Sharrock, *John Bunyan*, p. 141.

28. In Sharrock (ed.), *Casebook*, pp. 109–10, 111–12.

29. Isaac Ambrose, *Media: The Middle Things* (3rd edn, 1657), p. 73.

30. *A Mapp shewing the order and causes of salvation and damnation* ([1664?]) in G. Offor (ed.), *The Works of John Bunyan,* 3 vols (Glasgow, Edinburgh, and London, 1862), iii. 558. Systematic analyses of the process of regeneration and characterizations of the true Christian may be found throughout Bunyan's theological works: see, for example, *Saved By Grace* ([1676?]) in *Works*, ed. Offor, i. 336–61, esp. pp. 350–4; *The Doctrine of the Law and Grace Unfolded* (1659), in ibid. i. 492–575, esp. pp. 540–59 (this passage includes an early account of Bunyan's own experience and a version, in dialogue, of the arguments later to be given to Ignorance); *A Discourse upon the Pharisee and the Publicane* (1685), in ibid, ii. 215–77.

31. See on this B. J. Mandel, 'Bunyan and the autobiographer's artistic purpose', *Criticism*, x (1968), pp. 225–43; Owen Watkins, *The Puritan Experience* (1972), pp. 9, 37–49, 101–20.

32. Arthur Dent, *The Plaine Man's Path-way to Heaven* (16th impression, 1617), pp. 30–31.

33. N. H. Keeble (ed.), *The Autobiography of Richard Baxter* (1974), p. 103.

34. Ibid., pp. 10–11.

35. Thus, he wrote that 'the intimate Transactions of God upon men's Souls' are 'the life' of biographies (in [Theodosia Alleine *et al.*], *The Life of Joseph Alleine* (1672), p. 5) and yet omitted from his own autobiography any 'particular account of heart-occurrences and God's operations on me' as 'unsavoury' and irrelevant (*Autobiography*, p. 103).

36. L. B. Wright, 'William Perkins', *Huntingdon Library Quarterly*, iii (1940), p. 196.

37. In Thomas Gouge, *Christian Directions* (1664), appendix, pp. 80–81.

38. On the disconcerting literary character of *The Pilgrim's Progress* see Wolfgang Iser's excellent analysis in the first chapter of *The Implied Reader* (1974).

39. *Paradise Lost*, ix. 13–41; xii. 565–71; xii. 585–7.

Bunyan and the Confines of
the Mind

VINCENT NEWEY

The Pilgrim's Progress presents one quite obvious difficulty for
the would-be interpreter in our time. Coleridge, though
preferring 'the Bunyan of Parnassus', can yet talk respectfully
of 'the Bunyan of the Conventicle' and recommend his
masterpiece as excellently 'teaching and enforcing the whole
saving truth according to the mind that was in Jesus Christ'.[1]
Except in very special circumstances such a recommendation
is now out of the question. The problem is, how, precisely,
are we to relate to a work seemingly so firmly rooted in
assumptions that are in general no longer assumed? No one
could deny the basic claim of Philip Rieff's statement that
'The long period of deconversion, which first broke the
surface of . . . history at the time of the French Revolution,
appears all but ended';[2] and in setting out to explore the
interest and importance of *The Pilgrim's Progress* in an all but
deconverted world it would no doubt be safest to concentrate
the search on 'Bunyan of Parnassus', the Bunyan for example
whose language is a triumph of naturalness and frugal
sublimity, whose proto-novelistic characters are not infre-
quently (in Coleridge's phrase) 'as real persons', whose
genius took nourishment from the life around him and
refined the potential of English folk-culture into the art of
mimetic and imaginative realism. These features are
prominent among those praised by F. R. Leavis, who affords
The Pilgrim's Progress the status of a 'living classic' on the
additional grounds that it offers a vivifying 'reminder of
human nature . . . and human need'.[3]

My own approach will by no means exclude such areas,
but I aim to take a broader view. I shall be concerned above
all with the psychological and experiential truth embodied
in the work, and to some ·extent with reading its
psycho-historical message (that is, its meaning in relation to

the larger history of the Mind). To put it another way, I shall
be looking at both the essential character and later significance of the vision of the individual's existence, or
'being-in-the-world', expressed in Part I of Bunyan's classic.
We need to get behind the religio-theological ingredients and
suppositions of *The Pilgrim's Progress*; yet they cannot be
altogether ignored, if only because our 'deconversion' makes
us not less but more conscious of them. To confront them,
however, is to become aware, surprisingly enough, of a
certain *anti*-religious tendency in the work: we see not only
our distance from the past, our modernity, but also prophecies of that modernity, of a world without the Divine and
without inviolable corporate frameworks of Faith, where
each man must self-consciously struggle for stability and a
sense of purpose. Let us begin at Doubting Castle, a
prison-house of the self, with God conspicuous by His
absence and the emphasis falling, as it usually does in Part I,
on the vulnerability and answering strength of the individual
himself.

CHRISTIAN AT DOUBTING CASTLE

Of the many occasions on which Christian finds himself
shut-in or his way barred his imprisonment at Doubting
Castle is perhaps the most fraught with the possibility of
terminal disaster. Whereas in the fight with Apollyon he puts
his energy all into surviving, in this episode he almost
becomes the agent of his own destruction. He reaches the
very verge of self-slaughter; self-slaughter in two senses, for
not merely, on a narrative level, does Christian contemplate
suicide ('Christian again seemed to be for doing it') but, on a
psychological level, his whole predicament derives from
within. Giant Despair materializes out of the pilgrims' guilt
at having left the true path for 'the easier going' and their
forgetting of God's mercy—impulses such as, more
hardened, had confined the 'man of despair' at Interpreter's
house to his iron cage, from which he everlastingly shouts 'I
cannot get out' (p. 66). Formally, of course, the enemy lies
without: Christian and Hopeful stray into the grounds of
Giant Despair, and the Giant represents in part the oppressive

power of the landowning classes; they are 'forced to go, because he was stronger than they'. But the Giant is primarily an externalization, or projection, of inner pressures: 'They also had little to say, for they knew themselves in a fault. The Giant *therefore* drove them before him . . .' (p. 152, italics mine). Clothed by the imagination, their fear and hopelessness springs to active and independent life, beats them, and locks them in a dungeon.[4] Although religio-theological, as well as social, concerns remain crucially present, Bunyan's main haunt is the mind itself and, at this point, particularly the mind's 'capacity' for, not so much lapsing into, as actually generating states of potentially inescapable impasse.

Yet the pilgrims do escape. To a sense of psychic insecurity Bunyan's vision opposes a strong conviction of mental resilience and resourcefulness. First, however, there is a struggle, partly between reason and imagination and partly between positive and negative reasoning. The threat of morbid fancies, so starkly portrayed in the way Despair shows them 'the bones and skulls of those . . . already dispatched', and the attraction of the Giant's 'counsel' to do away with themselves are resisted by careful deliberation and studied appeals to the lessons of the past. 'Let us consider again, that all the law is not in the hand of Giant Despair', 'Remember how thou playedst the man at Vanity Fair', says Hopeful, Christian's better self; 'thus did [Hopeful] moderate the mind of his brother' (p. 154). The mind holds out against its own deadlier impulsions—and finally breaks free from them:

> Well, on Saturday about midnight they began to pray, and continued in prayer till almost break of day. Now a little before it was day, good Christian . . . brake out in this passionate speech, 'What a fool,' quoth he, 'am I, thus to lie in a stinking dungeon, when I may as well walk at liberty. I have a key in my bosom, called promise, that will (I am persuaded) open any lock in Doubting-Castle.' Then said Hopeful, 'That's good news; good brother pluck it out of thy bosom, and try.'   (p. 156)

Bunyan's *brake out* is exactly right, since Christian's passionate outburst is also a bursting-out from deadlock, from an apparently irresolvable cycle of mental thrust and parry.

Stanley Fish, echoing U. M. Kaufmann, sees the act of liberation, the remembering of the key of promise, as 'wholly discontinuous with' the preceding 'sequence of events' and 'morass of verification';[5] and indeed it is true that it relates to what has gone before as a *recoil*, a sudden exercise of the will and memory which lifts Christian out of the circle of stress, endurance, and inconclusive consolations. But in a sense it is in fact wholly continuous with the main episode. For one thing, the narrative prepares us for the escape when Mrs Diffidence, who has persistently goaded Despair on to greater efforts, herself begins to 'fear . . . that they live in hope . . . or that they have pick-locks about them'. The matter of authorial signs and strategies, however, is best left for the moment, though it is worth noting that Bunyan is here clearly aiming at a linear and progressive effect rather than, as Fish suggests, at subverting such effects. What I would stress is that 'Christian at Doubting Castle' is from beginning to end a psycho-drama in which emphasis is increasingly placed on the individual's ability to live by his own devices, which means overcoming his own weaknesses and the formidable challenge of the shadow side of his psyche. The means of escape are always there once Hopeful and Christian start to 'consult between themselves' and especially once they start remembering; all that it needs to make the Giant Despair dissolve into 'fits' is for one of them to recall the right thing, the key of promise. An intervention by God would create a real and radical discontinuity in the 'sequence of events', but miracles and divine influences are nowhere in the picture. The key to open the prison is situated just as entirely within the individual ('in my bosom') as the despair that shuts him in and the stabilizing thoughts that allow him to hold on.

It is possible now to attempt some provisional generalizations. Bunyan would seem to be more the celebrant of man and experience than of God and absolute Truth. Of course, he is concerned with doctrine and gospel-laws in the episode; as a leading interpreter says, when Christian rediscovers the key 'Bunyan makes his theological point . . . Scripture showed that the promises of God's covenant with him prevented his repentance from being rejected'.[6] It would be wrong, nevertheless, to contend (as perhaps the critic's statement does) that the theology and the didacticism are primary. The bias of the entire episode is away from 'believing' to 'being'—from Logos to the word, Scripture to text, the divine to the human. And it is not only in the sheer dominance of psycho-drama that this is seen. For it is striking how far Bunyan passes over the religious and theological possibilities of that drama and its setting; he refuses to specify or elaborate on what the 'promise' might be and refuses to transform the literal 'break of day' into a metaphor of spiritual illumination or the influx of redemptive light. We remain in the common light of an ordinary Sunday morning, with an image of an unexceptional man saving himself through a personal act of will and self-counselling: 'What a fool,' quoth he, 'am I . . .'. Moreover, we must never forget that *The Pilgrim's Progress* is cast all in the form of a dream. We return with Christian to clear-sightedness but we are still witnessing a dream; and dreams are subjective and interpretable. They may open up the recesses and workings of the mind, teach us to perceive life more vividly and intensely, and even, when analysed, offer access to more fruitful and stable existence, yet they can have no total claims to our assent and no status as objective truth. By its very form *The Pilgrim's Progress* encourages us to *be* and *experience*, rather than to commit ourselves to any dogma or faith.

It must be said that a particular religion—what we loosely call Puritanism or radical Protestantism—*is* everywhere present in *The Pilgrim's Progress*. The Doubting Castle episode reflects a number of its central emphases: the raising of *logos* over *mythos*, of the word and the understanding over ritual and vision (except where the vision is of heavenly joys); the importance of personal history, as opposed to custom and the traditions of the Church, as a means of stabilizing the individual present (in comforting Christian with memories of his former triumphs Hopeful is advising him as Richard Baxter had advised the wavering convert—to 'Call forth thy own recorded experience, . . . Remember what discoveries of thy state thou hast made formerly in the walks of self-examination'); the conviction that, even in a world of rigid predestination, the salvation or damnation of the soul was still the responsibility of the individual—a conviction memorably expressed by the latter-day Puritan William Cowper in the couplet 'Charge not, with light sufficient and left free, / Your wilful suicide on God's decree', and one which, together with the fact that assurance of election and grace was ultimately a matter of the heart subject to no verification through reasoning from externals, accounts for the ontological anxiety and strenuous self-consciousness to be found in many Puritan writers.[7] To note these features of Puritanism, however, is to realize all the more forcefully that *The Pilgrim's Progress* is not a religious work if by religion we understand a thoroughgoing commitment to and involvement with Deity, Spirit, and sacred Dogma. Inasmuch as it focuses so urgently on the self and its condition Puritanism is, we might say, already religion humanized. *The Pilgrim's Progress* pushes this orientation to its limits. The point can be usefully developed by reference to the fight with Apollyon, not least because that episode raises an apparent objection to the view that Bunyan reduces the status of God in favour of Man and the centrality of 'belief' in favour of 'being'.

Before moving to the Valley of Humiliation and other settings, though, we may recall that Christ himself, the nucleus of normative religious experience, has little felt presence in *The Pilgrim's Progress*. Even at the Cross there is scant sense of the power and mystery of the Redeemer. What we see is a character, Christian, weeping thankfully at being eased of his burden: '"He hath given me rest, by his sorrow, and life, by his death." Then he stood still a while, to look and wonder; for it was very surprising to him that the sight of the Cross should thus ease him of his burden' (p. 70). A theological point is made (Christ releases us of our burden of sin) and Christian's response implies something of the incomprehensible efficacy of Christ, yet the focus of interest is Christian the man and the situation in which he is the chief actor, and not only his feelings of liberation and desire for rest (not, we notice, a desire for a closer walk or communion with Christ) but also, taking the event proleptically as part of the work's larger structure, the astute irony that the Cross is nearer the start than the end of his troubles. Stanley Fish contends that the overriding motive of the work is to affirm the 'primacy' of 'the way of Christ' over 'the way of the self'.[8] He admits, on the other hand, that the rule '*I* am the way' is 'nowhere given'. It is nowhere given because Bunyan is by no means so preoccupied with it. It is an ingredient, albeit a highly significant ingredient, in a creation whose impulse is neither deeply religious nor overwhelmingly didactic but principally an inventive, fascinated, shrewd, and always at bottom earnest, engagement with the individual and his interior life. While the shape, components and preferred values of his vision are naturally determined by his religion and its doctrines, these latter do not constitute either its vital principle or the boundaries of its meaning.

SELF AS SUBJECT AND CENTRE

The phrase 'But as God would have it' which marks the turning-point of the struggle with Apollyon, who is just about to aim his last blow against a Christian beginning to 'despair of life' (pp. 93–4), is superficially a straightforward reflection of, and incentive to, belief in the Almighty, the all-controlling deity without whose intervention Christian would have fallen. In fact, the effect is not so simple. God has been removed from his superior heaven and placed familiarly in the authorial consciousness and in a text which demands to be read, not as a statement of Truth, but as a representation of experience, a fiction. The reader is given the option, whether he likes it or not, of seeing the author himself as the only true agency behind the events, and of seeing God as existing only within the structural design and dream-vision of the artist-creator. Similarly, *logos*—the biblical verses by which Christian overcomes Apollyon—is located in a narrative and in the mind of a character, and thus becomes true and potent in relation to the situation immediately portrayed rather than in any absolute sense. To fictionalize is to secularize, and an incentive to doubt; those of Bunyan's pious contemporaries who objected to his use of wit, fancy, and 'romance' were more than humourless prigs—they knew in their bones that *The Pilgrim's Progress* was dangerous stuff.[9] More ambitious than Philip Rieff, Erich Heller tracks back the processes of our deconversion to the 'demythologizing' animus of Protestantism: in the dispute between Luther and Zwingli over whether the bread and wine are really the body and blood of Christ or 'mere symbols' we can conveniently register the division of mind and soul, reality and truth, world and spirit, experience and belief, act and faith which is our fateful inheritance (and our *dis*inheritance).[10] When did God die? is a dangerous question—it is as if He has had at least nine lives. Yet Heller undoubtedly has a point; and in 'de-numenizing' God and 'de-sanctifying' the Word Bunyan both participates in and (in view of his immense influence) gives impetus to a dynamic that has left us largely god-less and without faith—proud, sophisticated, sometimes despairing adventurers seeking our treasure within the consciousness (psycho-analysis), or by stepping 'barefoot into reality' (Wallace Stevens), or in the emotional lessons or intriguing structures of the text itself, or wherever it might be found.[11]

Perhaps, god-less as we are, we feel closest to Christian when his God is a *deus absconditus*—at the River of Death, for example, where to Hopeful's 'Brother, I see the Gate, and men standing by it to receive us' Christian replies ' 'Tis you, 'tis you they wait for, you have been Hopeful ever since I knew you . . . he hath brought me into the snare and hath left me' (p. 199). If we find this poignant—or the piercingly matter-of-fact reaction of the narrator to being shut out from the Celestial City ('And after that they shut up the Gates: which when I had seen, I wished myself among them', p. 204)—then it is in part because we know deep-down what it is to be dispossessed of heaven and of visionary unselfconsciousness. But our response is a complex, or rather composite, one. Christian's urgent desire (' 'Tis you, 'tis you . . .') and sense of desertion are curiously inspirational as witness to the simple profundity and 'magic' of the human heart. And there is a gentle wit, a tactful effect of comedy, in the pun on Hopeful—of course 'hopeful' has been 'Hopeful' ever since Christian knew him—and in the fact that Christian fails to see that Hopeful is really his own better self. The Preface to *The Second Part of The Pilgrim's Progress* shows well enough that Bunyan was conscious of his ability to capture that peculiar quality in life which makes 'One's fancy checkle

while his heart doth ache' (p. 215). Here his writing, its
strange calculus, its balancing of pathos and pleasure, loss and
sober delight, infuses a quiet but solid strength. In the feeling
apprehension of experience, through fiction, lies a possible
'salvation'. Why bother about heaven when we have an earth
to look upon? That is the question *The Pilgrim's Progress*
continually implies, despite its investment in thoughts of the
Celestial City.

Critics often refer to the Puritan's distrust of this-worldly
('carnal') perception, as opposed to other-worldly ('spiritual')
perception or the treating of this world as a repository of
'images or shadows of divine things'.[12] Indeed, *The Pilgrim's
Progress* does abound with a respect for what Thomas Sherman terms 'the obligation upon heavenly minds to
spiritualize the several objects they behold'—for instance, the
educative and emblematic readings of experience that take
place at Interpreter's House, the paradisal landscape of Beulah, and Evangelist's advice to Christian and Faithful to 'let
the Kingdom be always before you' (p. 123).[13] It is also true,
however, that *The Pilgrim's Progress* largely depends upon a
singular fascination with, and concentration upon, things of
this world. The characters of By-Ends, Worldly-Wiseman,
Atheist, and Ignorance are pertinent in this respect: Bunyan's
greatness derives from a capacity for affording spectacular
realization to positions that run counter to his own accepted
ethos. Or there is Vanity Fair, where he displays a gift—it *is*
something given rather than worked for—akin to that of
Carlyle and Dickens for experiencing persons, objects and
events in an oneiric, near-spectral dimension.[14] Thus the
inhabitants of the Fair become presences in a phantasmagoric
festival of malice: ' "Hang him, hang him," said Mr Heady.
"A sorry scrub," said Mr High-mind. "My heart riseth
against him," said Mr Enmity [in a gross parody of the idiom
of Dissent] . . .' (p. 134). The destruction of Faithful has the
extreme physicality of nightmare: 'first they scourged him,
then they buffeted him, then they lanced his flesh with
knives . . .'. This death-scene is *carnal* in a precise sense; but
the entire episode is one in which imaginative capital is put
wholeheartedly into a contemplation of the world, the flesh,
and the devil (whose inauguration of the Fair is earlier

described). It is alive with realistic detail, yet subdued to unity by a compulsive vision of the devilish that is actually an inversion of spiritualizing vision.

But it is in his treatment of Christian and his companions that Bunyan is most emphatically involved with this world—with the self, with being-in-the-world. Before they enter the town of Vanity, Evangelist tells the pilgrims that 'bonds and afflictions abide *in you*' (p. 124, italics mine). How true this is. For the Puritan, faith can be no less of a challenge and difficulty than sin. As it turns out, however, Vanity Fair itself is something of an exception among the major trials. There is no drama or tension, because there is no doubt, no uncertainty, no pressure from within. Christian and Faithful merely affirm their consent to the bonds that abide in them, by resisting temptation and accepting the 'irons' and 'chains' of their enemies. Like the Lady in *Comus* they keep a resolute distance from their 'seducers'. To attempts to entice them with the vanities of 'the world'—'What will ye buy?'—they reply demurely 'We buy the truth' (p. 127). Faithful similarly answers his accusers' efforts to engage him in debate with a plain determination not to play their game—'what rule, or laws, or custom, or people, were flat against the Word of God, are diametrically opposite to Christianity' (p. 132).[15]

To be a pilgrim at Vanity Fair, then, is a relatively easy matter of occupying a set position over against external hostility and assaults. Evangelist warns Christian and Faithful to 'look well to your own hearts, and to the lusts thereof' (p. 123), but thereafter the question of inner struggle and danger never arises; they merely proceed by the rule Evangelist gives them—'be you faithful unto death'. More often *The Pilgrim's Progress* views the life of the pilgrim-individual psychologically, as a continual battle with oneself. In the great experiential episodes—Doubting Castle, the fight with Apollyon, the Valley of the Shadow, the River of Death—we discover the essential aloneness of the Puritan, hazardous yet dynamic. Although he spoke directly to God, God was also infinitely remote and impenetrably veiled; unaccountable, He might or might not 'favour' the individual as He pleased—or rather, at bottom, as the individual was able in himself to feel that he was 'favoured'. Relief for pilgrims there may be (the

Palace Beautiful), forearming and instruction there may be (Interpreter's House), Help there may be at the Slough of Despond, but in the final analysis man must *make his own way*, else fall into a state of psychic arrestment like the living-dead who wander endlessly among the tombstones, or the Man of Despair imprisoned in his cage, or the man enclosed within the limits of his own apocalyptic imagination who forever dreams and re-dreams the Day of Judgement. So precarious is the way of the self that the most commonplace 'weakness' can suddenly transform a benign resting-place into a place of horror and perplexity, a premature terminus, as when Christian loses his roll by falling asleep in the 'pleasant Arbour, made by the Lord of the Hill for the refreshing of weary Pilgrims' (p. 74). And yet Christian is plainly as much a victim of the lack of any unequivocal sign and guidance as of his own 'sleeping'. So it is throughout: his difficulty derives from the absence of given certitudes, from his 'aloneness', and emerges as constant pressure from within. (Perhaps the clearest example of this absence is the way the Shepherds of the Delectable Mountains turn Christian's request for advice back upon the questioner: 'Is the way safe or dangerous? Safe for those for whom it is to be safe, *but transgressors shall fall therein*', p. 158.)[16] But the same difficulty is, in the overcoming, also the source of his greatness. That phrase, 'As God would have it', makes the victory over Apollyon no less Christian's own. He triumphs because he recovers his strength—his strength in the Lord, but still *his* strength. His nimbleness in reaching for his sword just as he is about to be crushed turns into a nimbleness of mind, and *sword* becomes *words*: '. . . and he caught it, saying "Rejoice not against me, O mine enemy! when I fall I shall arise," and with *that* gave him a deadly thrust' (p. 94, italics mine). This efficacious cry, needless to say, represents a saving reliance on *logos*, both God and Scripture (the biblical text continues with 'I will look unto the Lord'). Simultaneously, however, it claims glory for the protagonist himself—the *I* who falls and rises, the *we* who are 'more than conquerers through him that loved us'. The Valley of Humiliation is not so aptly named, either here, where Christian assertively defeats the fiery demon of spiri-

tual doubt by an act of will and memory (recollection of a
text), or in the earlier battle of words with Apollyon where in
acknowledging his infirmities ('All this is true, and much
more', he says to the demon's accusations of fainthearted-
ness, despondency, and unbelief, p. 92) he worthily integrates
and overcomes the unworthier side of his personality. The
Lord's triumph is his triumph, dependence on *logos*
self-dependence; and the defeat of Apollyon is the defeat of
the devil within himself.

Much the same can be said of the Valley of the Shadow of
Death. The shadow that threatens to engulf him is, like
Despair or Apollyon, the shadow side of the psyche—the
darkness within, the vortex of deadly fears and imaginings.
Physical peril—'flame and smoke . . . sparks and hideous
noises'—soon transforms into inward peril: 'he heard doleful
voices, and rushings to and fro, so that sometimes he thought
he should be torn in pieces . . . and coming to a place where
he thought he heard a company of fiends coming forward to
meet him, he stopped' (p. 97). The emphasis on *thought*
directs attention from outer to inner, suggesting that the
fiends are *all in the mind.* Yet they are no less real for that.
Christian is halted (*stopped*) by incipiently terminal psychological threat—what Wordsworth calls in a similar crisis 'the
fear that kills'[17]—but then by a recoil-in-continuity like that
we saw in the Doubting Castle episode he escapes, at the very
point of destruction ('when they [the fiends] were come even
almost at him'), through an act of memory and resolve,
effected in the recollection of a text ('I will walk in the
strength of the Lord God') but already foreshadowed in
immediately preceding reflections and rationalization ('he
remembered also how he had already vanquished many a
danger . . . so he resolved to go on'). Again one might wish
to stress the element of faith in this act—that Christian breaks
out because he sees at last by the light of divine wisdom, the
Lord God.[18] None the less, the effort (like the peril) is still
personal, and the action 'self-centred' in the broadest sense.
The mind is still lord and master, both as subject and saviour.

The modernity of *The Pilgrim's Progress*, and of the Puritanism behind it, lies above all in the fact that they make
every man, however ordinary, a potential existentialist hero,

or a potential neurotic—survivor or one immured within the confines of the mind and oppressed by madness. Crusoe and Richardson's Clarissa, even Gulliver, the poet Cowper and the poet of Wordsworth's *Resolution and Independence*, Pip and Little Nell, twentieth-century 'heroes' such as the narrator of Joseph Heller's *Something Happened* (1974) whose first words are 'I get the willies when I see closed doors'—none of them Prince Hamlet, nor was meant to be—are all Christian's heirs.[19] But is *survivor* really the word to describe Bunyan's hero? It would seem so from the passages we have considered, where being-in-the-world consists of being constantly shut in and constantly breaking out, always halting and always coming through, ever falling into the morass and ever emerging afresh. The 'victories' we have been considering are all inconclusive—repeated moments of release and of temporary psychological poise along a line of continuing tension.

To stop there, however, would be to ignore at least two dominant aspects of the work: the climactic arrival at the Celestial City, which shows that Christian, and the author-traveller, *have* been journeying to some purpose, some transcendent goal; and the fact that Christian changes inwardly in the course of his pilgrimage. These are the features we must now tackle, carrying forward with us one last point about the earlier episodes. Though each moment of release and its aftermath are 'positive'—being celebrative of the individual's strength and suggestive of an ideal stability, a balanced and conscious selfhood which allows for recognition of 'other' (the Lord)—yet they have a tantalizingly 'negative' side. 'I have a key in my bosom', 'Rejoice not against me . . .', 'I will give thanks to him that hath delivered me', 'I will walk in the strength of the Lord God': the states Christian attains in his 'victories' are states of *minimal feeling*, relatively low in joy, without sublimity. Christian's struggles are an inspiring tribute to human resoluteness, will, clear-sightedness, and sanity, as well as faith, but they involve and issue in an evacuation of the mind's imaginative and, in some measure, emotional life. And that evacuation necessarily also takes place within the narrative which embodies the 'movement' of his mind. For example, the Valley of the Shadow of Death progressively loses its compelling life as the light of victory and faith begins to shine: the 'doleful voices and rushings too and fro' give way to static objects, 'snares, traps, gins . . . pits, pitfalls' (p. 99). While Stanley Fish may be right to interpret the 'sun' that rises when Christian leaves the Valley as the 'Son' himself,[20] what is striking is that in comparison even with other *logos*-oriented and *mythos*-rejecting Puritans—Sherman and Jonathan Edwards, or later James Hervey[21]—so little is made of the image. There is no bright counterpart to the mysterious darkness. Christian does not leave the Valley expatiating on the glories of a symbolic landscape, he goes out reciting a text: *His candle shineth on my head, and by his light I go through darkness. The Pilgrim's Progress* is as a whole rich in imagination, drama, and feeling, but on one level its intentional direction is towards their sacrifice. This becomes specially noticeable when we look at Christian's over-all development—that is, Bunyan's vision of psychological 'progress' and the achievement of 'optimum' being. As we shall see, both hero and work advance to a state of valuable but, for the reader, in some ways regrettable sobriety and equanimity. Much is gained, not a little relinquished.

'INDIVIDUATION'

John R. Knott counters Fish's provocative claim that *The Pilgrim's Progress* is 'anti-progressive' as a narrative and as a reading experience by demonstrating a movement whereby Christian is brought, through an 'awakening of the senses' to fuller awareness of the bliss he finally inherits at the Celestial City. Certainly, in the later stages of the work the hero undergoes a quickening of the spirit; on the Delectable Mountains and particularly in Beulah he experiences freedom, sensuous delights, and passionate longing for the divine ('If you see my Beloved, tell him that I am sick of love', p. 196) which anticipate, and prepare him for, the joys of the New Jerusalem, the fruits of salvation.[22] There has, however, already been another manifest 'progress' within *The Pilgrim's Progress*. That Christian almost 'goes under' at the last obstacle of all, the River of Death, does not mean that he remains always the same person as when he floundered at the Slough of Despond. The Christian who converses with Atheist, Ignorance, and Hopeful just before and during the walk over the Enchanted Ground—a section of the work almost totally ignored by critics—is very different from the Christian who had run through the City of Destruction, his fingers in his ears, screaming 'Life, life, eternal life', or who had quaked helplessly before Evangelist after falling easy victim to the arguments of Worldly-Wiseman ('Woe is me, for I am undone'), or who had been always learning (as from Interpreter and Piety) and never thinking for himself. Looking back, we are conscious of a definite psychological advance on Christian's part, and not least an advance in self-sufficiency.

At one extreme of the mind's journey is the oppression of madness: Christian's 'frenzy distemper' at the beginning of the work, though an ultimately profitable breakdown of the present self so that a new self can emerge, is a real neurosis of which the symptoms are withdrawal from family, violent outbursts ('a lamentable cry . . . What shall I do?', crying *What shall I do to be saved?*'), obsession with death ('I am condemned to die'), and a paralysis of will due to irresistible compulsions which have no direction in which to flow ('I saw also that he looked this way, and that way, as if he would run; yet he stood still . . . he could not tell which way to go', p. 40). There is no bolder spectacle of incipient insanity in literature (and no one except a Puritan like Bunyan could perhaps have created it—a Puritan, that is, who was able to recover in concrete and imagined form his own first period of 'soul-trouble', of initial disorientation and alienation from 'the world'). But the difference between the two questions quoted above—'What shall I do?' and '*What shall I do to be saved?*'—signifies that psychological progress starts almost at once, in that Christian has come vaguely to realize that he needs somehow to be delivered from his great distress; whereupon Evangelist—not so much a type of the preacher as prototype of the modern psychoanalyst—enters to release him from his paralysis, with the cryptic advice to make for 'yonder shining light'. The mind's journey ends, on the Enchanted Ground, in a state of sober, informed, wise passiveness—a state of knowledge and contentment, based in submission to the fact that no man is secure and nothing of one's fate can be known for sure. Christian's response to the story of Little-faith is a good example:

> I myself have been engaged as this Little-faith was, and I found it a terrible thing. These three villains [Faint-heart, Mistrust and Guilt] set upon me . . . I would, as the saying is, have given my life for a penny; but that, as God would have it, I was clothed with armour of proof. Ay, and yet, though I was so harnessed, I found it hard work to quit myself like a man; no man can tell what in that combat attends us . . . Since the lion and the bear hath not as yet devoured me, I hope God will also deliver us from the next uncircumcised Philistine.   (pp. 168–9, 171)

This passage brings together the salient features of what might be called the 'individuated' Christian. He is knowing yet humble in the face of his own weakness and vulnerability. He has become his own Evangelist, commenting upon and interpreting experience—just as in the conversation with Ignorance he assumes, quite instinctively, the role of teacher, albeit to deaf ears. The tone, the whole 'feel' of the lines, implies a stable, unanxious personality, especially beside, for example, the earlier hurried, hesitant, fearfully eager conversation with Piety (p. 81). Far from looking for repose in this life, as he did at the Cross, he now accepts the precariousness and uncertainty of the 'believer's' spiritual condition and the road he must travel: Faint-heart, Mistrust, and Guilt may assail any man at any time; all is in God's hands—the phrase 'as God would have it' is now a natural part of his own consciousness; former deliverances offer hope, but only hope, of deliverance from future trials; he is as yet 'alive', but fears 'we are not got beyond all danger' (p. 171).

In the exchanges with Atheist and Ignorance, too, Christian and Hopeful show a similar conscious tolerance of the limits of their knowledge and security. Atheist trusts to the evidence of his senses; he will no longer seek for the Celestial City because he 'see[s] it not'. Christian and Hopeful, on the other hand, are happy to relinquish all idea of certitude and 'walk by faith' (p. 175). Christian makes claims to knowledge—'I go on *knowing* that we have belief of truth, and no lie is of the truth'—but what the knowledge amounts to is, as the simple equating of truth with 'truth' in the second half of this quotation implies, a ready admission of the relative insignificance of human understanding. It is Ignorance that knows—or thinks he knows—it all: 'I believe that Christ died for sinners, and that I shall be justified before God from the curse through his gracious acceptance of my obedience to his law . . . so shall I be justified' (p. 187). These are the words of an over-certain man. Christian and Hopeful, for all their lengthy and reasoned attacks on Ignorance, have no such scheme for salvation. The whole weight of what they say falls firmly on the side of the importance of recognizing one's *ignorance*: God 'knows us better than we know ourselves, and can see sin in us when and where we can see none in ourselves . . .' (p. 187); 'no man can know Jesus Christ but by the revelation of the Father: yea, and faith too, by which the soul layeth hold upon Christ (*if it be right*) must be wrought by the exceeding greatness of his mighty power' (p. 189, italics mine). That 'if it be right' is the phrase of one who realizes that a position of complete assurance is out of the question.

Now, although it is not possible to trace a detailed, step-by-step process of psychological change in *The Pilgrim's Progress*, one is communicated none the less by a series of broad differentiations. Between our two extremes of paralysis/disorientation and wise passiveness, and in addition to signs already mentioned, lie, for example: the shift from journey as fleeing to journey as seeking;[23] personal deciphering of inscriptions and cautionary spectacles (Lot's wife, those who die at Demas's mine) replacing the need to have everything explained; the growth in capability signalled by the differences between the Slough of Despond, where Christian is rescued by Help, the fight with Apollyon, where we register both the idea of God's will and Christian's own strength, and Doubting Castle, where, with whatever difficulty, Christian finds the means of his escape directly within himself. Nor need we in fact be troubled by the absence of any clear-cut linear progression. Reversals, falls, haltings are part and parcel of any psychological journey, as they are of any life. Such journeys are never easy, never *straight-forward*:

> . . . it can be a tortuous and slippery path, and it can at times simply seem to lead round in circles; experience has shown, however, that a truer description would be that of a spiral. In this journey the traveller must first meet with his shadow, and learn to live with this formidable and often terrifying aspect of himself: there is no wholeness without a recognition of the opposites. He will meet, too, with the archetypes of the collective unconscious, and face the danger of succumbing to their peculiar fascination. If he is fortunate he will in the end find 'the treasure hard to attain'. . . . One cannot be certain that the goal will be reached, there are too many hazards by the way.[24]

This, Frieda Fordham's description of Jung's Individuation Process, would serve in many respects as a perfect account of Christian's pilgrimage: the circlings round to the same point, which are yet parts of an advance; the confrontations with 'often terrifying aspects' of the self—Apollyon, Despair—that must be faced and resisted, and that are also archetypes of the collective unconscious; the uncertainty that the goal will ever be reached; the danger of coming to a standstill in an identification with an archetypal personality, for in escaping Apollyon and Despair he overcomes the temptation of yielding his own emergent identity up to theirs. Moreover, we find in *The Pilgrim's Progress* a strong emphasis on the necessity of deliberately bringing to the surface, and facing, one's fears and sinfulness—the latent 'shadow'—before personal wholeness can be attained; a failure to value their terrors and 'sickness' is among the major errors of those whose 'minds are not changed' (p. 193) and who never reach the state of balance represented in Christian and Hopeful on the Enchanted Ground and foreshadowed all along in the turning-points of Christian's great battles—a state merging self-assertion with self-abnegation, self-sufficiency with recognition of a power greater than self (God).

   To place Jungian psychology and Bunyan side by side is of course to be reminded that the former has its roots in religion.

None the less, the interconnection undoubtedly throws into relief the underlying modernity of *The Pilgrim's Progress*. Beneath the often antique idiom of the discussions on the Enchanted Ground we register an exemplum of the individual emerged whole and stable out of a field of forces often dominated by hostile but educative psychic pressures. If extreme Protestantism opened a Pandora's box of aloneness, anxiety, and inner conflict by depriving man of his trust in ritual and tradition, it also produced, above all in its masterpiece, a saving sense that the box was after all full of riches and that order was still within man's compass. The importance of *The Pilgrim's Progress* resides not only in its influence on specific literary works of psychological ordeal and progress—*The Prelude, Great Expectations, The Old Curiosity Shop*—but in its anticipation of a characteristic conception of being-in-the-world of which these works are themselves, in their way, central expressions. Bunyan was the first to contemplate, and offer up for contemplation, the individual's tortuous and slippery path through the spectacular and peopled confines of this world and through the confines of the mind. No writer more patently prophesies what has become our own instinctive version of the problems and possibilities, the very nature, of human existence.

However much we may respect and understand the patient privacy of Christian and his companion on the Enchanted Ground, though, we are thankful that the work does not end there. Too much has been renounced. Their 'individuation' is synonymous with the elimination of inner tension and all extravagant urges, while in the artefact that presents it experience has largely given way to words, life-and-death confrontations to conversation, psycho-drama to psychological example. But there remains the other more important goal: the Celestial City, the *telos* to which the whole pilgrimage has been directed. In comparison with Jung, Bunyan is, on one point, very much a representative of religion old-style, for his 'treasure hard to attain' exists beyond consciousness, in the heaven beyond death. Only there, where men 'may . . . look their Redeemer in the face with joy', can the individual find 'completion'; only there can Self be truly fulfilled in a communion with Other. Ultimate value and terminus are thus located by Bunyan outside and above the confines of this world and the confines of the mind. At least that is theoretically so. In practice *The Pilgrim's Progress* actually ends in a vigorous commitment to those confines—to experience, life, and perception.

THE CELESTIAL CITY AND IGNORANCE'S REVENGE

The Pilgrim's Progress has not one climax but several. The first, the River of Death, is at once an ending (the *natural* terminus of Christian's journey), a pivot, and a break-through. It is not, as it might seem, a simple repetition of former trials suggestive of an anti-progressive literary structure; rather, it repeats the previous major conflicts in a single, conclusive moment of impasse, struggle and release. Psycho-drama floods back; we re-experience the events of the past in a brief span, as Christian himself re-experiences all the old pressures and displays all his old vulnerability. The 'great darkness' of the Valley of the Shadow again falls upon him, and with it the 'apparitions of hobgoblins and evil spirits'; the forgetfulness and despair of Doubting Castle return ('he could neither remember nor orderly talk'); even the despondent sin-consciousness of the Slough re-emerges ('For my sins he hath brought me into the snare'). When it comes, however, the breaking-out is different. We have not so much a victory of will or steadfastness, of personal effort linked to reliance on the Word, as of feeling, religious impulse, and spiritual 'seeing': '"Be of good cheer, Jesus Christ maketh thee whole." And with that, Christian brake out with a loud voice, "Oh I see him again!"' (p. 199). For the first time intensity is not lost in the movement from darkness to light, conflict to order or poise, but sustained in changed, redirected, form. And at last imagination is valued directly—in the 'seeing' of Christ—instead of being presented as something which must be overcome, something dangerous. As we move across the barrier from this world to the next, there is definite promise of a new freedom and sublimity—for hero, author, and reader alike.[25]

In Blake's view, the promise is fulfilled in visionary transcendence; for he must have the arrival at the Celestial

City pre-eminently in mind when saying that *The Pilgrim's Progress* is a 'Fable' containing 'Vision'.[26] By 'Vision' Blake means imaginative perception of the 'Infinite and Eternal', as distinguished from the 'Finaite and Temporal', and it can certainly be said that such perception, of a kind, does operate in this climactic episode:

> Now I saw in my dream, that these two men went in at the Gate; and lo, as they entered they were transfigured, and they had raiment put on that shone like gold . . . Then I heard in my dream, that all the bells in the City rang again for joy; and that it was said unto them, 'Enter ye into the joy of your Lord.' . . . I looked in after them; and behold, the City shone like the sun, the streets also were paved with gold, and in them walked many men with crowns. . .   (pp. 203–4)

We last glimpse Christian and Hopeful—now called simply 'two men' because they have been stripped of their earthly identities—blending into a festive chorus of saints and angels singing 'Holy, Holy, Holy', able to look their 'Redeemer in the face with joy'. Anyone who has been interior to the Dissenting tradition (as Blake himself was) will understand that this would have struck a resonant chord in the hearts of seventeenth-century Puritans and those who came after, and would have prompted 'visions splendid' of the heavenly Kingdom. Neither can the general reader fail to feel the joy, urgency, and triumphant ideality of this portrayal of the pilgrims' transfigurement and apotheosis, so long as he does not indulge a particular disrespect for the Puritan imagination and its biblical sources.

Yet to designate the episode exclusively one of the 'great triumphs of the Puritan imagination', as John R. Knott does,[27] and draw attention to its special sort of 'vision' (for it is not the sustained and sophisticated 'vision' of Dante or Milton, or for that matter of Blake's own Prophetic Books), is in fact reductive of the complexity of Bunyan's achievement and somewhat untrue to its nature. In the first place, this part of *The Pilgrim's Progress*, like the rest, endures on account of Bunyan's gifted mastery of the word and the procedures of communication, and his sheer creative zest. He turns religion into art:

> They therefore went up here with much agility and speed, though the foundation upon which the City was framed was higher than the clouds. They therefore went up through the regions of the air, sweetly talking as they went, being comforted because they safely got over the River. . .   (p. 200)

> There you shall not see again such things as you saw when you were in the lower region upon the earth, to wit, sorrow, sickness, affliction, and death, *for the former things are passed away*.   (p. 200)

> . . . the very sight was to them that could behold it as if Heaven itself was come down to meet them. Thus therefore they walked on together . . . And now were these two men, as 'twere, in Heaven, before they came at it; being swallowed up with the sight of angels . . .   (p. 202)

The unbroken advance and mounting excitement, the easy rhythms and sense of space, the positive exclusion of sorrow and affliction, the approach of a welcoming Heaven where before there had been only elusive intimations ('they thought they saw something like the Gate', p. 161), the unselfconsciousness that makes mental barriers impossible, engulfment with the sight of angels rather than immurement in the confines of doubt or solitary constriction to the narrow way of faith: the episode is all part of the fable, the culmination of a narrative/oneiric drama which is purposefully recalled and of which the major impressions, movements and psycho-physical structures and events are reversed.[28] No less important to note is the increased presence of the author-dreamer himself, impressed upon us by frequent references to the act of dreaming and beholding and such phrases as 'as 'twere', 'as if' or 'as they entered'. Whatever claims might be made for the reality of Heaven and life-after-death, and whatever feeling the devout might bring to and find satisfied in the revelation, we are neither required nor asked to believe in them, except by a willing suspension of disbelief. We are offered, and persuasively involved in, experience—the end of a story and a narrator's dream. The progress-into-vision is but part of Bunyan's, Puritanism's, and religion's progress-into-literature—the displacement of Truth by the relative, life-interpreting 'truths' of fiction.

The Gates of Heaven close and we are brought down to earth. But our disenchantment does not last long. As one door to experience shuts so another opens, and in comes Ignorance to furnish a final surprise, a drama as memorable as any we have witnessed on our way through the book. Crossing the River with ominous ease ('he soon got over'), and climbing up through empty space, he seeks entrance to immortality:

> But he was asked . . . 'Whence came you, and what would you have?' He answered, 'I have eat and drink in the presence of the King, and he has taught in our streets.' Then they asked him for his certificate, that they might go in and show it to the King. So he fumbled in his bosom for one and found none. Then said they, 'Have you none?' But the man answered never a word.   (p. 204)

So the two Shining Ones 'take Ignorance and bind him hand and foot, and have him away' to the opening to Hell, and 'put him in there'. In consigning Ignorance to Hell Bunyan of course adheres to a creed—the harsh Calvinist doctrine of 'predestination' and 'reprobation'. Ignorance is a 'castaway' with no 'certificate'. It can be argued indeed that Ignorance, Atheist, By-Ends, Worldly-Wiseman, and the rest were created only to fill positions that must be transcended by the 'chosen' pilgrims or to be condemned as a matter of course. An awkward last question is raised for the admirer of Bunyan: in the end aren't the validity and breadth of his interpretation of life, and of his commitment to experience, restricted by a categorizing and moralistic stance *vis-à-vis* humanity? Ground must be conceded. Yet we should also remember that these characters, and Ignorance especially, have had their revenge, and ask exactly why. Though turned away from Heaven, Ignorance has gained a kind of immortality. Even Atheist lives on, still walking cheerfully 'back again' from whence he came, our ears still ringing with that 'very great laughter' with which he greets the idea that there is a Celestial City, and our heads still echoing with that magnificent truism which Christian and Hopeful fail to detect—'There is no such place as you dream of *in all this world*' (p. 174, italics mine). Needless to say, we can see Atheist in a light very different from that available to Bunyan's contemporaries; that the assumptions in which *The Pilgrim's Progress* is rooted are no longer generally assumed allows us broader sympathies. But the collapse of the work's controlling beliefs—whether we think of religion itself or of the more precise Calvinist scheme of salvation—can account only for a shift in attitude towards such figures, and not for the vividness of their continuing presence. What gives them 'immortality' is Bunyan's creativity, appetite for life, and instinctive embrace of experience. He was restricted by his creed but was not its victim. As Ignorance is damned on theological and moral grounds he is redeemed through art—which is to say through Bunyan's imaginative grasp of his situation. As it comes out in the text, his damnation is neither something relished nor something regretted. It is a fact to which Bunyan responds with both sympathy and acceptance; there *is* a pathos in that picture of Ignorance fumbling for his roll and in that silence ('But the man answered never a word') which speaks volumes about his vulnerability and despair, although the pathos does nothing to excuse his inadequacies or to challenge the rightness of his being cast down to Hell.[29] The whole paragraph is so wonderfully pointed in its assent to the inevitability of what happens (seen notably in the business-like binding of Ignorance 'hand and foot' by the two Shining Ones), yet at the same time so moving in its understatement and sense of Ignorance's helplessness. It is the event that really matters to author and reader alike. Being-in-the-world or going out, the arduous way to Heaven or the primrose path to Hell, all is grist to the one and food to the other. Like every great artist Bunyan can even snatch affirmation out of the jaws of negation; he takes as much delight in depicting an Ignorance damned as in portraying a Christian saved.

NOTES

1. Roberta Florence Brinkley (ed.), *Coleridge on the Seventeenth Century* (Duke University Press, 1955), pp. 475–6; reprinted in R. Sharrock (ed.), *The Pilgrim's Progress: A Casebook* (London, 1976), pp. 52–3 (hereafter *Casebook*).

2. Philip Rieff, *The Triumph of the Therapeutic* (1966; Penguin University Books, Harmondsworth, 1973), pp. 1–2.

3. Leavis's important essay appears as an 'afterword' to the Signet Classics edition of *The Pilgrim's Progress* (New York and London, 1964) and in *'Anna Karenina' and Other Essays* (London, 1967).

4. This and related points were germinated in a reading of Stanley E. Fish's brilliantly suggestive 'Progress in *The Pilgrim's Progress'*, *Self-Consuming Artifacts* (Berkeley and London, 1972). My interpretation of Bunyan is, however, essentially opposed to Fish's, which puts forward the thesis that *The Pilgrim's Progress* is 'anti-progressive' both as a narrative and as a reading experience, the linear form of the work constituting a danger for the reader and the pilgrim because it 'spatializes' and 'trivializes' the 'way' of Christ's 'I am the way'.

5. Fish, op. cit., pp. 257–8; cf. U. Milo Kaufmann, *The Pilgrim's Progress and Traditions in Puritan Meditation* (New Haven, 1966), p. 198.

6. R. Sharrock (ed.), *The Pilgrim's Progress* (Penguin English Library, Harmondsworth, 1965), p. 376, n. 9.

7. See Richard Baxter, *The Saints Everlasting Rest* (4th edn, London, 1653), Part 4, pp. 187–90; William Cowper, *Truth*, ll. 19–20. Apart from salvation as the responsibility of the individual, the emphases here noted are all described in detail by U. M. Kaufmann, op. cit., *passim*. Recapitulation of and reflection on previous events—the treatment of personal history as inspirational *logos*—have a substantial presence in *The Pilgrim's Progress*; at the House Beautiful, for example, Christian is made to recall his pilgrimage for his own and his listeners' edification, while at Doubting Castle, the Valley of the Shadow of Death, and the River of Death the past becomes a source of 'evidences' (of courage and former 'deliverances') to be used against present doubt and weakness. But no amount of recollection or reasoning can bring complete inner assurance; the shift from agonizing circularities of thought and contemplation to a sudden act of will by which faith and hope are renewed (for the time being at least) is a *topos* of Puritan experiential literature (see Kaufmann, pp. 197 ff.) and appears in works as well-known as Milton's *Lycidas* (the abrupt excursus into 'redemptive vision' with the apotheosis of Lycidas) and Wordsworth's *Resolution and Independence* (see n. 17 below). Bunyan's *Grace Abounding* is the richest record we have of the Puritan's habitual self-consciousness, anxiety about personal 'sinfulness', and 'great fears of perishing for ever' (Preface)—and of his capacity for finding stability through retrospection, the ordering of experience, and resolute faith.

8. Fish, op. cit., pp. 228–9.

9. See R. Sharrock, *John Bunyan* (London, 1968), p. 139.

10. Erich Heller, *The Hazard of Modern Poetry* (Cambridge, 1953);

selection reprinted in Giles B. Gunn (ed.), *Literature and Religion* (London, 1971), pp. 168–76.

11. For particularly incisive investigation of this dominant psycho-historical trend, see Heller, op. cit.; Philip Rieff, op. cit.; J. Hillis Miller, *The Disappearance of God* (Cambridge, Mass., 1963) and *Poets of Reality* (Cambridge, Mass., 1965); and, writing from an orthodox religious standpoint, Nathan A. Scott, *Negative Capability: Studies in the New Literature and the Religious Situation* (New Haven, 1969).

12. The distinction between the two kinds of perception underlies the argument of both Fish's 'Progress in *The Pilgrim's Progress*' and John R. Knott's reply, 'Bunyan's gospel day: a reading of *The Pilgrim's Progress*', *English Literary Renaissance,* iii (1973), pp. 443–61 (reprinted in *Casebook*, pp. 221–43).

13. Sherman's words form part of the opening paragraph of his 'remedial' *Second Part of The Pilgrim's Progress* (1684).

14. For this and other connections between Bunyan and Dickens, see n. 19 below.

15. Thus the episode is a significant early example of what Raymond Williams terms 'that separation of virtue from any practically available world that is a feature of the later phases of Puritanism and still later Romanticism'; *The Country and the City* (London, 1973; Paladin edn, 1975), p. 84. It must also be said, however, that together with Puritanism's rejection of 'the world' goes not only a concomitant penetration of the psychology of the individual but, later, the great Cowperian and Wordsworthian pursuit of value in the communion between mind and nature, a saving intercourse between self and the 'active universe'.

16. Cf. John R. Knott's analysis of this passage, 'Bunyan's gospel day', *Casebook*, pp. 224–5.

17. *Resolution and Independence,* l. 113. For detailed discussion of the intimate relation between the content and strategies of this poem and those of Puritan psycho-experiential narratives, see my 'Wordsworth, Bunyan and the Puritan Mind', *English Literary History,* xli (1974), pp. 219–24.

18. As Stanley Fish does; op. cit., pp. 245–6.

19. Dickens's continuation of Bunyan deserves special note. Q. D. Leavis (F. R. and Q. D. Leavis, *Dickens the Novelist* (London, 1970), pp. 320–2) points for instance to the close parallel between Pip's encounter with Orlick at the sluice-house (*Great Expectations*, chap. liii) and Christian's fight with Apollyon in order to emphasize that Pip's drama is a drama of the 'inner self'; Pip must admit his past 'sins' and hope for forgiveness, as a step in the process of shedding his acquired egotism and false views of life. Dickens took from Bunyan, then, both the idea of the individual life being a spiritual pilgrimage and a naturalistic-symbolic mode of presenting that pilgrimage. This mode depends crucially upon the imaginative ability, mentioned earlier in relation to Vanity Fair but present throughout *The Pilgrim's Progress*, for making 'characters', objects and scenes among which the hero moves into embodiments of invisible forces, either good or evil, 'aiding' or hostile. *The Old Curiosity Shop*, which is profoundly indebted to *The Pilgrim's Progress*, offers perhaps the clearest

example in Dickens of this psycho-dramatic use of landscape and figures; the City from which Nell flees (the City of Destruction) and the Fair (Vanity Fair) and industrial Midlands (Valley of the Shadow) through which she travels are at once realistic settings and oneirically conceived places of soul-trial, 'threats' and 'spiritual dangers' that she faces and overcomes in her progress to the promised land of inward repose (the transcending of desperate loneliness and of the darkness of her distraught imagination in the 'Valley of the Shadow' at the end of chapter xliii is singularly Bunyanesque). The novel also supplies an apt comment on heroism: '. . . has this child heroically persevered under all doubts and dangers, struggled with . . . suffering, upheld and sustained by strong affection and the consciousness of rectitude alone? And yet the world is full of such heroism' (chap. xlvi). The reference to 'strong affection'—Nell's love for her grandfather—reminds us that Dickens's vision of being-in-the-world is more completely 'humanized' than that of his predecessor. And he can find moral and spiritual prowess even in a child. Yet Nell's triumphant perseverance, and her constant near-arrestment by 'doubts and dangers', are plainly in the image of Christian's own.

20. Fish, op. cit., p. 246.
21. 'Behold him coming forth from the chambers of the east. See, the clouds, like floating curtains, are thrown back at the approach. With what refulgent   majesty   does   he   walk   abroad!   . . .   the   sun   of righteousness!'—James Hervey, 'Reflections on a Flower-garden', *Meditations and Contemplations* (1748; London, 1812), pp. 84–5. Hervey's *Meditations* are the climax of a long tradition of 'heavenly' and 'spiritualized' meditation taking in many of the leading Puritan writers (see Kaufmann, op. cit., pp. 133–50, 186–7). The beginning of Sherman's *Second Part of The Pilgrim's Progress* is only relatively less effusive: '. . . the earth clothed in rich and glorious attire to rejoice and triumph for the return of her shining bridegroom'.
22. Knott, op. cit., pp. 235–9.
23. See section 2 of Philip Edwards, 'The Journey in *The Pilgrim's Progress*' in the present volume.
24. Frieda   Fordham,   *An   Introduction   to   Jung's   Psychology* (Harmondsworth, 1966), p. 79.
25. It might be argued that such a promise has already been made in the description of Beulah (pp. 195–7), where we move with Christian through the spacious vineyards and gardens of the King, whence there is a 'perfect view' of the Celestial City. What is most conspicuous, however, is that this foretaste of Heaven leaves Christian under as much pressure as ever; the sight of the City brings on an almost unbearable 'sickness', a yearning for something still out of reach. At the River of Death his passionate feelings are of something gained: 'Oh I see him again!' In the crossing, tension, dark imaginings, and 'troublesome thoughts' are displaced by secure expectancy and perception of the divine—both within Christian and within the work itself. The River is a *threshold*, Beulah but an *approach*.
26. 'A vision of the Last Judgment', in Geoffrey Keynes (ed.), *Poetry and Prose of William Blake* (Nonesuch Press, London, 1961), p. 638.

27. Knott, op. cit., p. 240.

28. And at the same time the motifs emergent in the landscape of Beulah are confirmed and expanded (see n. 25 above).

29. Maurice Hussey, 'Bunyan's "Mr Ignorance"', *Modern Language Review*, xliv (1949), pp. 483–9 gives a careful account of the moral grounds on which Bunyan's devout readers would have felt Ignorance's 'punishment' to be just, as the rightful destiny of a 'hypocrite'. But to limit the passage to a sweeping of 'the last devil . . . into Hell', as Hussey does, is seriously to underestimate Bunyan.

Life and Story in
The Pilgrim's Progress[1]

ROGER SHARROCK

In our post-industrial and technological age we have witnessed a progressive secularization of culture, and it would be
no use pretending that Bunyan's masterpiece any longer plays
as important a part in the mind of English civilization as it did
at least down to the Victorian age. The book has suffered from
the displacement of the centrality of the Bible in education just
as other literature has suffered from the decline in the
knowledge of the classics. Yet *The Pilgrim's Progress* both as
Christian statement and as imaginative creation is still profoundly there for all those of us who would wish to
contemplate the permanent outlines of our culture and make
sense of the present by seeing it in relation to the past and thus
not become lost in the waste land of its ephemeralities.

When Bunyan issued *The Second Part of The Pilgrim's Progress*
in 1684 he could already boast that the First Part had been
translated into several languages; in the prefatory verses he
says:

> My pilgrim's book has travelled sea and land,
> Yet could I never come to understand,
> That it was slighted, or turned out of door
> By any kingdom, were they rich or poor.
>   In France and Flanders where men kill each other
> My pilgrim is esteemed a friend, a brother.
>   In Holland too, 'tis said, as I am told,
> My pilgrim is with some, worth more than gold.
>   Highlanders, and wild-Irish can agree,
> My pilgrim should familiar with them be.
>   'Tis in New England under such advance,
> Receives there so much loving countenance,
> As to be trimmed, new clothed and decked with gems
>   . . . (p. 213)

In the Elstow Moot Hall at Bunyan's birthplace there is a permanent exhibition of editions of the allegory, many of them missionary editions, in hundreds of languages from all over the world. Here in one is Christian equipped like a Samurai warrior fighting an Apollyon in the guise of a Chinese dragon; in another designed for readers in Sea-Dyak some mid-Victorian engravings have been reproduced so that the readers can contemplate late romantic landscapes, idealized Puritan maidens, abundant lace and steeple-crowned hats. Bunyan criticism has always been confronted by a paradox: the contrast between the universal appeal thus demonstrated and the uncompromising dogmatism of the author's religious belief. Bunyan wrote a book to express the views on God, man, and salvation of an English seventeenth-century Particular Baptist and created a work for the world which has appealed even to those of other religions than Christianity or even of no religion (it played a role for instance among the liberalizing tendencies in Islam in the nineteenth century and in the last generation it found no more eloquent spokesman and defender than the late F. R. Leavis).

One approach to the paradox, initiated by the Romantics and some later critics, has been to attribute the success of the book to a happy accident of untutored genius. Coleridge's early statement of this view is well-known: 'His piety was baffled by his genius, and the Bunyan of Parnassus had the better of the Bunyan of the Conventicle.'[2] But elsewhere Coleridge had to acknowledge the importance of the theological framework when he described *The Pilgrim's Progress* as 'incomparably the best *Summa theologiae evangelicae* ever produced by a writer not miraculously inspired';[3] and he had been anticipated by a writer in *The Gentleman's Magazine* in 1765 reviewing *Some Account of the Imprisonment of Mr John Bunyan*:

> a work of imagination . . . illustrating a particular set of religious principles . . . it contains a most excellent epitome and illustration of the Calvinistic divinity under an allegory highly entertaining and affecting . . .[4]

So we may move from the image of Bunyan as the author of one great isolated work of the imagination to a different

image: that of an author of a large body of works of
evangelical piety, arousing sermons, books on the doctrine
of grace, conduct manuals and books of controversy,
among which *The Pilgrim's Progress* is simply an outstanding
example. 'He was Sixty years old, and here are Sixty Pieces
of his labours', as his first editor, Charles Doe, the comb-
maker of Southwark, said.[5] It seems likely that this was
Bunyan's own attitude to his work, and certainly there are
many factors which make it impossible to draw a hard and
fast line between the allegory and the other books. There
are often the same vivid and homely metaphors in the
minor works as in the fiction. In *Saved by Grace* the work of
divine grace in the heart is compared to burning oil on to
which the Devil is fruitlessly pouring water to extinguish it.
We encounter the same similitude as one of the emblem
pictures in the Interpreter's gallery in the First Part of *The
Pilgrim's Progress*. In *Some Gospel Truths Opened* Bunyan,
addressing the doubting Christian, says, 'Thou art left in the
mire', just as Christian at the beginning of his journey sank
into the Slough of Despond; and in *Come and Welcome to
Jesus Christ* the sinner is eased of his burden just as Christian
was when he arrived at the Cross. Everywhere, in allegory
and sermon writings, there are the echoes of the common
life of an England still predominantly agricultural. On the
gathering in of souls he instances the cry of the women at
harvest time, 'Poor gleaning, poor gleaning'. Or there are
common human images that do not belong to any particular
time or place: 'You know that when children fall down in
the dirt, they do usually before they go home make their
clothes as clean as they can, for fear their parents should
chide them . . .' (*The Doctrine of the Law and Grace Unfolded*).[6]

But the relationship of allegory and treatises works in both
directions. As well as the play of similitude in the sermons
something of their formal structure is carried over into the
fiction. This is most pronounced in the First Part. When
Christian and Faithful and Hopeful converse together about
their soul experience or when Christian and Hopeful contro-
vert Ignorance the manner of their conversation is a formal
discourse often arranged under numbered heads as in the

sermons. Bunyan is deeply influenced by the Puritan and Calvinist principle that any biblical text must present a single clear and unambiguous meaning and that this must apply also to parables and similitudes. Thus in *The Barren Fig-Tree: or, the Doom and Downfall of the Fruitless Professor* (1682) Bunyan first quotes the parable (Luke 13: 6–9):

> A certain man had a fig-tree planted in his vineyard; and he came and sought fruit thereon, and found none. Then said he unto the dresser of his vineyard, Behold, these three years I come seeking fruit on this fig tree, and find none; cut it down; why cumbereth it the ground? And he answering said unto him, Lord, let it alone this year also, till I shall dig about it, and dung it; and if it bear fruit, well: and if not, then after that thou shalt cut it down.[7]

Bunyan then goes on to state that there are two things to be taken notice of in parables, the metaphors, and the doctrines or mysteries couched under them. Each metaphorical element is analysed and listed. 1. A certain man. 2. A vineyard. 3. A fig-tree, barren or fruitless. 4. A dresser. 5. Three years. Then comes the explanation of the meanings. '1. By the man in the parable . . . is meant God the Father. 2. By the vineyard . . . his church. 3. By the fig-tree a professor. 4. By the dresser, the Lord Jesus. 5. By the three years is meant the patience of God, that for a time he extendeth to barren professors.' The numbering of arguments extends to many of the static passages of discourse that lie between the episodes of adventure, challenge, and temptation in *The Pilgrim's Progress*. Thus at Christian's second meeting with Evangelist after he has allowed Wordly-Wiseman to turn him out of the way, Evangelist tells him:

> Now there are three things in this man's counsel that thou must utterly abhor.
>   1. His turning thee out of the way.
>   2. His labouring to render the Cross odious to thee.
>   3. And his setting thy feet in that way that leadeth unto the administration of death.   (pp. 53–4)

He then proceeds to give reasons supported by Scripture texts for these three branches of error. Thus under the second head the Cross is to be preferred before the treasures in Egypt (Hebrews 11: 25, 26) and because he that will save his life shall lose it (Mark 8: 34), the marginal gloss adding three more supporting texts. Likewise in the episode of By-Ends and his friends, after his first brush with Christian and Hopeful, By-Ends proposes his time-serving principles in a formal question to his friends which is then discussed like a scholastic proposition:

> Suppose a man, a minister, or a tradesman, etc., should have an advantage lie before him to get the good blessings of this life, yet so as that he can by no means come by them except in appearance at least he becomes extraordinary zealous in some points of religion that he meddled not with before: may he not use this means to attain his end, and yet be a right honest man? (p. 140)

To this Mr Money-love propounds a reasoned answer, citing first the particular case of a minister under four numbered heads and then that of a tradesman under three; the third head for the minister is again subdivded into three:

> 3. Now as for his complying with the temper of his people, by deserting, to serve them, some of his principles, this argueth, 1. That he is of a self-denying temper. 2. Of a sweet and winning deportment. 3. And so more fit for the ministerial function.   (p. 141)

It will be noticed that some of these divisions are rhetorical rather than logical; satiric irony creates a kind of parody of scholastic reasoning. But when Mr Hold-the-world propounds the same question to Christian and Hopeful the former's indignant answer first takes the form of a spirited introduction, 'Nor do we find any other than heathens, hypocrites, devils and witches that are of this opinion'. These categories are then listed and illustrated under four heads—the story of Hamor and Shechem desiring the daughter and cattle of Jacob (Genesis 34), the hypocritical

Pharisees, Judas the Devil who was 'religious for the bag', and Simon Magus ('Simon the witch', Acts 8: 19–22); then there is a fifth section of summary and denunciation again referring to Judas selling his master and summing up the error of By-Ends and his friends as being 'heathenish, hypocritical and devilish, and your reward will be according to your works'. Then there is a masterly dramatic stroke: the utter silence of the routed hypocrites. 'Then they stood staring one upon another, but had not wherewith to answer Christian.' So we see that in spite of the drama and satiric humour, Christian's reply is as structured, as firmly logical and biblical as Evangelist's earlier rebuke to him. It is the same in the long discourse of Christian and Hopeful after Ignorance has parted from them: then Christian enumerates nine distinct and progressive stages in the falling away of the apostate.

Bunyan's preaching and expository technique is old-fashioned in comparison with that of Barrow or South or Tillotson. The slow opening of the text, the phrase by phrase progression of the argument, the laboured reasons and 'uses', all these features have a traditional logic that looks back to Calvin and beyond him to the Middle Ages. It may seem to the modern reader at times that the virtues of language, of personal urgency and of natural metaphor, are imprisoned in a scholastic straightjacket. Paradoxically our ecumenical age is likely to be repelled less by uncouthness or a narrow theological bias than by a highly structured and detailed form of verbal argument with which we have lost touch since the late seventeenth century. In terms of system of thought Bunyan comes at the end of a tradition. In the same manner he writes the last English emblem book, *A Book for Boys and Girls*, employing with instinctive sympathy a form based on the union of picture and text which had become degraded and dismissed from court and study to the nursery. Allegory itself is in decline in the period and once more Bunyan comes late in the development of a tradition when it is already on the verge of eclipse: *Piers Plowman*, *The Faerie Queene*, *The Holy War*. In Swift's tale of the three brothers in *A Tale of a Tub* we are in a different world where the large suggestiveness of spiritual and psychological entities gives way to the precise labelling of political and ecclesiastical types. Bunyan's allegory does of course already exhibit a tendency to substitute realistic types for archetypal vices and virtues. 'Not Honesty in the abstract, but Honest is my name', says that splendid character when he is first encountered (p. 300).

So far I have paid attention to some of the elements in *The Pilgrim's Progress* which are less dramatic, closer to evangelical sermonizing, only marginally allegorical (what real difference can be made out between By-Ends and Hold-the-world?) and likely to prove the hardest with which the modern ordinary reader can come to terms. Now I want to turn once more to what is permanent and powerful in the appeal of the book. And here I want to suggest that Bunyan's critics have sometimes done him a disservice by inviting us to look backwards or forwards when regarding him, back to the Middle Ages or forward to the modern realistic novel. Early scholars like J. B. Wharey and Harold Golder drew attention to the obvious links between *The Pilgrim's Progress* and certain episodes in the romances or in a medieval pilgrimage narrative like Deguileville's *Pélérinage de la vie humaine*, while a number of writers have treated Bunyan in his humorous vignettes or in the social realism of *Badman* as a precursor of Defoe and the early novel. As Gwilym O. Griffith wrote fifty years ago:

> . . . who is so familiar with it all—the nervous, homely dialogue, the deft delineation, the variety of human types, the wealth of humour, pathos, satire and compassion—as to fail to see that Bunyan, among other things of yet greater import, is the first of our modern novelists? Not Dickens himself, with a like compass, will give us a richer gallery of living, unforgettable types.[8]

It is my contention that this looking backwards or forwards to establish Bunyan's literary origins or the works up to which he was leading is liable in either case to divert our attention from the central themes of the book, not because it prevents concentration on the synchronic Restoration Bunyan but because it does not go far enough backwards or forwards. *The Pilgrim's Progress* is not an imitation of a chivalric romance and it is not the first modern novel, because, at any rate in Part I, it has the features of that very ancient but long-lasting form the story, something growing out of oral narrative like the fairy- or folk-tale. The novel isolates us in the particularity of an individual life like no other life; the story on the other hand speaks of general shared human experience and is therefore more difficult to be told or repeated in an age which has divided human experience by peculiar cruelties and peculiar indulgences. The story depends, as Walter Benjamin has finely said, on communicable experience.[9] Christian in the Slough of Despond or with the shepherds on the Delectable Mountains may not be a figure easy to identify with like the sensational images of the novel but his experience is communicable. With experience in the story comes wisdom, common truths to communicate, and this, if I may draw on Benjamin again, is of two kinds: that of a man living for some time in a settled place and grounded in a settled tradition, like a master craftsman, and that of the travelling man who brings back strange experiences from far places, like a sailor or a travelling journeyman.[10] Now Bunyan's position as, not a vagabond but a travelling tinker like his father working within a limited area of the Bedfordshire countryside, made him a master of both these kinds of experience, the strange things from farther off, like the highway robbery of Little-faith on the dangerous public roads ('His face was as white as a clout') and the things handed down within a household or a neighbourhood like the gentle home-keeping relationship of Christiana and Mercy in Part II. And his later experience as 'Bishop' Bunyan, pastor of Bedford Meeting and indefatigable traveller and messenger to the outlying congregations in Cambridgeshire, Hertfordshire and elsewhere, preserved his faculty of presenting both the two wisdoms of story-telling, the strange knowledge acquired afar off, and the understanding gained through years of experience of what it was to remain still and entertain nearer home the eccentric weaknesses of Mr Despondency and his daughter Much-afraid.

A story, even a fairy tale, is useful and contains counsel. This is why Bunyan's dogmatism and his scholastic interchanges are absorbed in the narrative and may be proved acceptable to the reader. In the novel we do not look for wisdom but for novelty, even for up-to-date information about the behaviour of people in North Yorkshire in the mid ninteenth century or north Oxford in the twentieth. The wisdom of the story, by contrast, is profound and subtle and can often be interpreted in different ways: it is conveyed within the story which is not a mere vehicle for it. Thus we have the mysterious beauty of Mr Despondency's daughter Much-afraid at the River of Death: 'His daughter went through the River singing, but none could understand what she said' (p. 370). In relation to her previous character this certainly teaches us, if literature can be said to teach, but how or what?

By relating Bunyan like this to the traditional popular tale as it is found in the *Arabian Nights* or *Robinson Crusoe* (which is not really a novel) or the *Haus-Märchen* of the brothers Grimm one is giving him back to the audience of children and simple people he enjoyed in the eighteenth and nineteenth centuries. In those periods the supremacy of the novel as the acceptable form of realistic fiction among sophisticated people made men forget that the realm of the story was both wider and deeper and had much earlier origins than either the novel or its ancestor the romance. W. P. Ker has a striking passage early in his *Epic and Romance* when he quotes Aristotle's analysis of the plot of the *Odyssey* purporting to show its likeness to the realistic novel of his own time:

> A man is abroad for many years, persecuted by Poseidon and alone; meantime the suitors of his wife are wasting his estate and plotting against his son; after many perils by sea he returns to his own country and discovers himself to his friends. He falls on his enemies and destroys them, and so comes to his own again.[11]

Ker has to admit that the reference to Poseidon a little spoils his analogy, and he would have to notice that many of the perils are supernatural, monsters and enchantresses, though treated in the single clear light of the Mediterranean world.

But it seems worth attempting a similarly dry and condensed account of Part I of *The Pilgrim's Progress*:

> A certain man reads a book which tells him he is living in the City of Destruction. He leaves it in sadness of mind, abandoning his family. A man (Evangelist) points out to him the right way which he must follow to reach the Celestial City. He has many setbacks and perils on the road, and suffers temptation from those who are not going the right way. But he is aided by two good companions, Faithful and then after Faithful's death Hopeful. In spite of having to pass through the Valley of the Shadow of Death and being incarcerated in Doubting Castle, he and Hopeful with further help from Evangelist finally reach the River of Death and are borne across it to enjoy an eternity in the Celestial City.

The *Odyssey* is both more folk tale and less novel than Ker would admit but we can now begin to see its likenesses to and differences from Bunyan's allegory and therefore the ways in which Bunyan conforms to the traditional form of the story or radically alters it. First of all, Odysseus, like most good folk tale heroes, departs from home to come back to it in the end, overcoming a final danger or betrayal on his arrival. Christian leaves his home for good and travels to the Celestial City which is his true home. Yet there are many common features. There are the adventures and obstacles along the way and the general notion of a significant journey or quest. Vladimir Propp in his study of Russian folk tales provided an analysis of form and function which applies to all such stories and is relevant also to Bunyan. Propp noticed that the hero at the beginning of the tale is suffering some kind of lack or deprivation which causes him to leave home. Either he is a seeker in quest of his fortune, or a sufferer persecuted by some villainy, or both.[12] Christian's position certainly reflects both features of the folk hero, the active and passive; as Claude Brémond has more recently described him, he is both *agent* and *patient*.[13] He has listened to the word of God and is acting on it but is a sufferer from countless sources from the time of his setting out. Important in most folk stories is the Helper who is usually the giver of a precious gift to assist the hero in his quest; this role in *The Pilgrim's Progress* is played by Evangelist whose gift is his recurrent unfolding of the truth of Scripture; to a secondary degree the role of Helper is also played by the Interpreter who makes a gift of the symbolic pictures in his house and by the women representative of virtues who refresh and then arm Christian in the House Beautiful. Faithful and Hopeful are equal companions rather than particular helpers; here one is reminded of some remarkable parallels with one of the earliest documents of our civilization, that sombre and elegiac work that has been named the *Epic of Gilgamesh*: in that work we have the touching relationship between Gilgamesh and his companion Enkidu who pursue the quest together.

When the hero, with or without his companion, has been prepared or armed by the Helper or giver of gifts, as Christian is at the House Beautiful, after his earlier instruction, there usually ensues a conflict with an evil power or creature in which the hero is successful. In the *Epic of Gilgamesh*, although Enkidu is at first unwilling, Gilgamesh embarks on a forest journey through the Land of Cedars and declares: 'Because of the evil that is in the land, we will go to the forest and destroy the evil; for in the forest lives Humbaba whose name is "Hugeness"', a ferocious giant. Gilgamesh is overcome by weakness before his fight as Christian is during it, but at last arms himself as Christian had done before sallying forth:

> At length Gilgamesh heard him; he put on his breast-plate, 'The Voice of Heroes', of thirty shekels' weight; he put it on as though it had been a light garment that he carried, and it covered him altogether.[14]

Humbaba as described by Enkidu is much like Apollyon. 'O my lord, you do not know this monster, and that is the reason you are not afraid. I who know him, I am terrified. His teeth are dragon's fangs, his countenance is like a lion, his charge is the rushing of the flood, with his look he crushes alike the trees of the forest and reeds in the swamp.' Apollyon has a mouth like a lion and wings like a dragon. 'Out of his belly came Fire and Smoke', and Humbaba too can blaze forth fire. The common features rest in common however wide the cultural separation and despite the fact that Apollyon is not purely legendary but a projection of the Devil as slayer of souls. Finally, to complete the parallels between the two works, there is a search for the source of everlasting life by Gilgamesh in which he has to pass through the great mountain whose name is Mashu which guards the rising and the setting sun. There is a remarkable resemblance to the terror of darkness which Christian undergoes in the Valley of the Shadow of Death:

> When he had gone one league the darkness became thick around him, for there was no light, he could see nothing ahead and nothing behind him. After two leagues the darkness was thick and there was no light, he could see nothing ahead and nothing behind him. After three leagues the darkness was thick, and there was no light, he could see nothing ahead and nothing behind him . . .[15]

And so with incremental repetition until Gilgamesh emerges from the mountain: 'After ten leagues the end was near. After eleven leagues the dawn light appeared. At the end of twelve leagues the sun streamed out.' The Valley of the Shadow of Death is 'as dark as pitch', and the dreamer says of Christian: 'Thus he went on, and I heard him here sigh bitterly: for, besides the dangers mentioned above, the path way was here so dark, that oft times when he lift up his foot to set forward, he knew not where, or upon what he should set it next' (p. 97). The darkness is dissolved by the morning when Christian can look back in safety on 'the hobgoblins, and satyrs, and dragons of the pit' that have tormented him. But here the archetypal terror of womb-like darkness which the hero has to struggle through to reach rebirth has been reinterpreted in the light of Bunyan's biblical imagination. He has started with a main theme drawn from Psalm 23: 4: 'Though I walk through the valley of the shadow of death, I will fear none ill, for thou art with me', and superimposed on it two other images from texts in order to express the turning of darkness into morning and the light which discovers to him the creatures of the pit when he looks back: Amos 5: 8: 'He hath turned the shadow of death into the morning' and Job 12: 22: 'He discovereth deep things out of darkness, and bringeth out to light the shadow of death.'

Bunyan's transformation in this manner of the folk-tale themes means that we can make only a partial application of the categories of Propp to *The Pilgrim's Progress*. But there are throughout the work marked parallels to the invariants and variables of Propp's classification. At the beginning the City of Destruction is the equivalent of the folk story beginning 'in a certain kingdom'. Christian is the member of a family but he is a father, not the usual younger son with his secular cleverness or good fortune. There are prophecies and forewarnings from Evangelist at his various appearances. Christian is in one sense, like the folk-tale hero, a fully formed character who does not develop, the development being in the ups and downs of the narrative; Christian is making the same mistakes and showing the same weaknesses quite late in the story, as when he falls into the hands of Giant Despair. But this is strongly qualified by Bunyan's limited realism, as when Christian plays the older and more experienced pilgrim to Hopeful's tyro: 'Thou speakest like one on whose head is the shell to this day.' There is the violation of an interdiction, rebuked by Evangelist after the encounter with Worldly-Wiseman. The episodes of Apollyon and Doubting Castle represent the first and second appearances of the villain, and Wordly-Wiseman as a minor villain is the type who acts by means of persuasion. The role of the Helper is shared between Evangelist, the Interpreter, and 'an hand with some of the leaves of the Tree of Life' which revive Christian during his fight with Apollyon. At the House Beautiful there is the customary provision for the journey of the hero. Ignorance right up to his exposure and doom at the end corresponds to the role of the false hero; Hopeful and Christian's conversation with him and discussion of him afterwards illustrate the desire to distinguish a false hero or pilgrim from a true one, now subordinated to a theological model (Propp's Table VII). The transfiguration of Christian and his companion at the end when they enter the Celestial City ('and lo, as they entered, they were transfigured, and they had raiment put on that shone like gold') bears a general resemblance to the anagnorisis of the folk hero when after disguise or obscurity he is revealed in his true colours at the end (as for instance, to take a familiar English example, when in the Middle English Breton lay *Sir Orfeo* Orfeo in his beggar harper's dress is recognized by his steward in the hall); but again the Christian patterning turns the folk material in an entirely new direction since Sir Orfeo and other heroes return to what they were to possess their rightful inheritance or kingdom while Christian and Hopeful are transformed into citizens of a heavenly country:

> These all died in faith . . . and confessed that they were strangers and pilgrims on the earth.
>
> For they that say such things declare plainly that they seek a country.
>
> And truly, if they had been mindful of that country from whence they came out, they might have had opportunity to have returned.
>
> But now they desire a better country, that is, an heavenly: wherefore God is not ashamed to be called their God: for he hath prepared for them a city.

It is in words similar to these from Hebrews 11: 13–16 that Christian and Faithful tell the inhabitants of Vanity Fair that they are strangers and pilgrims on the earth and have no part in their community.

Thus the folk-tale elements of the First Part are interpenetrated at every point by the passionate involvement of Bunyan's Calvinist Christianity. In the terms employed by Northrop Frye there is an interplay of myth and fable, the myth constituted by a Calvinist reading of the Bible sustains and transforms the folk-tale themes.[16] The journey through a dark forest or descent into the underworld, the overcoming of a monster, the helpers, opponents and companions, even the entry into a land of heart's desire, are subtly changed into something different but there is still a profitable tension between the elements that saves *The Pilgrim's Progress* from the limitations of the tract. Northrop Frye has spoken elsewhere of this problem as one of the central dilemmas of literature: 'If literature is didactic it tends to injure its own integrity; if it ceases wholly to be didactic, it tends to injure its own seriousness.'[17]

There is another blend of modes which may sometimes seem to furnish a clash rather than a blending. This lies in the Puritan schema of emblematic signs and episodes each of which is indubitably related to a single recognizable and unambiguous meaning and the continuities of character and adventure-plot. Often the two approaches cross each other. The relationship of Christiana and Mercy in Part II is touching and interesting in itself; she accompanies Christiana on pilgrimage as a friend and there is a considerable softening of the atmosphere from that at the beginning of the First Part when Christian puts his fingers in his ears so as not to hear the cries of his abandoned wife and children as he runs away shouting 'Life, life, eternal life'. When Mercy comes to the Wicket Gate (Christ) she fears for her reception and faints away:

> 'O Sir,' said she, [to the Keeper of the Gate] 'I am faint, there is scarce life left in me.' But he answered that one once said, *'When my soul fainted within me, I remembered the Lord, and my prayer came in unto thee, into thy holy temple.* Fear not, but stand upon thy feet, and tell me wherefore thou art come.'
>
> *Mercy.* I am come, for that unto which I was never invited, as my friend Christiana was. Hers was from the King, and mine was but from her, wherefore I fear I presume.
>
> 'Did she desire thee to come with her to this place?'
>
> *Mercy.* Yes. And as my Lord sees, I am come. And if there is any grace and forgiveness of sins to spare, I beseech that I thy poor handmaid may be partaker thereof.
>
> Then he took her again by the hand, and led her gently in, and said : 'I pray for all them that believe on me, by what means soever they come unto me.'
>
> (pp. 236–7)

Yet in spite of the emotional contrast between the two passages, and indeed between the worlds of feeling in Part I and Part II, both are equally Biblical in the support the author calls upon in his marginal gloss. Christ answers Mercy in the words of Jonah 2: 7 on the soul fainting within him but remembering the Lord; and the apparently Manichean abandonment of family and civil society by Christian is simply a dramatization of Luke 14: 26: 'If any man come to me, and hate not his father, and mother, and wife, and children, and brethren, and sisters, yea, and his own life also, he cannot be my disciple.' The stress on mercy and hope for sinners in place of the uncompromising urgency of Part I is product of those years preceding the publication of Part II in 1684 when Bunyan the preacher was especially engaged in offering assurances to tender consciences in the church and through highly popular treatises like *Come and Welcome to Jesus Christ.*

It is as if there is a two-way traffic between the array of Scripture references in the margin and the text itself. Or perhaps one could say that what we have is a work in reversible parallel columns. If we lean over towards the side of doctrine, then the story is a human commentary on that greater story which is seen as the Scriptures setting out the way of salvation; this is in the spirit of Bunyan's closing verses, '. . . Look within my veil, Turn up my metaphors': the allegory becomes a commentary and the marginalia become the text, a particular evangelical thesaurus or collocation of the Old and New Testaments in their application from God to man. If we 'read Bunyan for the story' the marginalia remain references like the footnote references giving sources but the balance is now such that the spiritual life of the sources has been fully embodied in the narrative. For the time of its reading we then have a work that does not merely illustrate truth but incorporates it. This of course was the great fear and objection of early critics of *The Pilgrim's Progress* on theological grounds, like the T.S. who issued a dull and improving Second Part of his own; we should notice their perception of a certain aesthetic truth about the alarming totality and conviction of the work of art—its seriousness as creation, in fact—as well as simply recognizing their theological narrowness.

The relation of the successive episodes of Christian's pilgrimage to the stages of Bunyan's conversion as he describes them in *Grace Abounding* provides a thread of development which unites diverse episodes, pastoral, heroic, or realistic, and their interconnecting static passages of godly debate. I do not wish to discuss this very important aspect because I have written about it elsewhere. It suffices to say that all the stages of a soul's progress as charted by three generations of Puritan psychologists are there; from Destruction to the Cross and the Cross to the Delectable Mountains we have them, conviction of sin, legality, justification, santification, and growth in grace. I am more conerned with other aspects of the narrative form of the work, its qualities as fable and the strange ways in which other qualities pull it in contrary directions.

These latter directions become apparent in those parts of the narrative where Bunyan shows a suprising tendency to throw away his fiction, to turn up his own metaphors, without leaving it to the reader, or to break with the wholeness of his fable entirely in order to bring out the myth of its meaning. Sometimes this is to be found in those marginal notes which are not Scripture references. Evangelist's advice to Christian to find the Gate by following the shining light is unnecessarily glossed 'Christ and the way to him cannot be found without the Word'; the vivid episode of Little-faith from whom the thieves take his spending money but not his jewels is superfluously glossed 'No great heart for God, where there is but Little faith. We have more courage when out, than when we are in.' The realism of the imprisonment of Faithful and Christian in Vanity Fair, their trial for treason and the execution of the former, is blurred by an unconvincing and incompletely explained release of Christian so that his story may be continued:

> But as for Christian, he had some respite, and was remanded back to prison; so he there remained for a space: but he that over-rules all things, having the power of their rage in his own hand, so wrought it about that Christian for that time escaped them, and went his way.   (p. 134)

Perhaps the most amusing of these instances of the clash between fable and single-minded theological meaning is when Christian obtains for himself and Hopeful their escape from Doubting Castle by simply remembering that as a convinced believer he has had the means of release from this spiritual malady of despair all the time in his possession:

> 'What a fool,' quoth he, 'am I, thus to lie in a stinking dungeon, when I may as well walk at liberty. I have a key in my bosom, called promise, that will (I am persuaded) open any lock in Doubting-Castle.'   (p. 156)

For a moment the giant story with its Jack and the Beanstalk convincingness lies in ruins, only to be revived again when the creaking of the gate as they open it awakes Giant Despair, 'who hastily rising to pursue his prisoners, felt his limbs to fail, for his fits took him again, so that he could by no means go after them'. In fact none of these breaks in the continuity of the pure allegorical fiction cause as much damage to the unity of the fable or confusion to the reader as might at first have been supposed. The reason, I suggest, is the presence of the dreamer throughout, who dreams like a dreamer in an actual dream, much more so than many of the witnesses of dream allegories. The relation of the traditional popular story to the dream is a close one: as in a dream all the characters are really aspects of the psyche of the hero, his hopes and fears, the self he aspires to, or the dark underside of his personality. The breaks and inconsistencies in *The Pilgrim's Progress* are justified by the inconsequentiality of the dream, its abrupt transitions and sudden interventions of fresh material. This is the way we should take the episode of Vanity Fair when something like a Restoration trial scene under a judge like Jeffreys is transformed into an early Christian martyrdom straight as it were from the early part of Foxe's *Acts and Monuments*.

I have been deliberately selective, concentrating on the narrative of *The Pilgrim's Progress* and hoping to elicit the mysterious but vital links between narrative in the traditional story and the springs of life itself. The long domination of the criticism of fiction by discussion of point of view and symbol, as in Henry James and E. M. Forster, their theory and practice, is giving way to a greater attention to the basic importance of the phenomenon or of the story itself. As Barbara Hardy has written, narrative is not just an invention of artists to order experience but 'a primary act of mind transferred to art from life itself . . . For we dream in narrative, daydream in narrative, remember, anticipate, hope, despair, believe, doubt, plan, revise, criticize, construct, gossip, learn, hate and love by narrative'.[18] Bunyan transfers narrative memory of his own belief and doubts to the half-conscious dreams of his prison period or to day-dreams as when in *Grace Abounding* he has to pass through a little door in a wall to reach the godly people of Bedford on the other side; then in a final stage life that has become memory and dream is transferred to art: so we have the Wicket Gate that is Christ and the different personages met along the road.

The reader is involved because Christian's progress is a reflection of the common human story, its hopes and fears. We live always at a single point of time with perspectives forwards and backwards: we have beginnings and endings. If life is story-shaped Bunyan's story takes us back deep into the issues of human life because it runs with a resolute naturalness and a dream-like vividness that ignore mere literary effects. That the First Part should end terribly with the fate of Ignorance, not with the trumpets and triumphs of the City, has been criticized on grounds of taste, but it has a power beyond the too easy ending with a celestial choir. Like a modern anti-novelist Bunyan exposes the illusions of 'literature'. In life itself there are no perfectly happy endings, and Part I of *The Pilgrim's Progress* ends, as do *Piers Plowman* and *The Holy War*, with the striving, the necessary continuation of the imperfect human struggle.

NOTES

1. This paper first appeared as the Thirty-Second Annual Lecture of the Friends of Dr Williams's Library (1978) and is reprinted here with the kind permission of the Trustees of the Library.
2. In *Table Talk*; Roberta Florence Brinkley (ed.), *Coleridge on the Seventeenth Century* (New York, 1968), p. 475.
3. *Literary Remains* (1838), iii. 398.
4. *The Gentleman's Magazine* (1765), p. 168.
5. *The Works of that Eminent Servant of Christ Mr. John Bunyan* (1692).
6. G. Offor (ed.), *The Works of John Bunyan* (1862), i. 556.
7. *Works*, ed. Offor, iii. 561.
8. Gwilym O. Griffith, *John Bunyan* (1927), p. 228.

9. Walter Benjamin, 'The Storyteller', in *Illuminations* (1970), pp. 83–109.

10. Ibid., pp. 84–5.

11. W. P. Ker, *Epic and Romance* (1908 edn), pp. 18–19.

12. Vladimir Propp, 'The morphology of the folk tale', *International Journal of American Linguistics* (Indiana University Research Centre in Anthropology, Folklore and Linguistics, Bloomington), vol. 24 (1958). Cf. Anne Wilson, *Traditional Romance and Tale* (1976), pp. 57 ff.

13. Claude Brémond, *Logique du Récit* (Paris, 1973), pp. 139–241.

14. *The Epic of Gilgamesh, An English Version*, with an Introduction by N. K. Sandars (1964), p. 78.

15. Ibid., p. 96.

16. Northrop Frye, *The Secular Scripture* (1976).

17. 'The Road of Excess', in Bernice Slate (ed.), *Myth and Symbol: Critical Approaches and Applications* (Lincoln, 1963), p. 14.

18. 'Towards a poetics of fiction: An approach through narrative', *Novel* (1968), p. 5. Cf. Stephen Crites, 'The narrative quality of fiction', *Journal of the American Academy of Religion* (1971), pp. 291–311, and Brian Wicker, *The Story-Shaped World: Fiction and Metaphysics; Some Variations on a Theme* (1975), pp. 33–49.

Dialogue and Debate in
The Pilgrim's Progress

DAVID SEED

Dialogue accounts for most of both parts of *The Pilgrim's Progress* in terms of sheer bulk. It is surprising that it has not received more critical attention. F. R. Leavis, for instance, has praised Bunyan's prose generally for its 'free idiomatic range and vividness', but he is mainly interested in its culturally symbolic value so that he can locate Bunyan in a vernacular tradition stretching back to the Middle Ages.[1] In fact Bunyan's use of dialogue shows an extremely sophisticated awareness of different levels of discourse and considerable skill at characterization. In histories of the English novel it is sometimes claimed that novelists were able to construct dialogue because they were either interested in theatre or were practising playwrights.[2] The example of Bunyan provides an important exception to this theory. His regional colloquialisms suggest that he wrote directly from life, but it is essential also to insist on his artistry. In his pacing and arrangement of dialogue he shows a fine sense of psychology in both speaker and listener. Of course we must not expect the kind of consistency that would come from an explicit theoretical awareness of his methods but Roger Sharrock's claim that he 'worked without any critical understanding of the potentialities of the various narrative forms he employed' needs to be resisted.[3] His skill at dialogue alone shows that the myth of Bunyan the semi-literate 'mechanick' has persisted too long.

The Puritan emphasis on individual responsibility for one's salvation led naturally to a view of life as being full of dangers. The convert was faced with the need to engage actively with the forces of evil. When, in *The Pilgrim's Progress*, Faithful sings 'let the pilgrims then be vigilant', this could stand as an exhortation for Puritan life generally. Nonconformist literature of Bunyan's period was full of metaphors of battle or striving, behind which lay the implication that the believer (or 'professor') was tested and proved by his capacity to survive ordeals.

The medium for these tests was often verbal. In May 1659 Bunyan was confronted in mid-sermon by the Revd Thomas Smith, professor of Arabic at Cambridge, who challenged his right to preach. Nothing daunted by his opponent's status, Bunyan exchanged biblical precedents with him.[4] The result was inconclusive, but the episode demonstrates that if ability in debate was necessary to the Puritan convert, it was positively essential to the preacher. Debate then was a fact of life to Bunyan, whether in the printed or spoken word.

It is hardly surprising that Bunyan's religious activities should have brought him into conflict with the law. The Nonconformist sects generally put a heavy stress on preaching, and in 1626 an Act was passed prohibiting either preaching or writing on controversial issues.[5] The story of Bunyan's arrest and imprisonment in 1660 is well known but his own account of his hearings far less so. *A Relation of the Imprisonment of Mr. John Bunyan, Minister of the Gospel at Bedford, in November, 1660*, published in 1765 as a supplement to *Grace Abounding*, shows at one and the same time Bunyan's skill at constructing dialogue and the Puritan's need to be successful in debate. Here Bunyan displays exactly the same fearlessness in the face of authority that he had shown in his meeting with Thomas Smith. He emerges as a courageous man of principle, one unwilling to compromise no matter what physical hardship he might have to endure.

His account of the Bedford hearings is almost comically flattering to himself, partly because Bunyan presents most of it in reported speech, which constantly reminds the reader that he is shaping the materials, summarizing and selecting speech. But perhaps the most impressive part of *A Relation* is the conversation between Bunyan and the local Clerk of the Peace, a certain Mr Cobb—impressive above all because it demonstrates Bunyan's ability to capture the natural inflexions of speech. Cobb tries to persuade Bunyan to observe the law, but Bunyan is wily and evasive. He declares his allegiance to the king and Cobb comments:

> Well, said he, I do not profess myself to be a man that can dispute; but this I say, truly, neighbour *Bunyan*, I would have you consider this matter seriously, and submit yourself; you may have your liberty to exhort your neighbour in private discourse, so be you do not call together an assembly of people; and truly you may do much good to the church of Christ, if you would go this way; and this you may do, and the law not abridge you of it. It is your private meetings that the law is against.
>
> *Bun.* Sir, said I, if I may do good to one by my discourse, why may I not do good to two? And if to two, why not to four, and so to eight, &c.
>
> *Cobb.* I, saith he, and to a hundred, I warrant you.
>
> *Bun.* Yes, Sir, said I, I think I should not be forbid to do as much good as I can.
>
> *Cobb.* But, saith he, you may but pretend to do good, and indeed, notwithstanding, do harm, by seducing the people; you are therefore denied your meeting so many together, lest you should do harm.
>
> *Bun.* And yet, said I, you say the law tolerates me to discourse with my neighbour; surely there is no law tolerates me to seduce any one; therefore if I may by the law discourse with one, surely it is to do him good; and if I by discoursing may do good to one, surely, by the same law, I may do good to many.
>
> *Cobb.* The law, saith he, doth expressly forbid your private meetings, therefore they are not to be tolerated.[6]

It is obvious from this passage that Cobb is a plain man. He is speaking as one neighbour to another, offering friendly advice. Bunyan's defiance, however, so obviously annoys him that Bunyan in turn understates his own actions (he is only 'doing good'). Cobb then tries to explain, rather crudely. The thinking behind the law. In this he is outwitted by Bunyan, only to fall back, no doubt with irritation, on a plain assertion of the law.

The direct speech admirably catches Cobb's mixed tone of

sympathy and disapproval. He even seems to respect 'good-man Bunyan', as he calls him. Bunyan himself, on the other hand, goes through an amazingly varied series of stances. He shows himself to be articulate; he cleverly deflects the claims of the civil authorities; and he professes humility although he constantly demonstrates a pride in argument. Disingenuously he declares 'Truly Sir . . . I do not desire to commend myself, but to think meanly of myself' (i. 58). Whatever he professes, Bunyan nevertheless carries the day. For all Cobb's friendliness, Bunyan is constantly on his guard, determined to resist his opponent and prove himself 'right'.

This example of dialogue/debate is public and external. But the Puritan might be subjected to assaults from within as well as without. The danger might come from the claims of a rival authority or another's plausibility; or it might come from personal weakness. A crucial text for understanding the psychological dimension of dialogue is Bunyan's spiritual autobiography, *Grace Abounding* (1666). Here he describes how, in the middle of a game, 'a voice did suddenly dart from heaven into my soul' (i. 8). This marks the first pang of Bunyan's conscience and throughout the work he engages in a private inner debate with these voices. The climactic moment of this debate is described as follows:

> . . . one morning as I did lie in my bed, I was . . . most fiercely assaulted with this temptation, *to sell, and part with Christ*; the wicked suggestion still running in my mind, *Sell him, sell him, sell him, sell him, sell him*, as fast as a man could speak: Against which also, in my mind, as at other times, I answered, *No, No, not for thousands, thousands, thousands.* . . .   (i. 23)

The metaphor of physical struggle merges with the notion of debate, the latter being emphasized by references to speech ('answered', 'speak') and by the typography (the italics are those of early editions). Although the debate is nominally internal ('in my mind'), the distinction between inner and outer collapses into irrelevance because Bunyan is using the formal convention of a 'voice' for both. The workings of his conscience are thus externalized into a kind of speech. In

Grace Abounding only the voices associated with the Devil take an active part in the debate; when God speaks it is to make authoritative statements. This process could be potentially terrifying to the convert because he is not sure of the origin of his own thoughts. We can see this in *The Pilgrim's Progress* when Christian is passing through the Valley of the Shadow. A demon suggests blasphemous thoughts to him and Christian, understandably unnerved, begins to think he is losing control over his own mind. Bunyan glosses this demon marginally as 'Satan'; but his works show that if Satan's purpose is one, his voices are many.

Various critics have paid tribute to Bunyan's capacity to externalize spiritual events through concrete images.[7] The same could be said of his use of dialogue which renders external the fears and trials experienced during and after conversion and thereby makes them more accessible to Bunyan's audience. To a twentieth-century reader the act of thought and the act of speech may seem poles apart. But because Bunyan uses the same formal convention for both, the distinction ceases to be important. Both are rendered in dialogue. Dialogue thus becomes a means of dramatizing self-examination as well as presenting confrontations with hostile agencies.

Broadly speaking the characters whom Christian meets on his journey fall into two categories: the tempters and the instructors. The tempters, such as Talkative or Mr Worldly-Wiseman, raise obstacles to Christian's pilgrimage, whereas the instructors help him to understand his own experiences. One of the main rhythms of Part I is that of an event being followed by a brief explanatory interlude. Because every event is a potential *exemplum* it must be ransacked for its significance; and this Christian is unable to do alone—at least in the early stages of his journey. So Help explains the Slough of Despond to Christian, Good Will instructs him on how to proceed once he has passed the Straight Gate, and the shepherds of the Delectable Mountains interpret the landscape before Christian and Hopeful. These encounters have the appearance of dialogues but the communication is fundamentally in one direction: Christian either receives knowledge or has his knowledge tested. At the beginning he is relatively passive and ignorant, but as his journey progresses he grows in understanding and in his powers of self-analysis. Thus when he loses his roll he is quite capable of interpreting the event for himself with appropriate biblical parallels.

A stage in the process is marked when Christian arrives at the Palace Beautiful. The damsel Piety invites him to give an account of his experiences which helps him to understand them retrospectively and at the same time gives moral benefit to his listeners. Like most of the conversations in *The Pilgrim's Progress* this one must be 'profitable' in that it must serve a direct moral aim. The dialogue Christian engages in has an edge since he is being put to a kind of test. His memory, motivation and powers of assimilation are being examined—unobtrusively, but examined none the less. This is particularly true when Charity inquires closely about his family. With such a name we might expect a gentle sentimental figure but the rapid interchange between question and answer suggests a legal interrogation or a catechism. Later in his journey Christian proves capable of explaining his experiences without any external compulsion, and this in turn suggests that he has grown in moral awareness.

The Shining One who releases Christian from Flatterer's net, the damsels of the Palace Beautiful and the other minor expository figures who appear in Part I all tend to speak with the same anonymous voice. They have no identifying peculiarities of speech quite simply because they all perform the same kind of function, namely to instruct or examine Christian. The only instructor who takes on any kind of 'character' is Evangelist, of whom Roger Sharrock rightly comments, 'he suggests an idealized portrait of some great spiritual preacher'.[8] He stays in the foreground of the narrative partly from the frequency of his appearances, and partly by the range of emotions he shows. Evangelist is of course a guide and instructor, but he directs Christian with solicitude at the beginning of his journey. This gentleness, however, does not prevent him from sternly upbraiding Christian when he has been diverted out of his way by Mr Worldly-Wiseman. He confronts Christian with an abrupt question, 'What doest thou here?' (p. 51)—a question which strikes the other speechless. Under the guise of accusing him, Evangelist forces Christian to retrace the steps by which he was led out of the way. By so doing Christian comes to understand how he went wrong. In other words Evangelist uses the question-and-answer sequence for a heuristic purpose: he wants to help Christian discover for himself how to practise Christian doctrine correctly. Once the latter has admitted his fault he is ripe for a homily which Evangelist proceeds to give him, firstly through a terrifyingly absolute statement about the fate of backsliders, and secondly through possible sources of hope for Christian. It is in his manipulation of Christian's reactions that Evangelist seems like an ideal preacher. And plainly he will only have an important part to play whilst Christian is relatively ignorant or unconfident. When he reappears shortly before the arrival at Vanity Fair it is largely to exhort the pilgrims (Christian has been joined by Faithful) and to predict future events.

Critics have commented frequently on Christian's isolation in Part I, but this has been rather over-stated.[9] Even before he meets Faithful, Christian has had the benefit of the anonymous instructors and of course Evangelist. When he emerges from the Valley of the Shadow and encounters Faithful, we are enabled to see Christian's character more fully from the way in which the two pilgrims hold 'sweet discourse' together and compare notes about their experiences. They can do this between themselves without any intermediary; and yet their conversations must be turned towards their moral improvement.

Apart from supplying companionship, Faithful also helps to define Christian dramatically. When the two meet, Christian shouts for the other to wait for him; Faithful does not; Christian runs ahead 'vain-gloriously' only to fall down helplessly until Faithful catches him up. This incident gives a clue to a tendency which Christian shows during his journey to Vanity Fair. For once *he* is asking the question instead of being examined and this leads him towards an assumption of superiority over Faithful. He gives some explanatory comments on the latter's narrative, but the episode which presents Christian most obviously in this new, and perhaps somewhat unflattering light is the encounter with Talkative. Faithful is particularly impressed by his plausible tongue and comments to Christian that Talkative would make a good pilgrim:

> *Christian.* At this Christian modestly smiled, and said, This man with whom you are taken will beguile with this tongue of his twenty of them that know him not.
>
> *Faithful.* Do you know him then?
>
> *Christian.* Know him! Yes, better than he knows himself.
>
> *Faithful.* Pray what is he?
>
> *Christian.* His name is Talkative, he dwelleth in our town; I wonder that you should be a stranger to him, only I consider that our town is large.
>
> *Faithful.* Whose son is he? And whereabouts doth he dwell?
>
> *Christian.* He is the son of one Saywell, he dwelt in Prating-row; and he is known of all that are acquainted with him, by the name of Talkative in Prating-row, and notwithstanding his fine tongue, he is but a sorry fellow.
>
> *Faithful.* Well, he seems to be a very pretty man.
>
> *Christian.* That is, to them that have not thorough acquaintance with him, for he is best abroad; . . .
>
> (pp. 112–13)

Christian's smile is hardly modest. It comes from the satisfaction of knowledge. In this exchange he presents himself as sophisticated and worldly-wise, in absolute contrast to Faithful's naïve credulousness. The way Christian contradicts his estimate of Talkative maximizes its impact rather than 'modestly' underplaying it. His opening remark to Faithful is deliberately quiet so as to surprise him all the more. When Faithful shows his surprise, Christian uses a device common to *The Pilgrim's Progress* in seizing on the key verb of another's speech and repeating it in an exclamatory way. Christian doubles the repetitive force of 'know'/'knows' by claiming an absolute knowledge of Talkative. This line is crucial for impressing Faithful, who then uses colloquial gap-fillers like 'well' or indications of respect like 'pray' (very common throughout the book), both being signs that he is ready to receive instruction from Christian. This dialogue then is at its most realistic and colloquial when Christian is trying to change Faithful's attitude. Once the change has been effected, Christian's words become less and less realistic. When he describes Talkative in the lines immediately following the quoted passage, he uses the compact epigrammatic antitheses of the seventeenth-century character books. Evidently Faithful learns his lesson, because he himself turns catechist in order to bring out Talkative's failings.

Faithful is never developed as a character, perhaps because it would distract us from his role as martyr. But, as if Bunyan had realized what profit and added drama could be gained from playing off another character against Christian, Hopeful is introduced as soon as Christian leaves Vanity Fair. He is explicitly described as a replacement for Faithful and a companion to Christian (p. 135). The resemblance is much closer than this however. Hopeful is also a naive figure. When Demas tempts them to visit his silver-mine he is childishly eager to go. Christian restrains him and then identifies Demas for his benefit. Considering the care with which Christian does this, it is extremely ironic that he should be the one to lead them into By-Path Meadow. When they get into difficulties both react predictably:

> Then Hopeful groaned in himself, saying, 'Oh that I had kept on my way!'
> *Christian.* Who could have thought that this path should have led us out of the way?
> *Hopeful.* I was afraid on't at very first, and therefore gave you that gentle caution. I would have spoke plainer, but that you are older than I.
> *Christian.* Good brother, be not offended, I am sorry I have brought thee out of the way . . . (p. 150)

Hopeful groans '*in himself*' for fear of seeming to criticize his elder and, as he thinks, better. Even when he does answer Christian's rather pathetic question to himself, he is deferential in his criticism, using the respectful pronoun 'you' (as to a superior). Christian apologizes, his apology is accepted, and then the two pilgrims can use the more intimate pronoun 'thee'.[10] This does not simply indicate that they are on more equal terms, but gives Hopeful his cue to take over the positive role, for it is he who resists the temptations of despair during their imprisonment in Doubting Castle. Despite his youth it is Hopeful who instructs Christian in this predicament, and not vice versa.

Hopeful, then, escapes being an abstraction for a variety of reasons. Firstly his speech is distinguished linguistically from Christian's in using far more colloquialisms. In the last passage quoted it makes quite a clear contrast, although this is not maintained consistently. When Hopeful is explaining the pitfalls of despair to Christian in Doubting Castle, his language becomes less colloquial, more formal with relatively elaborate syntax. The reason for this is not that Bunyan attempted to be realistic and failed, but that the importance of the local subject-matter changes the register in which Hopeful speaks. His language becomes more solemn in proportion to the subject. In exactly the same way the various pilgrims bid a formal adieu to each other in an elevated biblical language at the end of Part II. Their encounter with death marks the climax of their journey and lifts their language accordingly.

Apart from being a companion for Christian, Hopeful also acts as a dramatic foil to him. Their relationship is constantly shifting and this fluidity contributes to the realism of both figures. Once they have escaped from Doubting Castle, Christian regains his self-confidence and takes over the initiative by lecturing Hopeful about Little-faith. At one point he asks why Little-faith did not pawn his jewels. Christian's answer is prompt and sarcastic: 'Thou talkest like one upon whose head is the shell to this very day' (p. 166). This snub takes Hopeful aback and makes him ask 'Why art thou so tart, my brother?' The question reflects Hopeful's essential simplicity, but it is also unconsciously ironic for by this point Christian has gone back to his self-chosen role as guide and mentor to his companion. By no means could he be described as a 'brother'. The ironies continue to accumulate. Christian argues Hopeful down by sheer weight of biblical precedents and then compares him to Little-faith in being unable to withstand combat ('. . . I perceive by thee, my brother, . . . thou art but for a brush and then to yield' [p.

168]). His repetition of 'brother' is offensively patronizing and his criticism of Hopeful particularly misplaced since it was Hopeful who helped them out of Doubting Castle and it will be Hopeful who helps him across the River of Death. To crown it all, after boasting of his ability to resist opponents, Christian moralizes 'Let us never . . . vaunt as if we could do better' (p. 170).

These details imply that Bunyan is using Hopeful to expose weaknesses in Christian. The ironies and nuances mentioned above certainly make Christian seem realistic but less than admirable. They seriously damage his moral stature. For example, when Christian is talking to Atheist, he appears to believe him at first. Then, after Hopeful has warned him off, he claims he only did so to 'prove' (i.e. test) his companion. It is difficult to avoid reading this explanation sceptically since in general Christian treats Hopeful in an overweening, condescending way. Even as late as their journey across the Enchanted Ground he irritably asks Hopeful if he is weary of their 'discourse'. Christian at many points seems to be more interested in jockeying for a superior position in their dialogue than in its moral substance. Does this mean then that Bunyan wanted Christian's faults to be clearly visible? There is a constant uncertainty throughout the last half of Part I as to how far we should admire Christian or not.

The figures who have drawn critical praise for their realism have been the tempters in Part I. For the most part the instructors are anonymous (even though they are given names) because they use what Norman Page calls 'neutral speech'. This he glosses as 'stylistically undifferentiated, non-idiosyncratic dialogue which serves some other purpose than contributing to characterization'.[11] Their purpose of course is to comment on what has befallen Christian and to explain its significance, whereas such persons as Mr Worldly-Wiseman actually constitute threats to Christian every bit as serious as the physical obstacles he encounters. Mr Worldly-Wiseman greets Christian in a breezy friendly manner ('How now, good fellow', [p. 48]) and even offers him 'counsel'. His manner is insinuating and at this early stage in his journey Christian is not at all wary of such figures. Indeed he addresses Worldly-Wiseman as 'sir', as if speaking to his superior. His very name suggests that he has more knowledge than Christian and he uses this advantage to stress the physical dangers which Christian is heading for. Like most of the tempters in Part I he levels a prudential argument against Christian, contrasting domestic comfort with solitary danger. Having only just been pulled out of the Slough of Despond by Help, Christian mistakes his friendly tone and wanders off the straight path. His fundamental weakness at this point is in not being able to distinguish between a tempter and an instructor.

In the course of Christian's journey he demonstrates his moral and spiritual growth by his increasing ability to withstand such figures as Worldly-Wiseman. Although his meeting with Formalist and Hypocrisy happens soon afterwards, Christian is far less hesitant. He parries their legalistic arguments from custom and precedent, and draws his own moral conclusions from the incident. His firmness is important since Worldly-Wiseman had attacked not his beliefs but his character, accusing him of being weak and self-deluded.

Because the book's subject is religious, Christian must grow in moral stature (and fill out as a character) during his exchanges with the other figures. Apollyon, for instance, is remembered for his battle and horrific appearance. But these are relatively crude details compared with the subtlety of his dialogue with Christian. He challenges him with all the authoritative tone of a ruler, and much of their argument revolves around rival political claims of allegiance. As soon as Christian shows signs of resistance Apollyon slily shifts his ground to present himself as generous and lenient, asking only that Christian returns home. Their argument is inconclusive until Apollyon scores his most telling thrust when he accuses Christian of being faint-hearted and vainglorious. This stops Christian in his tracks, but only for a moment:

> All this is true, and much more, which thou hast left out; but the Prince whom I serve and honour is merciful and ready to forgive.   (p. 92)

By admitting the charges Christian has in effect answered them; and by retaining his faith in God he has demonstrated his constancy. The argument is typical of Part I in that Christian must win it in order to prove himself.

The general implication is that Christian's skill at debate is directly correlated to his spiritual stature. Growth in the one parallels an increase in the other. And since so much is at stake there is frequently more drama in the dialogues than their surface might suggest. Christian's confrontations with Apollyon and Mr Worldly-Wiseman are representative in that they test his moral strength rather than question his religious beliefs. The nearest to explicit theoretical debate comes in the dialogue with Ignorance but even here the latter's defeat in argument only confirms our awareness that he is deluded. This debate is of interest mainly because it plays ironically on the theme of knowledge rather than for abstract doctrinal issues which might be raised.

Roger Sharrock has commented that these various figures all represent states of mind, but that Bunyan has moulded them into 'lively minor characters'.[12] But Dorothy Van Ghent has pinned down Bunyan's method rather more closely:

> Bunyan's skill in swift characterization is of the very highest; he reproduces, on a person's first entrance into the tale, the precise and inevitable tone of voice, the mood of the verb, the idiom, and the syntactical rhythm which will put the speaker before us in his essential moral life, and which will cast upon the episode the energy and conviction of reality.[13]

Certain key qualities are insisted on here with admirable precision. Firstly, because most of the episodes are very brief, speed is of the essence; Bunyan can only pay attention to essentials. And secondly, this must be done through speech, since virtually no visual description is supplied. Thirdly, although the characters are realistic they are usually emblematic. In other words their speech identifies them as type-figures, not as full individuals.

The episodes with the different characters depend almost entirely on dialogue. Description is usually minimal —Ignorance, for instance, appears as 'a very brisk lad' (p. 162); and occasional gestures towards social definition are made by stating which town a character has come from. But for the most part their speech defines them, and in this Bunyan uses several devices. A character might make an arresting impression from his first words. Mr Worldly-Wiseman gives an immediate indication of his general manner from the hearty way he greets Christian. Similarly, Apollyon challenges him before they fight. And in Part II when Mr Great-heart wakes Old Honest he shouts out: 'What's the matter? Who are you? and what is your business here?' (p. 299). In all these cases the first impression is the correct one. Apollyon pretends to be generous but soon drops his mask; Old Honest shows himself to be bluff, direct, and dependable throughout his journey. In the briefer episodes a single mannerism or phrase might define the character. Obstinate's speech is full of exclamations and abusive epithets (he calls Christian variously 'crazed-headed', 'brain-sick', 'misled', and 'fantastical'), making very clear contrast with his more ingratiating companion Pliable. Formalist and Hypocrisy, who for practical purposes could be considered as one individual, use deceptively plain, matter-of-fact phrases ('if we are in, we are in' [p. 72]). Or lastly, Bunyan might allow a character to give himself away unconsciously. By-Ends, perhaps the only comic character of Part I, does this when he shows himself to be an absolute time-server. When Christian exposes him and then invites him to be a sincere convert, By-Ends's answer is an absurd inversion of true value: 'I shall never desert my old principles, since they are harmless and profitable' (p. 138). The term 'profitable' is an ironic echo of Christian's own vocabulary and is contradicted by 'harmless', just as By-Ends's general tone resembles that of the true convert. It is the gap between the sentiment and tone of voice which reveals him as a negative character.

Apart from particular devices of dialogue, Bunyan also shows his skill at combining moral purpose with characterization in his depiction of styles of speech. When Talkative meets Faithful and Christian, he expresses pleasure at having found travellers who appreciate good conversation:

I like you wonderful well, for your saying is full of

conviction; and I will add, what things so pleasant, and what so profitable, as to talk of the things of God?

What things so pleasant, that is, if a man hath any delight in thing that are wonderful, for instance, if a man doth delight to talk of the history or the mystery of things; or if a man doth love to talk of miracles, wonders, or signs, where shall he find things recorded so delightful, and so sweetly penned, as in the holy Scripture?

[Faithful agrees but with reservations.] That's true, but to be profited by such things in our talk should be that which we design.

Talkative. That is it that I said; for to talk of such things is most profitable, for by so doing, a man may get knowledge of many things.   (p. 111)

Faithful, as was suggested earlier, is rather naïve and accepts Talkative's flattery at its face value. But even Faithful is beginning to have doubts about him, doubts which prove to be eminently justified when his companion offers to talk about any subject at all. His syntax in the passage quoted becomes more and more cumulative. The second half of the first sentence is an explicit addition which includes two alternatives. The second sentence, in effect a grotesque repetition of the first, repeats phrases ('what things so pleasant') with or without modifications and also such terms as 'delight' or 'talk'. The syntax proffers a very broad range of alternatives; in piling phrase on phrase it seems designed to be as inclusive as possible. But by using whole or partial repetition Bunyan undermines the purpose of the statement. Talkative's verbosity is shown by a very careful and sophisticated play of vocabulary against syntax in his speech. Christian only identifies Talkative *after* he has begun to speak, thereby confirming the reader's impression, rather than anticipating it.

Talkative's efforts to be comprehensive are comically evident from the way in which he answers Faithful. He tries to engross the other's words in his own as if he wanted to dominate their conversation by sheer quantity. It is only with the help of Christian's warnings that Faithful can turn the tables on Talkative. He does this by constantly interrupting the other, until Talkative exclaims: 'You lie at the catch again, this is not for edification' (p. 118). He is partly right, for Faithful has been listening for vulnerable points which he can attack. But he misses the point in his second accusation. He cannot see the moral issues at stake since he measures discourse by purely internal standards. Good talk for him is quite independent of its moral worth and since this is the direct opposite to one of the book's main principles, it is essential that he should be defeated in argument, exposed and rejected.

The episode with Talkative fits into the larger question of Faithful's relation to Christian. By outwitting him in discourse Faithful proves himself in his and his companion's eyes. The care with which Bunyan orders the episode is, however, quite characteristic. Exactly the same care is exercised over the episodes with By-Ends and Ignorance. J. C. Forrest has brilliantly analysed the interplay between Ignorance and Hopeful:

> With an astonishing economy of line that adds a further dimension to the portrait, Bunyan here deftly sketches an eloquent chiaroscuro representing the truly hopeful man and the man who indulges a chimera, the sincerely humble man and the man whose modesty is a sham, the neighbor-loving holy man concerned for his fellow and the graceless man who takes his pleasure in walking alone.[14]

The final disclosure for Forrest comes when Ignorance stands exposed as a Pharisee. It is a moral conclusion. But Forrest argues convincingly that Bunyan adjusts the pace and sequence of events with the sophistication of a novelist in order to reach this end. His argument deals perhaps as much with plot as with dialogue but corroborates what has been suggested about the way we assimilate conversations such as that between Talkative and Faithful. Tone, texture, and order all perform crucial functions in the play of character against character in Part I.

When Bunyan began Part II of *The Pilgrim's Progress* he

attempted to combine two narrative modes: the dream and dialogue. It is the latter which is used the most in the opening pages. Mr Sagacity gives Bunyan a means of establishing a continuity between the two parts. He himself adopts the guise of a traveller unfamiliar with the surrounding district and he questions Sagacity about the reputation of Christian in the City of Destruction and about the subsequent fate of his wife Christiana. In this way both Bunyan and the reader are unobtrusively reminded of certain events and given a social context out of which Christiana's journey can grow. The conversation offers a means of understating the preliminary facts and of allowing information to emerge spontaneously. Sagacity's anecdotal style is quite appropriate to the social rumours he is recounting to Bunyan; but, having served this initial purpose, his subsequent abandonment goes virtually unnoticed.

Sagacity's descriptions point to one of the main differences between Part I and Part II. The latter, Roger Sharrock suggests, gives us 'a bustling, and on the whole a cheerful picture, of the life of a separatist church'.[15] The emphasis, in other words, is on the communal life of converts rather than on their individual destiny. This is reflected in the proliferation of characters; the landscape of Part II seems to be far more peopled. And the implied principle is pointed out explicitly by Mr Great-heart when he states that 'relations are our second self' (p. 351). Because the notion of responsibility has been broadened beyond the individual the narrative can take on more of a social texture.

We can see this difference in Bunyan's miniature character-studies. Feeble-mind, for instance, is rescued from the Giant Slay-good. The pilgrims then ask how he came to be there and who he is. As in Part I, Bunyan adjusts speech to character. Feeble-mind states apologetically:

> I am a man of no strength at all, of body, nor yet of mind, but would, if I could, though I can but crawl, spend my life in the pilgrim's way. (p. 323)

The elaborate conditioning and general care he takes over his words clearly suggests a nervous and ineffectual character. Within the group of pilgrims, Feeble-mind stands at the opposite extreme to the brief assertive phrasing of Valiant-for-Truth. Once again we receive an immediate impression of a character which must hint at actions that cannot be included in the narrative itself. Feeble-mind's timorous manner of speech gives sufficient explanation of how he fell into the giant's clutches; and Valiant-for-Truth's categorical assertion 'I . . . am going to the Celestial city' (p. 348) sums up his single-minded purpose and gives us a verbal demonstration of the spirit with which he fights off thieves.

This use of verbal styles is not new, but the order of each episode is. In Part II a character usually names himself to the pilgrims and then gives a narrative of how he came to be travelling. This Feeble-mind does and Old Honest then inquires about an acquaintance (suggested significantly by his speech). Here there is no hint of testing or verbal combat. In Part I Christian had to resist the vast majority of characters he met. Their faults were potentially dangerous because they might undermine his purpose. But Honest's words to Feeble-mind are friendly and mark his acceptance into the group. The typical rhythm of such episodes is quite different from Part I. The characters pose no threat so there is no need for debate. They are virtually all variations of a right-thinking convert, and so can be taken willingly into the group. This means that the character-studies in Part II have to be read differently. In Part I Christian (and the reader) was on the alert for signs of immorality. He was careful to look beneath the surface of a character's ostensible sentiments. And if any faults were uncovered this gave the cue for his rejection of that figure. In Part II, however, the characterization is both more explicit and less tense. Feeble-mind's strengths and weaknesses are immediately evident but this does not lead to condemnation or rejection. On the contrary, he is welcomed and Bunyan even provides him with an equally weak companion in the form of Mr Ready-to-halt. The main emphasis then is on the way in which the group steadily expands and on the relations formed, usually between pairs of characters, within the group.

The most important of these relations is that between Mercy and Christiana. Indeed her companionship with Mercy accounts for a high proportion of the dialogue in the opening sections. At first sight it looks as if Mercy is a second Hopeful. She is naïve, docile, and willing to submit to Christiana. She is even hired as the latter's servant. This does not mean, however, that she always occupies an inferior position. Soon after they enter the Wicket Gate they compare notes about their experiences in a summer-parlour:

> Christiana began, 'O Lord! How glad am I that we are got in hither!'
> *Mercy.* So you well may; but I of all have cause to leap for joy.
> *Christiana.* I thought one time as I stood at the Gate (because I had knocked and none did answer) that all our labour had been lost; specially when that ugly cur made such a heavy barking against us.
> *Mercy.* But my worst fears was after I saw that you was taken into his favour, and that I was left behind: Now thought I, 'tis fulfilled which is written. *Two women shall be grinding together; the one shall be taken, and the other left.* I had much ado to forbear crying out, 'Undone, undone'.
> And afraid I was to knock any more; but when I looked up, to what was written over the Gate, I took courage. I also thought that I must either knock again or die. So I knocked; but I cannot tell how, for my spirit now struggled betwixt life and death.
> *Christiana.* Can you not tell how you knocked?
> (pp. 237–8)

This is basically a conversation between equals who have both had terrifying experiences. Christiana was afraid of a fierce dog and Mercy that the gate would never open. Their discussion replaces the occasionally tedious retrospective instruction of Part I. It is noticeable what a heavy stress is put on emotions here at the expense of doctrinal explanation. Bunyan glosses this section in the margin quite simply as 'Talk between the Christians'. Christiana and Mercy do not watch for signs of weakness in each other to turn to their advantage; instead they admit and accept their vulnerability. Christiana makes no attempt to lord it over her companion and in fact diverts an embarrassing event into humour when

she reminds Mercy how hard she knocked at the gate. This is
the humour of sympathy not ironic condemnation (as in the
case of By-Ends). While we might agree that this kind of
conversation is more humane or morally better than those in
Part I, an element of drama has been lost. We wait expec-
tantly to see what will be the outcome of Christian's verbal
encounters because his success on his journey depends on his
success at defeating his opponents. Even if there is no doubt
that he will succeed finally at least we want to see *how* he will
do this. In the conversations of Part II nothing is at stake in
that way and so nothing hinges on their outcome. Mutual
toleration has excluded drama.

With the reduction of doctrinal discussion in Part II there
comes a corresponding increase in realism, which sometimes
means that dialogue modifies its function. During their stay
at the Palace Beautiful, Christiana's son Matthew falls sick
with gripes. Christiana naturally enough becomes very worried and is scarcely relieved when Samuel reminds her that
Matthew has eaten grapes from the Devil's garden. The
dialogue at this point forms part of a whole situation,
complementing the actions of the doctor (in making the
purge) and of Christiana (in trying to persuade Matthew to
take it):

> 'Come, come,' said the physician, 'you must take it.' 'It
> goes against my stomach,' said the boy. 'I must have
> you take it,' said his mother. 'I shall vomit it up again,'
> said the boy. 'Pray sir,' said Christiana to Mr Skill, 'how
> does it taste?' 'It has no ill taste,' said the doctor
> . . .   (pp. 280–1)

It is perfectly possible to read this episode without paying
any attention to its allegorical significance because Bunyan
captures so exactly the tones of anxiety (Christiana) and
reassurance (Mr Skill), and because the rapid dialogue diverts
the reader's attention away from the theoretical cause of
Matthew's gripes.

Christian's encounters are frequently presented as a conflict between a worldly and an other-worldly attitude, but in
cases like Matthew's illness or the gossiping of Christiana's
neighbours Bunyan has shifted his concern nearer to the

secular. His use of group scenes reflects this change, for we can scarcely get a sense of contrasting issues from them. Rather we see contrasts between social types whose differences are to be accepted (in the group of pilgrims), or whose hypocrisy has to be exposed, as in the case of Christiana's neighbours. Mrs Timorous pretends to be solicitous towards her but as soon as she returns home she summons all her cronies for a session of malicious gossip. Timorous recounts the news of Christiana's conversion, as her name suggests, without any overt comment, but this omission is amply rectified by Mrs Bat's-eyes' criticism of Christiana and Mrs Inconsiderate's impatient rejection of her:

> Away with such fantastical fools from the town; a good riddance, for my part, I say of her. Should she stay where she dwells, and retain this her mind, who could live quietly by her? For she will either be dumpish or un-neighbourly, or talk of such matters as no wise body can abide: wherefore, for my part, I shall never be sorry for her departure; let her go, and let better come in her room: 'twas never a good world since these whimsical fools dwelt in it. (p. 231)

Mrs Inconsiderate parallels Obstinate in her intolerant dismissal of what she sees as an anti-social attitude. Certainly she is speaking here with a very strong consciousness of her audience. She makes her main impact in her opening gesture but then pretends to be reasonable by describing the type she imagines Christiana to be. Although she ostensibly minimizes her outburst as purely personal opinion ('for my part' twice), in fact she discreetly congratulates herself on her social wisdom (who but she could be a 'wise body'?) and concludes her words with an epigrammatic phrase which reinforces this self-admiration.

The whole scene is ironic, but particularly Mrs Inconsiderate's charge against Christiana, since neighbourliness is a positive quality being asserted throughout Part II. Unwittingly, then, she raises one of the main themes of the book. Hospitality, neighbourliness in the broadest sense of solicitude for one's companions, is shown to be essential for the whole of Christiana's journey, and this is seen in the relaxed nature of the dialogues. They form conversations and never debates. Differences in tone and idiom are there simply to be enjoyed. The disputes of Part I have given way to mutual acceptance.

NOTES

1. F. R. Leavis, *'Anna Karenina' and Other Essays* (London, 1967), p. 41.

2. Cf., for example, Norman Page, *Speech in the English Novel* (London, 1973), p. 25.

3. Roger Sharrock, *John Bunyan* (2nd edn, London, 1968), p. 142.

4. John Brown, *John Bunyan* (revised edn, London, 1928), pp. 114–15.

5. Christopher Hill, *The Century of Revolution 1603–1704* (London, 1974), p. 79.

6. G. Offor (ed), *The Works of John Bunyan* (1862), i. 57–8. Page references to works other than *The Pilgrim's Progress* are to this edition.

7. Cf., among others, Roger Sharrock, *John Bunyan* (1968), pp. 89–90; Maurice Hussey, 'The humanism of John Bunyan' in B. Ford (ed.), *The Pelican Guide to English Literature*, 7 vols (Harmondsworth, 1956–61), iii. 221–2; Ernest A. Baker, *The History of the English Novel*, 10 vols (London, 1924–39), iii. 55–6; Dorothy Van Ghent, *The English Novel. Form and Function* (2nd edn, New York, 1961), p. 24.

8. Roger Sharrock, *John Bunyan* (1968), p. 77.

9. Cf., for example, Roger Sharrock, 'Introduction', *The Pilgrim's Progress* (Harmondsworth, 1965), p. 13; and Dorothy Van Ghent, op. cit., p. 25.

10. Cf. 'As the *you* became the mark of respect from inferior to superior . . ., the *thou* forms came to mark intimacy between family members and lovers, then developed as a mark of solidarity between speakers who shared a set of values' (Joseph M. Williams, *Origins of the English Language* [New York, 1975], pp. 248–9).

11. Norman Page, op. cit., p. 92.

12. Roger Sharrock, *John Bunyan* (1968), p. 75.

13. Dorothy Van Ghent, op. cit., p. 29.

14. J. C. Forrest, 'Bunyan's Ignorance and the flatterer: A study in the literary art of damnation', *Studies in Philology*, lx (1963), p. 18.

15. Roger Sharrock, *John Bunyan* (1968), p. 138.

Bunyan's Sense of Place

JAMES TURNER

> The spring being far advanced, the meadows being
> covered with a curious carpet of delightful green, and the
> earth clothed in rich and glorious attire to rejoice and
> triumph for the return of her shining bridegroom, the
> healthful air rendered more pleasing and delightful by
> the gentle winds then breathed from the south, impreg-
> nated with the exhilarating fragrancy of the variety of
> flowers and odoriferous plants over which they had
> passed, and ever blooming bush and flourishing grove
> plentifully stored with winged inhabitants, who with a
> delightful harmony sweetly sing forth their maker's
> praise and warble out their joyful welcomes to the gaudy
> spring, I one day took a walk in the fields to feast my eyes
> with the variety of delightful objects which that season
> of the year wherein the universe bears the nearest
> resemblance to the happy state wherein the immortal
> God at first created it liberally offers to the view of the
> admiring beholders, and thereby lays an irresistible
> obligation upon heavenly minds to spiritualize the
> several objects they behold, and satiate their happy souls
> with heavenly meditation, by affording them such
> innumerable occasions of contemplating the divine
> goodness.

These are the opening words of *The Second Part of the Pilgrim's
Progress* by Thomas Sherman, published in 1684 as a direct and
critical response to Bunyan's work. One commendatory
poem proclaimed that the pilgrim could now see by the
sunlight of Sherman's genius what previously had only been
glimpsed 'by Bunyan's candle' (f. A4v); Sherman was broad
and effulgent where Bunyan had been miserly and dark.
Breadth and accumulation are certainly indicated by Sherman's descriptive technique. He expatiates upon the landscape; in this opening sentence the Christian's walk with God
becomes the morning stroll of a tourist, collecting subordinate
clauses like souvenirs, each one testifying to some new
excellence or excitement of the place. His language has a
gift-shop quality and his imagery is decidedly superior; his

landscape is not merely a 'variety of delightful objects' but a glittering social occasion, irresistibly obliging. Both these effects are typical of seventeenth-century landscape description. The secular delight of walking through rich and varied scenery and recreating it in elevated words frequently serves to illustrate the plenitude of divine creation and the duty of Christians to 'spiritualize the several objects they behold' by meditation.[1] Sherman's opening sentence is an object-lesson in how to relate to the World and how to spread the Word.

Bunyan's opening sentence seems skeletal in comparison:

> As I walked through the wilderness of this world, I lighted on a certain place, where was a den; and I laid me down in that place to sleep; and as I slept I dreamed a dream. (p.39)

Both writers begin with a walk through the landscape and a divine vision, but their sense of place is as different as their social and doctrinal positions. Sherman was a General Baptist and clearly aimed at a high-class readership; his picture of the world is an *omnium gatherum* of delights. Bunyan's is minimal—a wilderness without, a prison within. His starkness, which Sherman and his friends saw as inadequacy, seems more like a deliberate artistic choice; the narrowness of the Way has already found a rhetorical form. Bunyan fends off the world, while Sherman gathers it into his fleecy embrace. Bunyan's descriptive style runs forward with its fingers in its ears; Sherman's takes a stroll through a park of its own making.

Bunyan's depiction of place is not always as laconic as this. Though he is never exhaustive, he does sometimes select vivid details and arrange them with some sense of space or scenic continuity. The Valley of the Shadow of Death, for example, combines perilous ground, murky atmosphere, and terrifying sounds whose effect on Christian comes to a crescendo 'about the middle' of the valley. Some of the pleasant places along the Way have catalogues of delights that resemble the traditional *locus amoenus*, and the Interpreter's garden (p. 250) is as regimented as an Elizabethan formal garden—a suitable image for the orderly social structure of the gathered church. The Enchanted Ground is not described at all in Part I, its effect is simply *given* as in a folk-tale or a dream; but in Part II it becomes a dark and tangled Gothic forest, interspersed with arbours that are all the more tempting because vividly described. Nevertheless, Bunyan often seems to undercut his own realism, to withdraw from a scene or place, to provide not even a frame for us to inscribe our daydreams but an absentmindedness which leads to contradiction.

One would have thought, for instance, that the Way would be a consistent image; it runs absolutely straight and due south from the bad to the blessed city, and any turning aside or bending, however slight, means certain damnation. Yet pilgrims do turn aside to stroll on the Delectable Mountains or to hunt giants (pp. 159, 321), and sometimes keeping to the prescribed straight course lands pilgrims in trouble. Christian makes for the Gate 'the next [i.e. nearest] way', as Evangelist instructed him, but thereby plunges into the Slough; and in Part II the party find a muddy pit straight in front of them, while the true road leads off to the right (p. 357)—an astonishing departure from Bunyan's original topography. 'Next ways'—here as elsewhere (pp. 163, 289) associated with expedience and shortsightedness—are not necessarily the same as 'straight paths'. Nor is directness a sufficient guarantee of correctness, as Christian and Hopeful find when they encounter a dual carriageway and must decide with no visible clues which track is the good one (p. 172). At several points the Way is an open road running past walls or fences that shut out the passer-by, but at other times it turns inside out and is itself walled like a garden, into which Formalist and Hypocrisy scramble like the biblical thief into the sheepfold (p. 72). Sometimes there is no wall at all: Christian sees Apollyon coming across the fields at a distance, and monsters, rapists, and hypocrites appear on the Way without any mention of how they gained access to it.

Single aspects of the road and the countryside through which it passes are selected as the requirements of the allegory arise, and they often resist combination into a homogeneous space. If we were to draw a map of the Way, it would emerge that the land of Conceit and the Flatterer's path must have been clearly visible from the Delectable

Mountains, and that Doubting Castle was a landmark for miles around, since its grounds are visible from the Hill Caution and in Beulah the pilgrims could not 'so much as see Doubting Castle' (p. 195), which implies that it *had been* clearly visible (and so easily avoided). The scale is also variable. The mouth of Hell is small enough to appear at a particular spot halfway through the Valley of the Shadow of Death, but we are also told that it is several miles long (pp. 97–8). Mount Calvary and the sepulchre could not be made to fit into the narrow fenced road where Christian encounters them; Mount Sinai must be placed 'hard by' Legality's house, and in bulk seems more like a steeple than a mountain; 'a wide field full of dark mountains' is something to stumble among rather than pant up; the Delectable Mountains are so compact that the pilgrims go 'up to' them without effort and walk 'to the end' of them as one would houses in a street—one hill is so small that it is located 'in a bottom' (pp. 58, 74, 157–61). Latitude, climate, and location are equally hard to fix: Stupidity lies in the frozen region four degrees north of the City of Destruction (pp. 300–1) and the journey south via the Delectable Mountains provides greater comfort the nearer the pilgrims get to their goal (p. 88), but bad lands may occur at any point along the route and are in no way affected by the latitude. The whole *Progress* takes place in a symbolic dream-land—except that the pilgrims actually visit Calvary, Jacob's ladder, the scene of the sacrifice of Isaac, and the plain of Sodom (pp. 69, 284–5, 337).

If we were to film *The Pilgrim's Progress* we would again encounter problems of discontinuity and contradiction. The opening scene takes place in daylight, since Christian is reading in the fields, but he steers towards a light. This in turn is forgotten by the time he reaches the Gate. The Valley of the Shadow of Death, presumably constituted by its darkness, is traversed in bright sunshine by everyone but Christian. The darkness which descends on the Enchanted Ground does not prevent the pilgrims from seeing into the arbours along the way (pp. 355–9). There are other problems, too. In Part I Bunyan walks through the wilderness, lies down in a den, and dreams of the City of Destruction, but in Part II his waking self visits a wood near that city and only begins his dream when he is lodged there; it is as if the author has wandered on to his own set and been caught by the cameras.

Special effects would be required to deal with the interiors, since they turn into exteriors without warning. In the Interpreter's House Christian is shown a series of rooms in which a significant scene is being enacted: he passes from the room with the fire to the grounds of a stately palace and on to 'a very dark room' and a 'chamber' with no apparent break in the narrative rhythm (pp. 64–7). In the House Beautiful Christiana is taken successively to a closet, to the place where Jacob's ladder goes up to heaven, to the actual mountain where Abraham offered up Isaac, and then immediately 'into the dining-room' (pp. 284–5).[2] Since none of these are pictures, it is clear that for Bunyan a 'room' was the basic unit of significant space, and may frame and contain 'places' which in reality must be more extensive than it. Wittgenstein stated that 'though a state of affairs that would contravene the laws of physics can be represented by us spatially, one that would contravene the laws of geometry cannot'. This is not true of Bunyan, whose outsides become insides, whose figures have several forms at once, and whose straight lines turn corners. And no lens could capture what his pilgrims see: the Delectable Mountains are so far from the House Beautiful that they can only be seen on a clear day, but Christian sees fruit and flowers there (p. 88); pilgrims make out the gate and the pavements of the Celestial City with the help of optical instruments, even though it is on a vast mountain above the clouds (pp. 161, 196–7, 200). It is clear that techniques like mapping and filming, ways of seeing which assume a three-dimensional continuum of space, cannot be applied to Bunyan's vision.

Critics have frequently noted topographical cinconsistencies in *The Pilgrim's Progress*. Practically everyone, for example, mentions the 'wide field full of dark mountains'. No one would now be so anachronistic as to force Bunyan into the mould of cinematic or novelistic realism and then complain that he does not fit; his failure to materialize is explained in terms of his limited experience (never having seen a mountain) or of his devotion to the doctrine that heavenly 'things to come' and earthly 'carnal sense' are 'strangers one to another' (p. 63). But this is still perceived as a lack, a self-consumption. Modern readers—the term may include dissatisfied contemporaries like Thomas Sherman—assume a Newtonian universe in which objects can be placed in a continuous grid of space and time. We expect artists and writers to represent space in forms which approximate to our perceptions or depart from them knowingly. Bunyan seems in this respect a child or a primitive.

These arguments are usefully summarized by David Harvey:

> Piaget and Inhelder [in *The Child's Conception of Space*] suggest that children automatically progress from perception of the topological characteristics of objects (characteristics such as proximity, separation, order, enclosure, and continuity), through perceptions which encompass perspective and projective relationships, to the ultimate ability to organize all objects in space in terms of some common spatial structure, such as a Euclidean system of co-ordinates . . . [They] are careful to distinguish, however, between the perception of space and the representation of space by means of imaginary concepts.

Representational ability progresses in the same way, but in 'many primitive societies' it is arrested at an earlier stage. Thus Cassirer claims that 'primitive peoples', though their perception of the concrete environment may be keen and precise, 'are unable to draw a map of [it], to hold it fast in a spatial schema'. These stages of development—which do help to describe Bunyan's work—should not be regarded as purely psychological phenomena. An individual's mental map is culturally determined, and reveals 'the ultimate values of a given social structure'; different classes and subgroups will have spatial concepts 'geared to the particular role which they perform in society'.[3] So we should see Bunyan's inconsistency not as a deficiency but as a specific product of the relation between him and his society. Furthermore, since we are dealing with a conscious artistic creation, we should see it as a critical response to that society.

Bunyan's social position was paradoxical and unstable. He was an outcast from the world in some ways, but in other ways had a real 'property' and interest in it. He was a despised itinerant manual worker, excluded from land-ownership, exposed to the rigours of the open road as he travelled and the violence of property-owners if he deviated; yet he was also a householder and artisan, descended from yeomen and small traders. His status was higher than common labourer, and like many wandering preachers he dissociated himself indignantly from the homeless poor (gentry and vagabonds are both Diabolonian). It is no accident that Bunyan's sense of place is problematic and contradictory—sometimes realistic and expansive and sometimes truncated almost to nothing, sometimes purely metaphorical and sometimes intensely literal, sometimes regarding places as hideous exemplifications of the world and its dangers and sometimes as delightful escapes from them.

It is certain, however, that Bunyan's places are related to a generalized concept of 'the World', and that he conceived the World in political and economic terms, as a hostile hierarchy of wealth and power founded on *place*—social position and landed estates. He saw place as property. The units of topographical space (heights and depths, lands, fields, hills, houses, and roads) are inseparable in Bunyan's imagination from the social means of their control, from lordship, tenure and sale, trespass actions and enclosure claims.

It may be objected that landscape in Bunyan is not a socialized image at all, but a crystallization of inner psychic conditions. However, 'inner landscape' means that some aspect of the material environment has been internalized: *The Pilgrim's Progress* could never have been written if Bunyan had obeyed Evangelist's instructions to 'let nothing that is on this side the other world get within you' (p. 123). The elements of his topography have social implications, and the inner states of the pilgrims are caused for the most part by social pressures. Bunyan certainly did refer to 'heights that build themselves up in us', as Roger Sharrock notes in his Oxford edition (p. 320), but he also wrote in the same passage that height signified the gigantic walls built 'of purpose to keep Israel out of his possession'. God is seen as a force counteracting this social injustice: 'but now, to support us against all these, . . . there is, for us a height in God'.[4] (Breadth likewise has a direct political significance: 'this breadth that is in God, it also overmatcheth that spreading and overspreading rage of men, that is sometimes as if it would swallow up the whole church of God' [*Works*, ii. 4].) The vertical height of Mount Sinai, set 'hard by' the manor-house of Mr Legality, is clearly a representation of the physical terror Bunyan felt at church steeples—vividly recorded in *Grace Abounding*. His fear of simultaneously being crushed from above and falling through the floor is repeated in the juxtaposition of the Slough and Mount Sinai, and strongly suggests the insecurity of the aspiring mechanic preacher under threat of being 'trodden down like mire in the streets' (p. 97). Worldly-Wiseman, seeing the mud on Christian's clothes, remarks that he had been meddling with things 'too high' for him (p. 49). Mount Sinai symbolizes the Law, which in Bunyan's mind meant both the old dispensation of Moses and the repression of his own day; Moses knocks Faithful to the ground and threatens to evict him by burning his house down (pp. 105–6), much as 'drunken, proud, rich and scornful Landlords' were denounced for doing in *A Few Sighs from Hell* (*Works*, iii. 677). Part II shows a slight relenting towards the ruling class when springs rising 'out of the tops of high hills' show Matthew that 'the Spirit of Grace shall spring up in some that are great and mighty, as well as in many that are poor and low' (p. 283). Height still has a specific social meaning, however.

Here then is one aspect of the dimension *height*. It is interesting to note that the Delectable Mountains, which represent not the things of this world but a token of the pilgrims' inheritance to come, are treated with no sense of height at all. Topographical realism suggests carnality. Likewise the Valley of the Shadow of Death—a negative apprehension of Christian's future prospects—is given no features of a valley, though the previous Valley of Humiliation is reached by a steep descent. The lowly but fertile valley was a traditional symbol of religious humility, conveniently conflated with low social status,[5] but Bunyan depicts not the state of Humility but the process of Humiliation. Discontent and Shame lurk in this valley and remind Faithful of its 'lack of honour', of the 'base and low estate and condition of those that were chiefly the pilgrims', the scorn of 'the mighty, rich and wise' for religion, and the folly of growing 'strange to the great' because of their vices (pp. 106–8). 'Humiliation' is thus assimilated to class-hatred and opposition.

Apollyon blocks the way like Giant Maul, or Grim who 'backs the lions' of repression; he looks disdainfully and threatens Christian in the high-handed and violent manner of a powerful employee. (As well as prosecuting sectarians, JPs' duties were to fix the wages of agricultural labourers below that of subsistence, so there is literal truth in Christian's remark that 'your service was hard, and your wages such that a man could not live on' [p. 90].) In this confrontation the land is both a setting and a bone of contention. Christian 'shoulders it with [his] adversary, saying, *Give place to me, that I may dwell*'—a text heavy with radical political implications.[6] Apollyon 'stroddl[ing] quite over the whole breadth of the way' is clearly identified with the giants who 'stand in the cross ways to cut off Israel from his possession' (*Works*, ii. 8). He tries to insist that Christian, having been born in his 'dominions', must work for his wages; James Harrington the political theorist argued that 'dominion', or property in land, was the foundation of empire,[7] and Apollyon is as much a great landowner as a king. Christian can only use the defence of the itinerant against the agents of private property: 'Apollyon, beware what you do, for I am in the King's highway' (p. 93). Giant Grim likewise appears as a militant defender of private land, and his confrontation with Great-heart echoes the struggles against private enclosures which raged throughout England in the 1650s:

> *Grim*. Will you slay me upon mine own ground?
> *Great-heart*. 'Tis the King's highway that we are in.
>   (p. 269)

It was frequently complained that roads in enclosed land were 'much unoccupied, and . . . almost all grown over with grass' (p. 268), as the Way had become at this point.

Giant Slay-good also asks 'why are you here on my ground?' (p. 322), and the whole Giant Despair episode is a

vivid reconstruction of a country estate as it is experienced
by those excluded from it:

> Now there was not far from the place where they lay, a
> castle, called Doubting Castle, the owner whereof was
> Giant Despair, and it was in his grounds they now
> were sleeping; wherefore he getting up in the morning
> early and walking up and down in his fields, caught
> Christian and Hopeful asleep in his grounds. Then with
> a grim and surly voice he bid them awake, and asked
> them whence they were and what they did in his
> grounds. They told him they were pilgrims, and that
> they had lost their way. Then said the Giant, 'You have
> this night trespassed on me, by trampling in, and lying
> on my grounds, and therefore you must go along with
> me.'   (p. 151)

Giant Despair's walking up and down in his fields suggests
Apollyon 'coming over the field' (p. 90) or the 'great ones
of the world' who 'go strutting up and down the streets' in
A Few Sighs (*Works*, iii. 676); these are the movements of
someone seeking to control the space he owns. He is 'surly'
like the 'disdainful, surly, rugged, proud' rich men who
persecute Baptists (*Works*, iii. 685) and 'falls to rating them
as if they were dogs', as Bunyan had been rated in *Dirt
Wip'd Off*.[8] His estate is marked by the stile and fence and
defended by the laws of trespass; only when the pilgrims
come to the King's highway again are they 'safe, because
they were out of his jurisdiction'. This episode teaches
'what 'twas to tread upon forbidden ground' (p.
157)—exactly the same phrase is used for the detour Christian made when tempted by the reasonable rents and easy
credit of Morality, only to be terrorized by the
steeple-mountain of the law (p. 56). Despair is less an
abstract or existential inner state than the emotional response of the poor Christian to repression and social contempt.

The horrors of Doubting Castle and By-path Meadow
are all the more intense by contrast with the place
before—'a meadow, curiously beautified with lilies and . . .
green all the year long' where the pilgrims ate and rested.

These good places, like the bad ones, are characterized in terms of economic possession:

> he that can tell
> What pleasant fruit, yea leaves, these trees do yield,
> Will soon sell all, that he may buy this field.
>
> (p. 149)

Two sorts of landownership are thus opposed: *carnal*, in which the pilgrims are treated as outcasts, and *spiritual*, in which they 'possess the brave country alone' and receive 'an inheritance incorruptible' (pp. 42, 45). For the weary pilgrims to ask 'whose delectable Mountains are these?' is not an 'improbable question' as J. R. Knott assumes;[9] in the same way Great-heart knows 'many labouring men that have got good estates' in the Valley of Humiliation, and Mercy claims that 'this Valley is that from whence also the King will give to his their vineyards' (pp. 289, 292). To 'spiritualize' the landscape, as Thomas Sherman exhorted his readers to do, is not to ignore the economic reality of a landowning society but to convert it to a new cause.

Bunyan belongs to a well-established tradition of making 'spiritual use' of the land by converting it to religious metaphor. The phrase is taken from Ralph Austen's *Spiritual Use of an Orchard* (1653), in which his own experiences and observations as a horticulturist are made to reveal holy matters. Austen was like Bunyan an artisan and a radical Puritan, but his imaginative use of the environment is rather different. His life's work was rooted in the land, and he accepts the working landscape in all its details. The relation between tenor and vehicle is thus a non-problematical one; like Thomas Sherman he selects from the physical world those features which 'bear the nearest resemblance to the happy state' of divine perfection. Spiritual use is thus equivalent to physical production, both 'working up' and extracting value from agricultural land. Austen, the self-employed improving tenant, represents the kind of Puritanism that led Weber and Tawney to formulate their views on the rise of capitalism; he sees the world in functional terms, while Sherman is decorative.

Then there are the gentleman-poets, who scrupulously

avoid any mention of hardship, work and rent when describing secular landscapes but lay heavy stress on them in their
religious imagery, creating an *inverted* landscape in which
they imagine the land from the point of view of their own
labourers and servants. For example, Sir William Denny's
Guide and Pilgrims Passe to the Land of the Living (1653),
strikingly similar in some ways to Bunyan's work, shows
nevertheless the attitudes of the rural ruling-class: towering
rocks, far from threatening, protect the Cell of Humility
from storms—the occasion for a pointed attack on the
militancy of the lower orders; the 'Slough' means 'the
plunges of disadvantages in the world'; the road is not merely
rough but piled high with flints over which the pilgrim must
walk barefoot; the low and fertile valley is not a place where
labouring men can 'get good estates' and regain a sense of
themselves, as Bunyan's Valley of Humiliation is (p. 291),
but a 'Farm of Self-Resignation' in which the tenant 'pays
himself for rent' and submits to the absolute power of his
landlord.[10] Spiritualization in Denny's case means idealiza-
tion of the existing social structure.

These authors have a metaphorics of landscape compatible
with their social position; if Talkative or Wordly-Wiseman
had written *The Pilgrim's Progress* it would read like Sherman
or Denny. They posit some collusion between this world and
the next. Bunyan repudiated this above all else; either you
have your cake in this world, like Dives or Passion, or you
have it in the next, like Lazarus or Patience. There can be no
compromises between Vanity Fair and the saints; 'Christianity and the customs of our town of Vanity [are] diametrically
opposite' (p. 130), and elsewhere this opposition is expressed
in economic terms:

> Riches and power, what is there more in the world? For
> money answereth all things—that is, all but soul
> concerns. . . . The Word . . . setteth covetousness and
> the fear of God in direct opposition.
>
> (*Works*, i. 107, 474)

Bunyan's landscape is inconsistent because it is made of
two incompatible kinds of land, related to each other not as
adjacent regions on a map, but as in trick-pictures where a

shape appears either as figure or ground but never both at once. Two incompatible 'jurisdictions' exist side by side, like matter and anti-matter, antipathetic but identical in structure. The Way is an idealized private estate in which the ragged and down-trodden pilgrim has 'a privileged place' (p. 245); Christ is the Lord of the Hill, the King whose highway is like a rich garden and who prosecutes hypocritical intruders for trespass. His régime is so lenient that his domain becomes a Land of Cokaigne in which estates are 'rent free',[11] inns never present the bill, and pilgrims share simultaneously in the benefits of communism and private property:

> Then he asked the name of the country; they said it was Immanuel's Land: 'and it is common', said they, 'as this Hill is to and for all the pilgrims'.   (p.88)

> And because this country [Beulah] was common for pilgrims, and because the orchards and vineyards that were here belonged to the King of the Celestial Country, therefore they were licensed to make bold with any of his things.   (p. 364)

In carnal space the poor pilgrims are hemmed in, their spatial envelopes restricted so severely that the enemy sometimes twitches their flesh and speaks with their own voices; but in these spiritual estates they enjoy lordship of the eye and foot, strolling with 'a pleasant prospect on every side' (p. 159), 'tracing and walking to and fro' in the valley at daybreak (p. 306). In these pleasure-grounds away from 'rattling with coaches' and 'rumbling with wheels', the pilgrims even begin to assume the attitudes of the landowner, the luxurious vagueness and pastoral complacency of traditional rural poetry:

> Our country birds . . . are very fine company for us when we are melancholy, also they make the woods and groves, and solitary places, places desirous to be in.
>   (p. 287)

> I will dare to say that, this [shepherd] boy lives a merrier life, and wears more of that herb called

hearts-ease in his bosom, than he that is clad in silk and velvet.   (p. 290)

The pilgrims' use of space while on the road is *vocational*—a single furrow—but in the palaces and vineyards prepared for their comfort it is *recreational*: they sample a variety of 'places' in casual arrangement. This landscape of alternate constriction and expansion, painful exclusion and privileged expatiation, first appears in *Grace Abounding* when Bunyan dreams of the Bedford congregation as a walled and sunlit estate on high ground, which he reaches by forcing his head and shoulders through a tiny gap. The same rhythm is kept up throughout *The Pilgrim's Progress*—narrow passages through the estates of the World, relieved by the delectable mountains, green meadows and goodly vineyards of *Canticles* and *Isaiah*.

These good lands, as I have mentioned, are depicted with an unfortunate lack of topographical realism. Bunyan seems to draw on real experience when he describes his pilgrims floundering in the mud of the Slough of Despond or the Enchanted Ground, struggling up the Hill Difficulty, cowering before Giant Despair, being mugged at Dead Man's Lane and suffocated in Demas's mine. Realism of texture and incident is permitted if it furthers the model of violent opposition between pilgrims and the world. Other kinds of realism are suppressed, however; the more highly evolved models of space, projective, perspective, or three-dimensional, are too strongly associated with techniques of dominion and control over property. In 'Adam Unparadis'd' Milton gave Gabriel the task of describing Eden, 'the angel Gabriel, as by his name signifying a prince of power, tracing paradise with a more free office'; he recognized that the liberty to trace paradise in verbal description implies domination and power, and transferred and magnified his worldly experience to create an image of the divine. Bunyan's relation to the land was one of bitter struggle and exclusion—he had no Horton to compose in. He could not achieve the rich breadth of Milton's Eden, nor the sauntering inclusiveness of Sherman's opening sentence, because it had no basis in his experience.

Moreover, Bunyon never makes use of the concept *landscape* or the panoramic effects of landscape painting, and though

Great-heart makes use of a 'book or map' in the Enchanted
Ground, it is never described or applied elsewhere; indeed his
own 'Map . . . of Salvation and Damnation' (1663) is not a
map at all but a rigid diagram. This is all the more striking
since contemporary writers were so keen on these
images—Richard Baxter, for example, refers to his religious
mentors as 'maps and landskips of the Holy Land'.[12] Bunyan's refusal here is based not on incompetence but on a
positive rejection of the carnal rationality which lies behind
mapping and surveying. (A parallel may be found in the
Quaker William Bayley, who claims that the Devil tempted
him to learn arithmetic and navigation: 'which things took
me up into an exceeding high mountain, showing glorious
promises of the preferment, riches and love of the world'.[13]
Navigation is linked with Christ's temptation on the mountain, since they are both temptations to master the world.)
The requirements of doctrine act against the multidimensio-
nal grasp of landscape. Sometimes in Bunyan space is reduced to a simple binary system: inside means salvation,
outside damnation; the left is sinister and the right is holy (for
example pp. 162, 220, 287, 357). Its dimensions in any case
vary according to the frame of mind of the pilgrim; so that
the journey is long or short, easy or rough depending on
Grace, the River of Death is deep or shallow according to
one's belief in the king of that place, and the pit vanishes with
prayer (pp. 158, 198, 295). When Christian, Formalist, and
Hypocrisy reach the bottom of the Hill Difficulty those who
try to reckon out the lie of the land in three dimensions are
immediately plunged into Danger and Destruction (p. 74).
Ignorance, likewise, offends against godliness by applying
topographical criteria to his journey:

> And as for the Gate that you talk of, all the world knows
> that that is a great way off of our country. I cannot think
> that any man in all our parts doth so much as know the way
> to it; nor need they matter whether they do or no, since we
> have, as you see, a fine, pleasant, green lane, that comes
> down from our country the next way into it.
>
> (pp. 162–3)

This is the man who is 'wise in his own conceit'.[14] Christian takes the parallel path through Giant Despair's meadow because it looks as if it leads in the right direction (p. 149), and the same thing happens at the Flatterer's junction, except that this time the path develops a curve (p. 172) and should consequently have been visibly wrong; the inconsistency is removed if we consider that for Bunyan *all* topographical empiricism is evil if it extends into a second dimension. While they are on the road his pilgrims are Line-landers, and if they stray they become morally blind. It is perfectly acceptable for Christian to reckon how far he might have to go through the Valley of the Shadow of Death or the Enchanted Ground (pp. 98, 191)—he can do that without leaving Line-land—but all other forms of carnal perception are illegitimate.

In *The Pilgrim's Progress* the more significant questions are answered in terms which are not simply less spatial than we expect, but entirely non-spatial. The pilgrims finally saw 'where they were' when the veil fell, not from their own eyes, but from the person of Flatterer (p. 172). *Where* is subsumed into *what*. Puzzling inconsistencies are removed if we thus despatialize the idea of location and movement. If Christian and Faithful have journeyed from a far country to the town of Vanity, how can they deal with its inhabitants as if they were lifelong neighbours (pp. 134, 180, 192)? The answer is that Vanity Fair and the City of Destruction are the same place, and progress between them is purely mental; indeed it begins with the realization 'that believing and coming [are] all one' (p. 182). How can humble pilgrims simultaneously 'live and trace these grounds' in the Valley of Humiliation and continue their pilgrimage (p. 291)? In the same way that Abraham and Isaac 'are now resting upon their beds, each one walking in his righteousness' (pp. 200–1). Walking in righteousness was an entirely despatialized concept; to *walk* did not have its present meaning,[15] and walking with God was a familiar concept in Puritan didactic manuals. Titles like John Owen's *Eshcol, or Rules of Direction For the Walking of Saints in Fellowship* (1646) or Edward Bury's *A Help to Holy Walking, or a Guide to Glory* (1675) indicate the tradition which Bunyan inherits.

Bunyan's pilgrims walk 'not by sight' but by words

(p. 356). To escape from the clutches of Flatterer they must use not their perceptions but their 'note of the way'. This, like Great-heart's map and the lamp he reads it by, signifies the Word. People find out 'where they are' by reading the memorials along the Way and by repeatedly rehearsing the sequence of places in their conversations until they are too familiar to write out in full. The only real space traversed by pilgrims is the verbal; the only pilgrim's progress which really exists is *The Pilgrim's Progress*, a progress-into-text whose greatest memorial—larger than the wayside monuments of Part II but serving the same purpose—is Bunyan's book itself: 'This book will make a traveller of thee' (p. 36).

In his introductory poem Bunyan also suggests that his landscape allegory will work like the art of memory in which 'places' (*loci*) are used as a grid to help recall images of things (*imagines*)—'art thou forgetful? Wouldest thou remember?' (p. 36). Other authors too had combined *loci and imagines* by taking this meaning of 'place' literally, basing their didactic poems on a landscape which like Bunyan's was partly symbolic and partly the historical Palestine: the heroine of Joseph Beaumont's *Psyche*, for example, is taken in a winged chariot to Mount Calvary in order

> that that prospect might
> Yield her with uncontrolled liberty
> Of Love's chief stations an open sight
> (1648, p. 221)

'Place' likewise meant the 'stations' or stages of an argument, as Christiana appreciates when she exlaims 'this place has been our second stage' (p. 257) or 'Behold, how fitly are the stages set! / For their relief that pilgrims are become' (p. 347). The word becomes concrete when she discovers a wooden stage erected by the wayside (p. 267). Bunyan's mind works by literalizing semantic associations. The places of the Interpreter's House and the Palace Beautiful, which seem so inconsistent and paradoxical to us, are quite homogeneous to Bunyan since they are all 'places' in the didactic and conceptual sense; the precise way in which they are places—whether they are rooms or stretches of open countryside—is of secondary importance, and he chooses rooms simply because that is more comforting and familiar to him, less tainted with topography. Discovering Bunyan's spatial system is like learning a new language; our phonemes are his allophones, and vice versa.

Bunyan thus appears in a way to have a consistent theory of place, linking its social, physical, and mnemonic senses. But the word had a further meaning in the seventeenth century. Bunyan, like Esau, was engaged in a search for a 'place of repentance', 'a place of comfort', meaning a text from the Bible. This sense of 'place'—a *locus* or passage in a text—is closely connected with the others; Bunyan's 'Map' of 1663, for example, showed not topographical outlines but biblical sentences of salvation and damnation arranged in a symmetrical diagram. Places are the physical manifestations of texts. The Hill Difficulty—'that difficult place' (p. 75)—represents the problems of reconciling contradictions in the Bible. The battle between Christian and Apollyon was fought with biblical texts, and left great scars on the ground when they 'made good their places against each other' (p. 292). The dark mountains are stumbling-blocks, like those assembled on pp. 352–3; William Denny described the Holy Hill of Contemplation in stanzas shaped like mountains (op. cit., pp. 286–92), but Bunyan's mountains *are* paragraphs. Biblical meaning may be compatible with topographical realism, but if there is any contradiction between them the Word will prevail. Bunyan's theory and practice of place is nicely summed up in the episode of Mount Marvel (p. 343), when the pilgrims 'looked, and behold at a distance a man that tumbled the hills about with words'.

Grace Abounding describes how Bunyan experienced sentences from the Bible as physical intrusions, acting on him as powerfully as Mount Sinai or Giant Despair did on the pilgrim. He was helpless in the face of contradictions, and spent months searching for a single quotation. He was no more in control of these verbal 'places' than Christian was of physical ones. But assurance of salvation gave him also a command over the Word, an ability to collect 'places' into meaningful patterns and expound them with eloquence. *The Pilgrim's Progress* is an expansion of his 'Map of Salvation and Damnation', an artistic concordance of Threats and Promises:

concordances for their use may be compared to the top of Pisgah, which, though itself was barren and rocky, yet it was able to show the discoveries of the whole land of Canaan.[16]

The splendid eloquence and spaciousness of the closing pages of each Part is a rhetorical representation of the moment when the godly enter into their inheritance, and a counterpart to the starkness and narrowness of the opening. *The Pilgrim's Progress* begins with the experience of someone 'wide as to God, but narrow for this world, lean in estates, but fat of soul'.[17] The greater assurance and control of space in Part II reflects the experience of pastoral care and leadership of his community; it was written, after all, to put his largely female congregation 'in their place'.[18] Each stage of his life and work is founded on a different relation to 'the Word'—exploratory, expository, and authoritative. Language is an estate he *can* master in this world. Thanks to this mastery *The Pilgrim's Progress*, the symbolic landscape of the landless, remained for two centuries one of the principal possessions of the dispossessed.

NOTES

1. Cf. John Barclay, *Icon Animorum* (1614), chap. 2; Joseph Hall, 'On a fair prospect', in *Occasional Meditations* (1633 edn); Barten Holyday, *A Survey of the World* (1661), f. A3.

2. Bunyan may have been influenced by didactic picture-books: for example in Comenius's *Orbis Pictus* (chap. 71 in Charles Hoole's English version of 1659) we see a cross-section of the interior of a house one of whose 'rooms' turns out to be a rectangular picture of the back yard.

3. D. Harvey, *Explanation in Geography* (London, 1969), pp. 193–4.

4. G. Offor (ed.), *The Works of John Bunyan* (1862), ii. 8.

5. Cf. William Habington, 'Et Exaltavit Humiles', in K. Allot (ed.), *Poems* (Liverpool, 1948), pp. 142–3: the 'humble man', assumed to be a 'Cottager', 'heaves up his head Like some rich vale whose fruits nere faile . . . '.

6. *Works*, iii. 515. Ralph Austen, proposing radical land reforms in the light of the coming 'gospel days' of 1653, uses these very words to describe the poor clamouring for land (preface to *A Treatise of Fruit-Trees* (1653)).

7. *Oceana* (1656), p. 4.

8. By Edward Fowler or an anonymous supporter (1672), f. A2v.

9. In 'Bunyan's gospel day', R. Sharrock (ed.), *The Pilgrim's Progress: A Casebook* (1976), p. 236.

10. In *Pelecanicidium* (1653), pp. 86, 103, 194, 200–1, 253.

11. *Works*, ii. 579; for communism, cf. also iii. 454, 543, and Mercy's contract in *Pilgrims Progress*, p. 232.

12. *Poetical Fragments* (1681), p. 17; cf. also pp. 24–25, where 'Map' and 'Glass' are equated. Bunyan does use the image of the telescope, but this is a narrow form of vision—contrast the 'multiplying glass' that Satan uses to magnify the things of the World in our sensual eyes (*Works*, i. 735).

13. *A Short Relation or Testimony of the Light of Christ in Me* (1659), p. 5.

14. In *Works*, iii. 463, Bunyan explains that the detailed plans of Solomon's Temple were dictated by God and not invented by Solomon, in order to forestall the criticism that Solomon gave way to his 'own humours or fancies'.

15. The physical act of walking was expressed by the verb *to go*, and *walk* was thus the vaguer term.

16. Robert Wickens, *A Compleat and Perfect Concordance* (1655), dedicatory epistle. Bunyan owned Vavasor Powell's *Concordance* (in which Promises and Threats are specially marked) and probably wrote one of his own.

17. Adapted from *Works*, i. 767—another use of spatial metaphor to represent the opposition between the world and religion.

18. *Works*, ii. 674.

The Journey in *The Pilgrim's Progress*

PHILIP EDWARDS

In his chapter on *The Pilgrim's Progress* in *Self-Consuming Artifacts* (Berkeley, 1972), Stanley Fish assumes that the word 'progress' in Bunyan's title has its modern sense of 'improvement' and that Bunyan's readers expect an allegory of journeying to imply that kind of advancement. In fact, Bunyan's 'progress', correctly quoted by the *Oxford English Dictionary* under sense 1, means, quite neutrally, travelling, a movement from one place to another, how Christian got from this world to the world which is to come. Bunyan's image of a journey is of great interest and value because travelling has a great many applications, of which improvement or achievement is only one. Since everyone who has ever lived has had the multiple experience of making a journey, Bunyan can rely on his readers' instinctive adjustment to each new application of the image as it is introduced. It is a basic error of Stanley Fish's position that Bunyan is always pulling the reins against the reader's mouth—that (as he concludes) so far as journeying is concerned, the insights which *The Pilgrim's Progress* yields 'are inseparable from the demonstration of the inadequacy of its own forms, which are also the forms of the reader's understanding' (op. cit., p. 264).

Certainly, as Fish indicates, on two notable occasions in the book pilgrims are themselves shown to be deceived by making false applications of the image of journeying. The first is when Formalist and Hypocrisy 'come tumbling over the wall' (p. 71) and argue with Christian that whatever short-cuts they may have taken they are in the same road as Christian and as near to Mount Sion as he is. The second is when Ignorance, having got to the end of the road, wrongly imagines he has arrived at the heavenly destination (p. 204). According to Fish, the mistake of these pilgrims is 'to believe too literally in the image of the journey' (op. cit., p. 261)—a mistake the reader himself is constantly tempted to make. It would be better to say that these pilgrims believe too literally in *one* use of the image of the journey. The whole power of both these passages, the latter so grim and frightening, lies in the very richness and versatility of the image, which make misinterpretation possible. The richness and versatility are fully apparent to the reader, and it is because of his co-operation that Bunyan is able in these two incidents to drive home his harsh doctrinal points.

Initially in *The Pilgrim's Progress* the journey is simply an escape. Some way out of the doomed City of Destruction has got to be found. Christian is informed that his city will be burned with fire, and he is determined to escape. 'Fly from the wrath to come', says the roll which Evangelist gives him (p. 41)—the marginal note indicating 'conviction of the necessity of flying'. But 'he could not tell which way to go'. Like any refugee, he has to choose in which direction to flee. 'Whither must I fly?' (p. 41). The choice of a direction inevitably involves the idea of a refuge or haven, and very soon the notion of going towards a place is added to the notion of fleeing from a place. Evangelist tells him to go towards the shining light which will lead him to the gate which he cannot see. The idea of escaping to a refuge is summed up in Christian's words when he is struggling in the Slough of Despond: 'I was bid go this way by a man called Evangelist, who directed me also to yonder Gate, that I might escape the wrath to come' (p. 46). At the gate Christian is to receive further instructions, but even before he has reached it, by the most natural and scarcely perceptible transition, the idea of seeking not merely an asylum but a permanent alternative home has been introduced. Christian speaks of 'that which I am seeking to enjoy'; 'I seek an inheritance, incorruptible, undefiled, and that fadeth not away' (p. 42).

So when Christian reaches the gate, the journey is seen as a balance between escape from and movement towards. His sentence to the gate-keeper, 'I come from the City of Destruction, but am going to Mount Sion' (p. 56), becomes a little later (p. 60): 'I am a man that am come from the City of Destruction, and am going to the Mount Sion.' The one cannot be without the other; journey as escape can have a Christian meaning only if a final destination is known and sought.

The idea of journey as pilgrimage is not introduced until surprisingly late, about a quarter of the way through the book (p. 80). The palace called Beautiful was built by the Lord of the Hill 'for the relief and security of pilgrims'. A little later Christian is asked what moved him to betake himself to 'a pilgrim's life'. By this new word a new perspective is given to the journey. The idea of escape is almost obliterated, and the emphasis falls on journeying towards a destination. The new perspective shows itself in a new version of what was formerly flight. His wife and family, he now says, 'were all of them utterly averse to my going on pilgrimage' (p. 84). Nothing was said about pilgrimage at the time. We shall all, he had then told his family, 'miserably come to ruin; except (the which yet I see not) some way of escape can be found, whereby we may be delivered' (p. 39). He began to run towards the shining light and his family cried to him to return. The difference in accent concerning the original occasion of the journey is observable at the end of the book (p. 203) when we are told that 'these pilgrims are come from the City of Destruction, for the love that they bear to the King of this place'.

While the concept of pilgrimage shifts the emphasis of the journey from the departure to the destination, the phrase 'a pilgrim's life' shows how strongly the journey itself is a centre of attention. Bunyan's use of the image of the pilgrim is deeply affected by the biblical phrase 'pilgrims and strangers'—a phrase he does not actually use until two-thirds of the way through the book (p. 127). This phrase occurs most strikingly in Hebrews 11: 13, where Paul speaks of those who died in faith before Christ; they dimly recognized the promises they had not received, 'and confessed that they were pilgrims and strangers on the earth. For they that say such things declare plainly that they seek a country.' This is Paul's interpretation of numerous Old Testament allusions to men being only sojourners or strangers upon earth. The phrase 'pilgrims and strangers' has little or nothing to do with a devotional journey towards a shrine. It implies wandering as aliens in this world. Our true home being elsewhere, our life on earth is a passage through a foreign land. So pilgrimage itself provides a twofold application of the image of the journey of wayfaring Christians; of alienation and of search. 'The men told them that they were strangers and pilgrims in the world, and that they were going to their own country, which was the heavenly Jerusalem' (p. 127).

The last sentence comes from the Vanity Fair episode, and it is necessary to pause here to reflect on the way in which the very existence of Vanity Fair depends upon the mutability of the journeying image. In discovering faith in Christ, Christian has escaped from the City of Destruction, reached the haven of the gate and entered into the way leading to heaven. In becoming a Christian he has become alienated from the unconverted, and the journey which was a flight from his fellows is now a journey among those fellows, who are now foreigners. The journey takes him to Vanity Fair, which is of course the very City of Destruction which he had left long before. It is a different city because Christian has become a different man. That city which he had once dwelt content-edly in, then fled from in fear, he now enters as a convinced Christian, ready to put up with whatever mockery, abuse, and violence may be directed at him. Faithful and Christian are no longer citizens of the City of Destruction; they are pilgrims and strangers in it. Their own town has become a place of hostility and persecution. The change is denoted not by a return (which would have done violence to other uses of the journey image) but by an arrival at a new city called Vanity. There never was any escape from the City; these refugees have to stay in it for the whole of their natural lives (p. 126). The alteration of the image of the journey from flight from a doomed city to arrival in a hostile city excell-ently conveys the transmutation of the self and consequently of one's surroundings in accepting Christianity.

The idea that the Christians are on a special journey of their own to their desired country is superimposed on a continuously underlying assumption that *all* life is a journey. When Christian 'sets out for Heaven' (p. 58), he is already far on in the journey of life. When in Part II Christiana and her children resolve to follow in Christian's path we have in our minds two different aspects of the journey image. Christian has completed his journey of life and is dead; the journey he made, however, was the journey of Christian commitment and Christian conduct. The two journeys are compatible: the Christian destination can only be reached by dying and the journey of life can only be finished by dying. Yet there is an awkwardness in the blending. In Part II it is almost impossible to resist the impression that Christian had left his family long before he died—soon, indeed, after his great cry of 'what shall I do to be saved?' The entangling of Journey A (the universal life-journey) with Journey B (the journey of Christian commitment) obscures the fact that Christian never really left his wife and children and quite prohibits description of the continuing tensions of a Christian in a hostile home. Christiana's decision to follow in Christian's footsteps is absurd in terms of Journey A (since following him is inescapable) and awkward in terms of Journey B (since physically he never left).

Adventure, keeping to the path, movement forward: Bunyan's journey continuously and successfully combines three distinct ideas. These are (a) the vicissitudes of a Christian's life, arising from external threat and inner disturbance, (b) obeying the strict demands of the true faith, and (c) advancing in the understanding and practice of the Christian life. In journeying, you encounter people good and bad; you pass through places good and bad. Christian's journey is one of trouble and endurance, and of special and exclusive favours. Journey as adventure accounts for a great many of the incidents in *The Pilgrim's Progress*, including the Slough of Despond and the Valley of the Shadow of Death. In journeying, you must also keep to the right path if you wish to get to your destination. 'I am in the King's highway, the way of holiness', says Christian magnificently, and journeying as path-keeping in the way of truth also accounts for many incidents, particularly those concerned with the narrowness or difficulty of the road (for example, pp. 59, 74) or with forks in the road where it is possible to take the wrong path (for example, pp. 74, 171–2). In journeying you do, if things go well, get nearer your destination. Christian's journey charts the progressive attainment of spiritual understanding and proficiency and the never-lessening danger of losing one's way, or one's determination, right up to the last mile. No journey is safer, no traveller more protected from losing his way, because the greater distance has already been travelled.

These three elements of spiritual travel combine well enough in Christian's single journey. There is, however, a fourth element to be added, and it makes the journey special indeed. Christian path-keeping (at least as Bunyan sees it) means not only keeping to the path but keeping the whole path. You can only get to the end of the road by travelling the whole of the road. You need a passport too and must give it in at the end (p. 165). In this aspect, far more than in the encountered marvels and horrors, Christian's journey is 'in the similitude of a dream'. Pilgrims start from various cities, but all must enter the way at the same wicket gate. As in a dream, or in a children's game, the journey is valueless and the destination unobtainable unless you have started from exactly the right point and made all the obligatory moves. Formalist, Hypocrisy, and Ignorance, one might say, fail to realize that in this one respect the journey-allegory of Christian salvation moves out of daylight rationality into a travelling experience resembling nightmare. Bunyan's readers, on the other hand, though they may have difficulty in accepting the severity of the doctrine, are only too aware that they have met this kind of journey before.

The final use of the journey image is the metaphor of arrival and welcome for the union of Christian with his maker. As at the beginning of the book the terror of a man seeking to escape gave great initial energy to the journey image, so the sheer satisfaction of the weary traveller reaching his destination and being welcomed invigorates the image at its conclusion:

> Drawing near to the City, they had yet a more perfect view thereof. It was builded of pearls and precious stones. . . . They walked on their way, and came yet nearer and nearer, where were orchards, vineyards, and

gardens, and their gates opened into the highway. . . .
They had the City itself in view, and they thought they
heard all the bells therein to ring, to welcome them
thereto.   (pp. 196, 202)

Bunyan's resourcefulness in recruiting every biblical image
that might be utilized in a journey allegory was extraordinary, and he combined them so skilfully that it seems the most
natural thing that Christian should flee from wrath, enter a
gate, tread a narrow path, be a pilgrim and stranger, walk
through the valley of the shadow of death, and enter into the
kingdom of heaven. Yet this compound journey, constantly
and imperceptibly changing its meaning, raises problems
when looked at closely. The unsophisticated reader can
probably find his way without help, but the critic is advised
to carry a proper map.

The Pilgrim's Progress:
Satire and Social Comment

BREAN S. HAMMOND

I

In its own time *The Pilgrim's Progress* was considered by some
to be unseemly. The Baptist T.S. (Thomas Sherman), for
example, produced his sequel to Bunyan's book as a corrective to its wit and levity; his version would 'deliver the whole
in such serious and spiritual phrases that may prevent that
lightness and laughter which the reading of some passages
therein may occasion in some vain and frothy minds'.[1] In the
poetic prologue to Part II, Bunyan himself felt it necessary to
defend the work from such accusations of unseriousness and
fictionality:

> But some there be that say he laughs too loud . . .
> . . . some love not the method of your first,
> Romance they count it, throw't away as dust . . .
>
> ANSWER
> One may (I think) say both his laughs and cries,
> May well be guessed at by his wat'ry eyes.
> Some things are of that nature as to make
> One's fancy checkle while his heart doth ache . . .
>   (pp. 214–15)

Our sympathy of course lies all with Bunyan, for the
passages to which T.S. objects are those that have an interest
for the reader beyond the requirements of allegorical example. At certain points the texture seems to thicken into a far
more precise and detailed mode than the relatively general
one demanded by the over-all conception of the work.
Among these are occasions on which the writing is propelled
by a vigorous thrust of social criticism, where the strength of

Bunyan's animus, firmly moored as it is in quotidian existence, creates mature satire.

The most accomplished satirical passage is the description of Vanity Fair. Here, Bunyan portrays and pillories corrupt institutions and the individuals who serve them in a way that provokes the hollow laughter of contempt. The town of Vanity, its fair, and the events that occur there are rendered in a heightened, semi-dramatic manner. Observation of detail is instinct with the author's own personality. While the allegory continues to be perfectly well served and the theme, 'all that cometh is vanity', well proved, there is about the description that graphic particularity of real life normally found in developed satire. There is a good deal of concrete information provided about the wares peddled, the side-shows on view and the organization of the stalls. There is traffic, literal and metaphorical, in 'houses, lands, trades, places, honours, preferments, titles . . . wives, husbands . . . blood, bodies, souls, silver, gold', and we can see 'jugglings, cheats, games, plays, fools, apes, knaves, and rogues' as well as 'thefts, murderers, adulteries, false-swearers', 'and that for nothing' as the author snidely comments (p. 125). A Jonsonian bustling energy is created by the simplest of syntactical structures—lists of nouns competing for a place in each sentence. The stalls are divided into different rows, each classified according to the nature of the commodity on offer, as was the case at the Stourbridge market that Bunyan knew. Eighteenth-century readers would find their pictorial appreciation of the scene sharpened by woodcuts or copperplate illustrations depicting it; in early editions, there are said to be engravings of Vanity Fair that include such specific features as handbills for Dryden's comedies affixed to the booths.[2] Such is the realistic set supplied for the drama of Faithful's martyrdom. Christian and Faithful are accorded the kind of welcome given to obvious outsiders in an incestuous, self-regarding community. Their summary imprisonment in an iron cage (a punishment actually suffered by the apostate Baptist minister and intimate of Bunyan's, John Child), their rough treatment at the hands of an incensed mob and their own Christian resignation in the face of all this are recounted with the conviction of personal experience. Bunyan neglects no details of the scene, even where his scrupulous observance of authenticity complicates the moral scheme. Thus, there are decent, humane citizens living in the town of Vanity who are outraged by the injustices done to the pilgrims and whose punishment is to be tarred with the same heretical brush. The passage is convincing, both socially and psychologically: the more patiently the victims bear their treatment, the more provocation they offer their tormentors.

Bunyan's account of the kangaroo court presided over by Lord Hate-good is conceivably a particular satire on the state trials sanctioned by Charles II. George Offor, Bunyan's nineteenth-century editor, has instanced the trial of Lady Alice Lisle, condemned to death by Judge Jeffreys, and such disgraceful travesties of justice as the trial of the Dissenters William Penn and William Mead, where intolerable pressure was put on the jury to convict.[3] Judge Jeffreys, 'the hanging judge', is a feasible identification for Hate-good, though I think it more likely that the scene's accuracy derives from Bunyan's experience of local rough justice rather than from his knowledge of abuse of the courts at a national level; the Bedfordshire justice who committed him to prison, Sir John Kelynge of Southhill, is a plausible candidate. Though there is scant evidence for specific identifications of this sort, the writing is of such a quality that it does *invite* speculation. The minutiae of the scene are perceived in sharp focus: 'one chanced mockingly, beholding the carriages of the men, to say unto them, "What will ye buy?" but they, looking gravely upon him, said, "We buy the truth"' (p. 127). This shrewd observation fuels the author's indignation against the institutionalized corruption of Vanity's leading citizens. Court procedure is manifestly irregular. Envy, the first witness, performs to order, brashly asserting his prepared-ness to 'enlarge my testimony against him' if he should escape the death penalty. Superstition and Pickthank provide testimony that is vague and useless—Faithful 'is a very pestilent fellow' who has been heard to 'speak things that ought not be spoke'—but they are given untrammelled licence by the Judge. Pickthank, seeing in the trial an opportunity to feather his own nest, shamelessly curries favour with the local potentate and the leading gentry, whom

Faithful is alleged to have calumniated. The Judge has determined to execute the prisoners before establishing their guilt. Indeed, since Pickthank's evidence attests that the Judge himself has been vilified by Faithful as an 'ungodly villain', Lord Hate-good is in no position to try the case.

A persuasive realism is achieved not only by the accurate mimesis of the events and atmosphere of a sham trial, but also by Bunyan's impressive use of dialogue. Vividly reproducing the contemporary abusive idiom, he sets up an incisive comic contrast in tone between the Judge's intemperance and Faithful's reserved, faintly ironic dignity:

> *Judge.* Thou runagate, heretic, and traitor, hast thou heard what these honest gentlemen have witnessed against thee?
> *Faithful.* May I speak a few words in my own defence?
> *Judge.* Sirrah, sirrah, thou deservest to live no longer, but to be slain immediately upon the place; yet that all men may see our gentleness towards thee, let us hear what thou hast to say.   (p. 132)

The Judge's 'gentleness' here is a masterly irony. His summing-up and citation of common-law precedents, all rulings given by pagan tyrants, continues the aura of burlesque and travesty. The jurymen themselves return not so much verdicts as impressionistic character-judgements on the prisoner that clearly demonstrate their prejudice and unfitness to serve: 'Then said Mr No-good, "Away with such a fellow from the earth." "Ay," said Mr Malice, "for I hate the very looks of him"' (p. 134). The final account of Faithful's execution comes to sound like Nashe's description of Zadoch the Jew's execution in *The Unfortunate Traveller* in its baroquely complicated extravagance: 'and first they scourged him, then they buffeted him, then they lanced his flesh with knives; after that they stoned him with stones, then pricked him with their swords; and last of all they burned him to ashes at the stake' (p. 134). As Bunyan says in the prologue, some experiences invite both a comic and a tragic response—we really do not know whether to laugh or cry at this point. Our reaction is then further complicated by the appearance of God's 'chariot and a couple of horses' ready to carry Faithful off to the Celestial City. While this may well come as an enormous relief to the reader, there is something irresistibly comic about Bunyan's having them waiting in the wings, outmanoeuvring the authorities of Vanity in their moment of triumph. The entire passage in fact strikes a serio-comic balance out of satiric indignation. Comedy results, not from any intentional light-heartedness on Bunyan's part, but from the grotesquerie of the events under description. At a trial like this, normal morality and propriety are perverted to such an extent that laughter is the only possible human response.

Realistic satire of this kind, agile, sophisticated, which ranges across the changing moods of its author's personality, can also be found in some of the characterization. To the extent that personification of abstractions always involves a dimension of fictionality, all of Bunyan's creations are 'characters'; and those that are given words to speak are endowed with a further degree of fictional life. In so far as the perspective on a character is critical, as it is with Obstinate, Pliable, Formalist and Hypocrisy, Mistrust, Timorous, Ignorance and others, the conception moves towards the satiric character-portrait. In these particular cases, however, Bunyan's prime interest lies in demonstrating that the character embodies a form of weakness, malfeasance, or wickedness that is at variance with biblical injunction; they are judged by a rigid criterion and there is little room for flexibility in Bunyan's treatment of them. But where the sins being allegorized are less doctrinal or spiritual lapses, and more forms of conduct that are self-indulgent and yet defended in the terms of a false theology, as in the case of Worldly-Wiseman and By-Ends, Bunyan invokes a very firm sense of identity and *milieu*. The whole life-style is up for criticism, not merely an isolable tenet of faith. Allegorical purposes are here hand-in-hand with those of satire, because showing what is *wrong* with being a Worldly-Wiseman depends on showing convincingly what it *is* to be one. With a character like By-Ends we cannot say that he contradicts this fundamental principle or that, but rather that his way of going about things is wrong. We need to show *how*, rather than show *that*—and this involves the author in utilizing his own experience, fully engaging his powers of observation. Again, precision, detail, and the accurate identification of a character within the social structure creates satiric portraits of great persuasion.[4]

By-Ends, whose 'great-grandfather was but a waterman', is a portrait of a social climber. His irritating habit of name-dropping and (we feel) bogus claims to be related to all the local gentry mark him out for an *arriviste* even though he now owns an estate and is elegantly clad. Like the jealous 'cits' of Restoration comedy, he fatuously insists on his wife's virtue and good-breeding:

> . . . my wife is a very virtuous woman, the daughter of a virtuous woman. She was my Lady Faining's daughter, therefore she came of a very honourable family, and is arrived to such a pitch of breeding that she knows how to carry it to all, even to prince and peasant. 'Tis true, we somewhat differ in religion from those of the stricter sort, yet but in two small points: first, we never strive against wind and tide; secondly, we are always most zealous when religion goes in his silver slippers; we love much to walk with him in the street if the sun shines and the people applaud it.
> (p. 136)

This manner of speech is close enough to that of a Sparkish or a Tattle, the imprudent fop who lacks wit enough to conceal the machinery of his own epic. There is a disarmingly brazen candour about his trimming philosophy: he does not scruple to be known as an opportunist who swims with the tide. We might well be reminded of Tattle's teaching Miss Pru to lie in *Love for Love*, behaviour similarly unselfconscious in its effrontery. Worldly-Wiseman's idiom is equally distinctive. He addresses the struggling Christian with an easy superiority—'How now, good fellow, whither away after this burdened manner?'—and the mealy-mouthed periphrasis of 'after this burdened manner' is an insult to Christian's fatigued condition. Metropolitan and suave, he treats Christian as a country clown. Calling attention to Christian's clothes besmirched by dirt from the Slough of Despond, he heaps scorn on the attempt to follow biblical teaching:

> . . . it is happened unto thee as to other weak men, who
> meddling with things too high for them, do suddenly
> fall into thy distractions; which distractions do not only
> unman men (as thine I perceive has done thee), but they
> run them upon desperate ventures, to obtain they know
> not what.   (p. 49)

Worldly-Wiseman speaks for all the world as though strict
Christian faith was an unsound trading proposition. Bunyan's sense of decorum does not fail him here. The
hypotactic, flowing manner of speech, down to the elegantly
rhetorical use of relative adjective and repeated noun ('which
distractions'), is well fitted to express Worldly-Wiseman's
counsel: always go to the shortest and easiest way to work as
regards salvation. There is a sugary blandishment about his
tone deriving from the assumed voice of experience: 'hear
me, I am older than thee'. His social position is clearly
superior to Christian's, perhaps that of a rich burgher or a
comfortable Latitudinarian preacher. Again, the texture of
the writing here is such that individual identifications are
tempting. Roger Sharrock has suggested that the capacious,
accommodating faith of a Latitudinarian like Edward Fowler, vicar of Northill and an adversary of Bunyan's, is perhaps
intended.[5]

As in the Vanity Fair episode, Bunyan's mimetic grasp of
conversational rhythms and powerful evocation of social
climate engages his entire personality. There are other
characterizations where these humanizing elements are
present to a lesser extent, notably Talkative and Atheist. Still
other figures in the work are denounced without being
treated satirically in the sense here discriminated, since they
present a threat that it would be dangerous to trivialize or to
expose to laughter. Of this kind are Apollyon and the Giant
Despair. But these are satirized in an older, less sophisticated
mode that we shall now proceed to discuss.

II

In an elastic sense of the term, most of *The Pilgrim's Progress* is
satirical; indeed satire of a kind is the staple diet of the prose.

The work as a whole does express the 'militant attitude to experience', in Northrop Frye's phrase, that is characteristic of satire. Christian frequently adopts a pugnacious posture before his enemies and, unless one thinks of Christianity in the full-blooded Pauline form, there is something surprising about his living his life by the Marquis of Queensberry rules: 'Apollyon, beware what you do, for I am in the King's highway, the way of holiness, therefore take heed to yourself' (p. 93). There is nothing in the slightest meek about this. In Part II, this militancy is carried even further. Mr Great-heart is as ready to punch a man's head as to clap him on the back and against the Giant Grim he strikes the first blow, before, we might think, he has tried all that persuasion can do.

This tone is accounted for by the fact that much of the work is dedicated to giving the rich and propertied their allegorical come-uppance. Apollyon is the 'prince and god' of the territory in which the City of Destruction is situated, but he is a harsh and neglectful master: 'I was born indeed in your dominions, but your service was hard, and your wages such as a man could not live on' (p. 90). In Vanity Fair, as we have seen, the oppressive authorities are all noble, and By-Ends aspires to their social position, his idiom an etiolated imitation of his betters. Worldly-Wiseman is a man of substance. The Giant Despair apprehends them for trespassing on his lands and the arbitrary punishment he metes out leaves them in no future doubt as to the distinction between *meum* and *tuum*. Helpless in the face of such brutality and power, the pilgrims are in the case of many a landless peasant or itinerant whose path has crossed that of a great lord. The Giant Grim also arrogates to his own use the King's highway, which he patrols with lions. But throughout the work it is made quite clear that these social abuses, the tyrannies of petty lordlings, will be righted in the hereafter. The tough, grainy texture of the writing derives from an uncompromising belief in a time when 'the first shall be last'. This, I would suggest, is part of what is understood by the 'key called Promise' that releases the pilgrims from Doubting Castle; but there are clearer indications of it. Faithful ascends to the Celestial City directly after his martyrdom. At the beginning

of Part II we learn from Sagacity of the rumour noised
abroad that Christian 'now walks in white' and 'has a chain
of gold about his neck', lives in 'a very rich and pleasant
dwelling at court', and that his Prince is asking very awkward questions about his ill-treatment while he was alive
(p. 221). In the House of the Interpreter the significance of
the man with the muck-rake is expounded: this-worldly
appetites carry the hearts of men away from God. In the
Valley of Humiliation, 'many labouring men have got good
estates . . . (for God resisteth the proud but gives more, more
grace to the humble)' (p. 289). Throughout this part biblical
texts extolling the virtues of simple poverty are cited. Giants
Grim and Slay-good are among those whose depredations on
the highway and on pilgrims are ended: Doubting Castle is
razed to the ground.

There is then a vein of social commentary running
through the entire work, an animus against the socially
advantaged that imparts to it its muscle and sinew. Christopher Hill has set *The Pilgrim's Progress* and its author in the
ambience of mid-seventeenth-century radical thought on
the basis of this social criticism, though his view is tem-
pered by the admission that 'Bunyan shared the social and
political attitudes of the radicals but not their theology'.[6]
With this I cannot agree. The tendency of the book's social
criticism is to my mind conservative—perhaps as conservative as is possible, short of actually defending Lord Hate-
good and his class of oppressors. In no sense does *The
Pilgrim's Progress* offer a programme of attack on the social
abuses it isolates, but rather its purpose is to allegorize the
hazardous and indirect spiritual journey away from this
world and its concerns. That Bunyan sees any form of
worldly commitment, even social reform, as secondary, is
clearly seen in Stand-fast's dealings with Madam Bubble on
the Enchanted Ground. This complaisant female, who 'always laugheth poor pilgrims to scorn, but highly com-
mends the rich' (p. 362) and who represents 'the world', is
given a wide berth by Stand-fast: she is not molested by
him, but goes her way in peace. Unlike the Levellers and
the Diggers, whose radicalism consists precisely in their
determinations to alter the here-and-now, Bunyan's hopes

are centred on the next world, not on this. It seems more plausible to me that his attack on the landowning and propertied classes derives from a more general moral and theological foundation—from the tradition of pre-Reformation pulpit preaching that is sometimes called satire.[7]

The case for the medieval origin of The Pilgrim's Progress was put by G. R. Owst many years ago, though his argument has not received the attention it deserves.[8] It rests on the considerable similarities that exist between Bunyan's work and medieval allegorical impersonations like William de Guileville's Le Pèlerinage de l'Homme and other sermons which deal with the progress of a pilgrim fleeing from a City of Destruction. Particularly close resemblances occur between The Pilgrim's Progress and a late fourteenth- or early fifteenth-century vernacular treatise on the Weye to Paradys, which dramatizes a burden-bearing pilgrim's journey to the Celestial City, narrowly avoiding a Slough of Hell en route and falling in with various personified abstractions sent by the Devil to mislead the true Christian. Though Bunyan is unlikely to have read specifically these works, the sermons he would have heard during a youth spent in the Bedfordshire village of Elstow were very likely to have been pre-Reformationary in character. In this rustic area, traditional forms of preaching, sermons medieval in spirit and structure, may well have lingered on unchanged into Bunyan's day;[9] and among the recognizable features of medieval sermons that are relevant to us here are the employment of allegory, the use of homely examples, and the vituperation of fashionable vices. Medieval homilists castigate clerical abuses, professional and business sharp-practice, social vices like swearing and wearing cosmetics and, with a fervour that can seem to be revolutionary, every kind of feudal oppression. Tyrants who suppress the poor are fiercely denounced, in the most extreme and violent terms. Very often, medieval preachers presented in lurid detail a vision of God's vengeance on the Day of Judgement, that effectively satisfied a crude sense of justice in the listener. This fierce passage from John Bromyard's Summa Predicantium (an anthology of fourteenth-century Mendicant preaching) is worth quoting at length:

Where are the evil lovers of the world [he asks] who a
little while ago were with us? Where are the evil princes
of the world, the kings, earls and other lords of estates,
who lived with pride and with great circumstance and
equipage, who used to keep many hounds and a numerous and evil retinue, who possessed great palaces, many
manors and broad lands with large rents, who nourished
their own bodies in delicacies and the pleasures of
gluttony and lust, who ruled their subjects harshly and
cruelly to obtain the aforesaid luxuries, and fleeced
them? Where, moreover, are the false wise men of the
world, the judges, assessors, advocates, swearers and
perjurers . . . who for bribes were wont to sell God and
the kingdom of heaven, and purchase hell? Where,
again, are the usurers, who used to make a penny out of
a farthing, and from eleven pence make twelve, and out
of a peck of wheat or its value make two or three pecks;
the false merchants, who knew how to deceive a man to
his face, . . . and the cruel executors who increased the
sorrows of widows? Where are the wicked ecclesiastics,
who showed the worst example to the people; where are
the haughty, where the envious, the lustful, the glutton-
ous and the other criminals? . . . You will find that, of all
their riches, their delicacies and the rest, they have
nothing; and the worms, as you will see, have their
bodies. . . . Their soul shall have, instead of palace and
hall and chamber, the deep lake of hell, with those that
go down into the depth thereof. In place of scented
baths, their body shall have a narrow pit in the earth;
and there they shall have a bath more black and foul than
any bath of pitch and sulphur. In place of a soft couch,
they shall have a bed more grievous and hard than all the
nails and spikes in the world; in place of inordinate
embraces, they will be able to have there the embraces of
the fiery brands of hell. . . . Instead of wives they shall
have toads; instead of a great retinue and throng of
followers, their body shall have a throng of worms and
their soul a throng of demons. Instead of large domain,
it shall be an eternal prison-house, cramped for both.
Instead of riches, poverty; instead of delights, punish-

ment; instead of honour, misery and contempt; instead
of laughter, weeping; insteady of gluttony and drunken-
ness, hunger and thirst without end; instead of excessive
gaming with dice and the like, grief; and *in place of the
torment which for a time they inflicted on others, they shall
have eternal torment*.[10]

Homilies like this were not intended to promote a spirit of
revolution. On the contrary, they were designed to effect a
kind of catharsis; listeners could indulge ritualized
revenge-fantasies in an institutionalized environment, the
better to endure their daily hardships.

The Pilgrim's Progress operates in the same way as social
commentary. There is nothing in the work quite as explicit as
this and other equally extreme thirteenth- and
fourteenth-century visions of Judgement Day, but Christian's entire journey, his progress from burdened, ragged
itinerant to celebrated guest of the Shining Ones in the
Celestial City, is a revenge-fantasy directed at Bunyan's own
persecutors and captors. The Celestial City is conceived by
Bunyan as the estate of the landless. Not only is the material
standard of living high, every need and want sumptuously
attended, down to 'an equipage fit to ride out with the King
of Glory' (p. 201), but the political organization is as egalitarian and democratic as is compatible with the full acceptance
of the Lord. Continuous contact with an approachable King
is stressed, because such free intercourse would be quite
unimaginable to the lowly pilgrims and not the least elysian
feature of the Celestial City. The pilgrims are promised full
participatory rights in the justiciary process, in marked
contrast to their muted position in the trial at Vanity: '. . .
when he shall sit upon the Throne of Judgement, you shall sit
by him; yea, and when he shall pass sentence upon all the
workers of iniquity, let them be angels or men, you also shall
have a voice in that judgement, because they were his and
your enemies' (p. 201). This threatening suggestion of retri-
butive justice is made more explicit in Part II. Mercy's
dream, in which she is apotheosized and exalted above those
who 'laughed at [her], called [her] fool and began to thrust
[her] about' (p. 272), represents in little the *peripeteia* that is

contained in the entire allegory of Christian's reaching the
Celestial City. Great-heart's muscular revenge wreaked on
Christian's enemies of Part I is a consummation demanded
by the work's theology, but also demanded by the author's
belief in an avenging deity: 'vengeance is mine, saith the
Lord, and I will repay'. At times, Bunyan can be as lurid as
Bromyard himself. When Mercy and Christiana come across
the place where Simple, Sloth, and Presumption are hanging
in chains, Mercy improvizes this little song, almost Brechtian
in its nastiness and a strange lyric for one called 'Mercy' to
sing:

> Now then, you three, hang there and be a sign
> To all that shall against the truth combine;
> And let him that comes after, fear this end,
> If unto pilgrims he is not a friend.   (p. 263)

Medieval homiletic tradition underprops Bunyan's criti-
que of the rich and propertied in *The Pilgrim's Progress*. The
pre-Reformation pulpit sermon that was in all probability
part of the youthful Bunyan's spiritual ecology, available
both in the sermons he would hear and in bound copies of
homily books, contains the fulmination against harsh
landlords, feudal barons, false stewards, and corrupt ecclesiastics that creates the combative, derisive tone of *The
Pilgrim's Progress*. Doubtless the book's animus against spiritual and social bullying *derives* from its author's contemporary experience, but insofar as it represents a substitute for,
rather than a form of political action, it is closer to medieval
reprobative preaching than to Winstanley. Acerbic satirical
writing very often does perform such a cathartic function;
personal vengeance is not an uncommon motive among
satirists, whose politics are very often strictly conservative.
Bunyan as satirist and social commentator is, I believe, a fine
exemplar of Eliot's symbiotic relationship between the originating genius and the tradition he inherits. His use of
allegory and personification is also medieval in origin, but in
this province it is Bunyan's innovation rather than indebtedness that impresses us. Where his experience, personality and
powers of observation are most potently combined, the
result is developed satire of a calibre previously undiscovered

in satiric prose—characters and scenes that have a lively precision and yet a general application, that are flexible and yet wide-ranging. Elsewhere, the castigatory spirit of the social critic imparts to the surface texture of the writing an uncompromising energy and excitement.

NOTES

1. Quoted in Roger Sharrock, *John Bunyan* (London, 1954, reissued 1968), p. 139.

2. See Northrop Frye, *The Secular Scripture: A Study of the Structure of Romance* (Cambridge, Mass., and London, 1976), p. 21.

3. George Offor (ed.), *The Works of John Bunyan* (1862), iii. 71.

4. The extent of Bunyan's influence on later novelists has not been sufficiently appreciated. Dickens arrives at a similar compromise between the allegorical and the real and may well owe something to Bunyan's characterization in the more developed passages of *The Pilgrim's Progress*. Like Bunyan's, his characters often serve the purpose of expressing their author's tenets of belief, while at the same time possessing a rich and independent life. Dickens was steeped in Bunyan's masterpiece and there is scarcely a novel that does not allude to it. In *Hard Times*, Bounderby is explicitly characterized as a latter-day Giant Despair: 'Stephen . . . turned about, and betook himself as in duty bound, to the red brick castle of the giant Bounderby.'

5. See Penguin edition of *The Pilgrim's Progress*, p. 375, n. 2.

6. Christopher Hill, *The World Turned Upside Down: Radical Ideas during the English Revolution* (Harmondsworth, 1975), p. 405.

7. A distinction can be drawn between this kind of reprobative invective and fully developed satire; see John Peter, *Complaint and Satire in Early English Literature* (Oxford, 1956), chap. 1, where the author designates the former mode and the vernacular verse that derives from it 'Complaint'. This term might be usefully borrowed and applied to Bunyan's social commentary in *The Pilgrim's Progress* and the term 'Satire' reserved for the fully developed passages discriminated in the first section of my essay.

8. G. R. Owst, *Literature and Pulpit in Medieval England* (Cambridge, 1933), pp. 97–109.

9. The Devotional manuals that we know Bunyan read, especially Arthur Dent's *The Plaine Mans Path-way to Heaven* (1601), are written in the medieval homily tradition.

10. Quoted in Owst, op. cit., pp. 293–4.

The Pilgrim's Progress and Allegory

BRIAN NELLIST

The Pilgrim's Progress is the last considerable work in English that all readers would agree to call an allegory. Other compositions, from *Gulliver's Travels* to *Animal Farm*, may have their claims but they require argument to substantiate them.[1] More than that, *The Pilgrim's Progress* is a popular allegory. This is the more surprising in that, since its demise, allegory has found apologists but has had few passionate defenders. Its operations are accused of being mechanical, especially by contrast with the density and suggestibility of symbol. Coleridge's discrimination between the two is the *locus classicus* of this criticism:

> Now an allegory is but a translation of abstract notions into a picture-language, which is in itself nothing but an abstraction from objects of the senses; the principal being more worthless even than its phantom proxy, both alike unsubstantial, and the former shapeless to boot. On the other hand a symbol . . . is characterised by a translucence of the special in the individual, or of the general in the especial, or of the universal in the general. Above all by a translucence of the external in and through the temporal. It always partakes of the reality which it renders intelligible; and while it enunciates the whole, abides itself as a living part in that unity, of which it is the representative.[2]

On inspection, this distinction looks loaded. By using terms like 'universal', 'reality', 'unity', and 'eternal', Coleridge manages to describe symbol as a form with direct access to knowledge, though it is a knowledge that the modern reader would feel to be less positive than Coleridge claims. Symbol is made to beg the very questions which are at issue, by its assumption that such 'knowledge' and a referential image can be at one. Allegory, by insisting on the distance between image and doctrine, at least honestly acknowledges that belief is not confirmed in any simple sense by experience.

This might seem, in its turn, to be unfair to symbol. All I want to do is to insist that they are separate literary epistemologies, as it were, and so to avoid the use of one to dismiss the other. Allegory directs our attention to the point of view which has gone to the making of a literary world. It manifests its selectivity by the distortions that it makes in the referential image ('shapeless to boot'). Symbol, by contrast, draws our attention to a moment of consciousness when image and viewpoint are subsumed. It is the seeing mind which authorizes symbol, where allegory takes its authority from what the mind sees. Traditional allegory is, by comparison with symbol, anti-individualist in its scope. It involves the assumption of some great typifying role: the scholar in Martianus Capella or Jean de Meun, the aristocratic lover in Guillaume de Lorris, the Body of Christ in Dante and Langland, the accomplished courtier in Spenser. Indeed, the demise of the mode may be attributed to social and intellectual changes which rendered such great collective images of human achievement not only unpopular but positively sinister. In so far as allegory survives in *Gulliver's Travels* it serves as a parody of over-systematic societies and thought-processes which obscure the individual's apprehension of truth. In Kafka's *Castle*, allegory has become the principal threat to the individual, whom it perplexes by offering a system without an interpretation, a nightmare that threatens the sanity of the mind.

The Pilgrim's Progress seems in many ways closer to such post-allegorical works than to traditional allegory. Its transformation of a literary form from within is similar to the relation of *Comus* to the court masque. Both are the only examples to survive for the unprofessional reader of modes which they are in effect destroying. At the centre of *The Pilgrim's Progress* there stands not a coherent body of thought or a process of developing reflection, as in traditional allegory, but a consciousness. What Christian perceives remains, like a symbol, shadowy in import and clear in valuation at the same time. His positive apprehensions are objects and locations which suggest more than they specify: the Wicket Gate, the Delectable Mountains, the River of Life. Doctrinal coherence is something attributed, on the other hand, to his enemies, Talkative, Ignorance, or Worldly-Wiseman. Much of the time he is resisting the claims of those collective images that allegory requires the reader to honour, such as husband, father, good citizen, scholar, even churchman. The only continuous relationship in the book is not with another person but with a thing, the road, and our concern is with an inner process of attentiveness. The Way itself behaves with a mysterious intimacy that makes it almost a part of the self. 'Is this the way to the Celestial City?' Christian asks the Shepherds on the Delectable Mountains, to receive the strange reply, 'You are just in *your* way' (p. 158, my italics), which, if the pun is intended, conflates Christian's just apprehensions with the road itself.

It is this placing of all significance in the interior processes of the hero which most sharply distinguishes the work from earlier allegory. Spenser's knights, for example, are shadowy creatures because they exist only to meet further segmentations of a way of life of which they are merely the central image.[3] Dante figures in his own poem as *poeta* principally to guarantee the truth of what he sees. But in Bunyan it is not so much what the hero sees that matters as his response to it and what he is in himself. The attendant allegories declare their significance with naïve directness because meaning resides not in them, as it partly would in Spenser and Dante, but in Christian's perceptions of them. The hero, moreover, has none of the magisterial claims of the great collective roles of allegory. Like the heroes of such post-allegories as *Gulliver* and *1984*, he has the individuality of the negligible man, bullied by the powers-that-be, whose only strength lies in thinking things out for himself. His value lies less in his expertise than in the depth and honesty of his feelings and the authenticity of his response.

Even if Bunyan was not familiar with any of the extended and sophisticated examples of allegory, he would know the developed similitudes used in the sermons of the day.[4] Like traditional allegory, these fix in the memory the abstract articulations of an argument by the analysis of a physical image. The analogy for the apprehension of truth becomes the right reading of objects in the physical world, for which, as in any act of good reading, we need to relate all the signs in the right sequence. More complex allegories may recognize the difficulty of this process but they do not reverse it. When Red Cross and Una, in the first canto of the *Faerie Queene*, take undue pleasure in the identity of the separate trees, they lose their way in the Wandering Wood and are brought to Error. In Bunyan, however, we start, not with a *selva oscura* of images but with bad places that declare their badness openly—the City of Destruction and the Slough of Despond. The 'reading' of them individually appears to present no problem at all. It is when Christian tries, so to speak, to construe these separate words into a sentence that perplexity starts. When he learns to turn the question 'What shall I do?' into the more specific 'What shall I do to be saved?', that is the result not of his tuition by images but of some prompting from within himself. His journey along the road produces no progressive comprehension of its phenomena. Bunyan uses allegory, oddly, to increase the sense of experiential perplexity. Traditional allegory creates a model of the world moving towards imaginative satisfaction, a species of utopia; *The Pilgrim's Progress* presents the world as a *dystopia*, permanently unredeemable to the mind. The River of Death sets a boundary to the realm of allegories as to the world, and in the Heavenly City the need for reading disappears since image and meaning are one.

One major problem for the reader of the book is how truth so individually derived can constitute an image of the generally true. Bunyan in Bedford gaol had good private reasons for presenting the world as a prison-house of rival allegorical certitudes threatening the individual consciousness. In earlier examples, however, allegory was itself the celebration of the authority of some great idea, so that the problem of authorization did not occur. The agent in such allegory was placed in his created world specifically to understand its laws. But Christian's law is, apparently, to keep himself uncontaminated by his world. Even if we assume he must always be right because he is elect, he himself is unconcerned with that election. We trust Christian in practice because of the honesty of his response. Unlike the order of priorities in traditional allegory, the feelings give authority to the doctrine, not the doctrine to the feelings.

This apparent subjectivism, we could argue, is verified by the persistent play of recognizable biblical image and analogy. The whole conception of the journey is sustained by centuries of usage, popular and sophisticated, of the New Testament imagery of *peregrinatio*, retrospectively read into the journey of Israel in the Old Testament. Yet images prove nothing. When we turn to Christian's use of the Bible itself, moreover, we observe that he uses it to confirm only what he already knows. Manifest cheats and heretics can be discomforted by apt quotation: St Paul puts paid to Talkative—'The Kingdom of God is not in word but in power' (p. 114).[5] In the hour of need the Bible provides analogy for Christian's condition but not the actual inspiration to his actions. In the victory over Apollyon he quotes Micah 1:7, 'Rejoice not against me, O mine enemy, when I fall I shall arise', before he cites St Paul's attribution of all conquest to Christ, 'We are more than conquerors through him that loved us' (p. 94). In Doubting Castle the Bible speaks no comfort to Christian himself, and in the River of Death it provides the language of his despair as well as of his renewing faith. Though scripture helps to make Christian's history representative, it is not the source of its validity. Similarly, the approving witnesses of his often repeated story save it from becoming pure phantasmagoria but give a support which is purely provisional.

Even the internal authorization bestowed on earlier allegory by the impersonal grandeur of inherited images and their continuous process of interlocking is deliberately reduced in *The Pilgrim's Progress*. The occasional positive moments of insight, it is true, provide a skeletal progression: Evangelist indicates the Wicket Gate; at the Wicket Gate Christian hears of Interpreter's House; from the Palace Beautiful he sees the Delectable Mountains; and from the Mountains he glimpses the Heavenly City. But in the major part of the progress the sinister figures seem to know nothing of one another. In Book I of the *Faerie Queene* the threatening presences gradually coalesce into a secret hierarchy, an other-world corporately engaged in the destruction of all good meaning. In Bunyan, Apollyon may claim to be Lord of the City of Destruction but nobody else seems to have heard of this prerogative. The figures all relate to Christian, not to each other. They are generated by his mind not by some autonomous figure of evil, like Archimago. Similarly, Bunyan restricts the larger resonances of his symbolic places, even Vanity Fair and the two dreadful Valleys.[6] Mythic associations would imply a centre of truth outside the consciousness of the hero himself.

This is evidence enough, I hope, for me to claim that Bunyan is writing a secondary form of allegory whose value is both to disguise and then to show forth the radical individualism of his position. Allegory enables Bunyan to fashion a special world where Christian can function successfully without his singularity provoking our protest. Just how well this works we can see by a comparison with *Grace Abounding*. This work is also a progress, though a negative progress into solitude and deprivation. It is also a study of an individualist sensibility. The hero's specialized condition is declared by the particularity of detail in the book and the constant use of superlatives. He is 'Chief of Sinners', 'meanest and most despised', 'the ungodliest fellow', 'most fearful', and so on.[7] The word 'all' is used with emphatic insistence, either to describe the inescapability of his condition 'all this while' or the separation between himself and the whole world ('I . . . counted the estate of everything that God had made far better than this dreadful state of mine').[8] The obsessional and unique nature of the experience, apparent in the style, is the book's chief subject. At the start we see him with his family, but it is the lowest in the land, and with friends, though he is their leader. We watch him progressively singled out for destruction (or salvation) by threatening bells and steeple and driven by guilt (or holiness) out of all social ties. His strange interior hauntings usurp the signs by which objective phenomena are usually recognized—spatial prepositions for instance. The happenings occur in mundane and public places and separate him from the comfort of what seems familiar and sociable.[9] Community survives only in the image of a group of old women sitting in the sun and talking of sin and grace, and even from that society he is excluded.[10] When he seeks companionship in the past and finds analogy for his sufferings in Luther, this temporary relief only prepares for the extrem-est stage of his despair and solitude. Ghostly figures—Esau, Cain, and Judas—begin to offer their unwelcome fellowship. Yet even this discovery of identity at the cost of damnation is qualified, for unlike them he has rejected the fruits of Christ's death. Even if the Saviour would wish to redeem him, He cannot: 'For my sin was not of the nature of theirs for whom he bled and died.'[11]

The difficulty for the reader lies in the status awarded to this strange mental journey. A peculiar pride is apparent in the singularity of his position, despite all the horror, and a conscious wilfulness in the passivity with which his mind is made a vacant field for the combat of salvation with despair.[12] The divine words that come to his aid are often obscure and in two critical instances are an uncanonical text from the Apocrypha and, secondly, phrases not in the Bible at all.[13] They constitute a new revelation made uniquely to the individual, transcending in power even the Word of God itself. The book's vitality, moreover, lies in its terror. With the restoration to community and the first use of the word 'we',[14] the work loses much of its strength. Are we, then, reading a confession or an apologia? Which of the languages of accountability do we trust? Does the work show the power of the devil, the perversity of the human heart, or an extraordinary operation of Providence? The value placed on the unanalysable uniqueness of the experience qualifies its claims as *exemplum*.

By using the language appropriate to a history, Bunyan turns *Grace Abounding* into something approaching a dream. By using a dream in *The Pilgrim's Progress*, he constructs a narrative with the substance of a history. The world of allegory, with its special and selective laws, confirms the centrality of the hero. The ordinary laws of probability operate against the experiences of *Grace Abounding*: 'These things may seem ridiculous to others, even as ridiculous as they were in themselves.'[15] The metaphysical anxieties that affect only the narrator in *Grace Abounding*, however, become universal in *The Pilgrim's Progress*. Even in the City of Destruction, although his family and friends ignore Christian's rags and burden they are roused by his prophecy of doom. They compound with their secret fears by despising Pliable for turning back from the Way. The concealment of actual malaise by apparent confidence is betrayed through a series of Freudian slips. Atheist, who has spent twenty years in search of heaven, now knows 'There is no such place as you dream of in *all this world*' (p. 174, my italics). Precisely—Christian himself would claim no more than that. When we read that Mr Envy in the trial at Vanity Fair accuses Faithful of denying the Christianity of the townsfolk, we are surprised that they claim to be believers at all, but we are more surprised to learn that Faithful had in fact merely indicated that what was opposed to the Word of God could not be Christian belief (p. 132). Faithful's apparently harmless proposition becomes a dangerous rebuke administered by the secret guilt of the men at the Fair. Christian is unique only in recognizing such guilt.

Thus, Bunyan exercises the customary privilege of allegory to present a selective obsession as though it were a universal law. What makes *The Pilgrim's Progress* secondary allegory is the nature of that law. If the reader brings to the work the reading habits appropriate to allegory he is surprised to discover that he cannot compose the images into a coherent order in themselves. They always carry him back to the introspective self of Christian. The latter's own consciousness generates the threatening figures who challenge and demonstrate his intelligence, courage, and capacity for survival. Yet if the reader, baffled like Christian by what is happening, changes his reading habits for those of the picaresque tale, no less does he find a calculated fracturing of the laws of narrative probability. Both modes, allegory and narrative, offer a confidence to the reader that Bunyan wishes to deny him. In Spenser the knight's road often lies between recognizable extremes—presumption and despair in Book I or the denial and excess of vitality in Book II—and the road provides an image of ascertainable truth. But in *The Pilgrim's Progress* the road is no safe middle way but itself leads into and through the fearful places. It springs on the reader the maximum number of surprises to bring him to the point where he realizes that it cannot be understood; it can only be followed.

Bunyan uses allegory as a trap. He is intent on withholding

from the reader just what the reader is expecting: clarification. In this respect the metaphor of the journey functions as it does in those two other popular, misread and nearly contemporary works, *Robinson Crusoe* and *Gulliver's Travels*. At a first approach we read and remember them all as a personal anthology of significant moments: the Slough of Despond, the fight with Apollyon, Vanity Fair, Doubting Castle. To return to them is often to discover with a shock how different the books are from our recollections of them. This experience is radically related to the image on which the books depend. They all describe visits to far countries which exhibit special and peculiar circumstances. We watch with pleasure a man like ourselves trying to adjust to puzzles they set him. But our detached delight in such alien marvels tends to turn to discomfiture when we discover that the apparently foreign is only another way of seeing the familiar. We end, like the confirmed traveller, estranged from our home-ground. To generations of Sunday-reading adolescents *The Pilgrim's Progress* must have offered the pleasure of a secret-service tale, written out of due season. The hero makes his way through apparently hostile territory, subject to oppressive powers, but in the service of a ruler who is the actual, if repudiated, governor of those lands, a graver ancestor of Kim.

The reader may protest at this point that the work is more coherent in its design than this account suggests. To forestall such legitimate rebuke, let me turn to the episode of Interpreter's House, which as an allegory within an allegory may be presumed to have a heuristic value. At the Wicket Gate, a step before it, Christian has been assured that he cannot miss his way. He scarcely seems to need the knowledge he seeks from Interpreter 'to help me in my journey'. Nevertheless, he is offered an ostensibly helpful series of emblems. Renaissance emblem had developed within two distinct traditions, the arcane and the moral. On the one hand it could be a means of rendering an esoteric truth through hieroglyphs, and on the other it was a way of presenting familiar proverbs with pictorial immediacy.[16] Interpreter, however, presents his emblems as though they were simple pictures but uses them to disconcert the beholder as though they were hieroglyphs. For example, Christian sees first a man with lifted eyes, book in hand, the world behind him, pleading with men, while a golden crown hangs over his head. 'Christian witness', we may think. The hero only confirms his naïvety in our eyes by asking, 'What means this?'. Yet the interpretation provided is more perplexing than the emblem itself: 'This is one of a thousand; he can beget children, travail in birth with children, and nurse them himself when they are born' (p. 60). This static figure, moreover, grotesquely distorted, eyes upwards, mouth on the level, back to the world ('Where is the audience, then?'), this is the authorized guide 'In all difficult places thou meetest with in the way'.

If the pictures are in themselves puzzling, their sequence increases our bemusement. We see next a man vigorously active with a broom in a dusty room ('Ah,' we think, 'Salvation starts with contrition'), yet his action only makes Christian choke as the dust flies into the air, until it is laid by a girl sprinkling water about ('Correction: contrition begins with salvation'). It is not that the images do not make theological sense. But the image is used to maximize the strangeness of the doctrine: the man who is apparently doing little is doing a great deal whereas the active servant is making bad worse. Moreover, it is not the doctrine as such that generates the sequence of emblems, it is its effect upon Christian's consciousness. It leads not to clarification, but to a see-saw between confidence and despondency.

This is the subject of the penultimate pair of pictures. In the first, we see a stately palace that attracts desire for entry, with men dressed in gold, walking on its roof. No sooner does Christian formulate the apparently required response, 'May we go in thither?', than he sees a crowd of men like himself, held back by fear. Expecting a cause, we see instead a secretary seated and ready to record the names of entrants. Only then does Christian observe, actually within the entrance, armed men ready 'to do the man that would enter what hurt and mischief they could'. No wonder Christian stands 'in a muse'. This apparently valid response is immediately contradicted by a bold fellow who rushes up, commands his name to be set in the book, draws a sword and, in a brutal affray, wins entry—upon which a pleasant voice calls out, 'Come in, come in / Eternal glory thou shalt win' (p. 65). If we recall that the Kingdom of Heaven is taken by storm, we may be the less surprised that Christian should say, 'I think verily I know the meaning of this.' But the emblem does not so much clarify the doctrine as raise doubts about the official role of the thugs at the gate and the character of the owner of the palace. Moreover, once we try to construe the sequence, the picture seems to recommend a confidence nearly Pelagian, though earlier images have speci-fied the worthlessness of merely human action.

The second emblem muddles any interpretative scheme still further. It shows a man in an iron cage. At first we see his imprisoning despair as the proper consequence of backslid-ing, an inconstancy that distinguishes him from the steadfast man at the gate. But then we recognize that the despair is itself the sin and that here steadfastness is directed suicidally against the self. In the face of such contradictory impressions Christian 'trembles', like the man in the last picture who dreamed of Doomsday. In Interpreter's House, Christian has learnt nothing but the value to be placed on an unresolvable contest of 'hope and fear' (p. 69). The allegories he has seen have robbed his mind of the peace of that doctrinal clarifica-tion that allegory usually pursues.

Throughout the book the movement of the interpreting mind from perplexity to explication is put into reverse. Whenever the reader thinks he understands, Bunyan extends the imagery to subvert understanding. He uses allegorical configurations to heighten the sense of absurdity. At the start, before he has a name to guide us, Christian is presented as a man dressed in rags and weighed down by a burden. Without hastening to identify their significance, Bunyan gives the man privileges over our attention precisely because he is in this state of guilt and destitution. Curiously, the neighbours do not even seem to notice that the burden is an awkward encumbrance when they put him to bed. Most allegories produce such local images which disappear when their significance is no longer central (one remembers Una's lamb in the *Faerie Queene*) or distort referential images at the command of doctrine. But Bunyan seeks nonsense out with the passion of a Lewis Carroll. The grotesque is not a consequence of his earnestness; his earnestness goes in search of the grotesque.

The phenomenon is used too extensively to be mere passing clumsiness. After the fight with Apollyon, a hand appears with healing leaves. Another allegorist would have sent an angel or at least given the hand a location; in *The Pilgrim's Progress* the unlocated fingers of Grace must float in the air. In the fight with Apollyon a sword will serve, but in the Valley of the Shadow Christian's weapon is All-prayer (solemnly delivered pages before in the armoury of the Palace Beautiful), allegorical significance without allegorical image, an apt but again grotesque weapon against ghostly enemies. Bunyan will emphasize the logic of narration only in order to break it by the logic of doctrine. In Vanity Fair Faithful is mangled in six different ways and reduced to a heap of ashes:

> Thus came Faithful to his end. Now, I saw that there stood behind the multitude a chariot and a couple of horses, waiting for Faithful, who (as soon as his adversaries had despatched him) was taken up into it.   (p. 134)

Elijah's analogous ascent in the fiery chariot is as clearly miraculous as this is matter-of-fact. The eye-witness verification, the dry enumeration of tortures, the locating of the chariot, the familiarity of 'a couple of horses', signal tonal veracity in the narrative just where all laws of narrative probability are being abrogated. Most strikingly of all, in Doubting Castle Christian discovers the key to his prison mysteriously round his own neck, though we have heard nothing of such a key before. Any allegory approached with the right degree of ignorance can be made to seem open to surrealist liberties; Bunyan, however, at times approaches parody in his use of the transformations that all allegory creates.

The consciousness of these procedures in a more specifically literary work would require the description, wit. The principle that governs the sequence and fashioning of the images in *The Pilgrim's Progress* is, basically, antithesis, and antithesis that parodies Christian's learning process. No sooner does he think he is in possession of some useful discovery than he meets that discovery changed into a new ignorance. As in *Gulliver's Travels*, and manifestly as not in the *Faerie Queene*, the images are related by a dialectic of irony. Christian starts his journey as a man who trusts a book more than his eyes but who still offers himself as guide to Pliable. Though he is dressed in rags he promises entry to a City where new garments 'Will make us shine like the sun'—and promptly falls into a slough. To read this as pride going before a fall is manifestly facile and to doubt that Christian is right to hope for glory is as manifestly false. Genuine knowledge prepares for a genuine ignorance: 'Ah! neighbour Christian, where are you now? Truly, said Christian, I do not know' (p. 45). Of the not knowing there seems no end. Help, one of those commissioned visitants to the mind's space who recur throughout the book, when he pulls Christian from the Slough, acknowledges that it has withstood the will of the King for sixteen hundred years.

The image generated antithetically by the slough parodies what we might expect to be Christian's response to that experience. Worldly-Wiseman arrives to offer in exchange for such degradation human dignity and social status. As a correction to the Pilgrim's confession of ignorance, he provides a systematic and instructed moralism. But when Christian follows his advice and approaches the Mountain of the Law, it threatens to fall on his head. We can only assume that the Slough was the better place to be in. He is visited now not by kindly Help but by a ferociously stern Evangelist. Doctrine puts restraints on our bemusement, of course ('Religious despondency is preferable to open heresy'), yet the effect upon the reader is not dissimilar to that of the restless play of irony in Swift's masterpiece.

In the sequence of antitheses every partial shelter for the interpreting mind becomes the ambush for a new threat. Allegory is transformed into a species of ordeal. At the Cross Christian's burden falls from him with astonishing ease, yet he immediately encounters a parody of this ease in the sleeping figures of Simple, Sloth, and Presumption and the abbreviation of the Way by Formalist and Hypocrisy. Learning the need for effort, he ascends the Hill of Difficulty with such energy that he falls asleep in the arbour on its summit.

On waking he rushes on full of guilt, only to meet Mistrust and Timorous in retreat from the lions. He summons his courage by thoughts of the Roll of Promise, to discover that he has lost it. So, like Timorous and Mistrust, he also has to retreat along the Way, like them in sorrow and self-mistrust, recognizing also his kinship with the figures of presumption that he thought he had dismissed: 'That I should sleep in the midst of difficulty' (p. 76).

The images in the book certainly do not lack ordering principle. It is not arbitrariness that distinguishes them from earlier allegory. It is rather that they are used to resist a process of generalization and to restrict access to any coherent body of knowledge. The allegories start into life, not at the command of an argument or a process of reflection, but in order to specify the moments of a psychic history. Taken out of context, for example, Talkative is an acute presentation of the temptation in any evolved system of belief to replace experience by technical jargon. In his *Essays* of 1805, John Foster, the Baptist, indicated this very danger in Evangelical faith.[17] Although Bunyan manifests this criticism through Talkative, he brings him into the landscape only after Christian has met Faithful and is first exposed to the perils of holy conversation. Their discourse is perfectly valid, yet it generates Talkative as a sinister parody. Like the other threatening presences, Talkative is imprisoned within an obsessional language which transforms the whole world into evidence for his point of view. Nothing exists except to furnish a good line of talk. The talk of Christian and Faithful has been particularized. It has described their distinct experiencing of the Way. Yet it materializes, as it were, a pseudo-body of generalization in Talkative, claiming the status of a knowledge beyond mere experience. The danger is proper purely to its context. The mirror-image of Talkative, in the second half of Christian's journey, is Ignorance, who attributes everything to experience and in relation to whom Christian and Hopeful occupy the earlier role of Talkative, demanding of him doctrinal discussion. There is no contradiction here because everything in this allegory is relative to the moments of Christian's experience. Most allegories are timeless in their operations, but in *The Pilgrim's Progress* meaning resides in temporal occasions. Christian's repetition of the events of his life does not turn into an argument understood, but remains a sequence of crises averted and critical moments survived.

This is to make *The Pilgrim's Progress* sound suspiciously close to the account I offered earlier of *Grace Abounding* and, indeed, in comparison with that work we can recognize another value to Bunyan of this particular transformation of allegory. In the autobiography, the reader is puzzled by the indeterminate status given to the experience. Is it near-damnation or the very shape of the saved life? In the allegory, this indeterminacy becomes not a side effect but the real issue. Christian's experiences induce in him a condition of nescience, bounded by hope and discouragement. Knowledge means submission to a succession of antitheses, always formulated in a fresh series, so that nothing can ever be predicted. Yet this labyrinth of ever occluded meanings produces in the end not terror but a state of resigned acceptance. It is the reprobate figures who are, in the main, in a hurry to reach a destination and who are cheerfully confident of their ability to read the signs. On the road to Doubting Castle, Christian asks Vain-Confidence where the track leads. 'To the Celestial Gate' comes back the reply, just before the speaker is dashed to pieces in the pit (p. 150). Formalist and Hypocrisy have the legal justifications for their trespass at their fingers' tips. The ancient custom of tumbling over the wall would be admitted 'as a thing legal, by any impartial judge' (p. 72). Christian answers not with an argument but by indicating the mysteriously redundant symbolism of election: his garments, his roll, and the mark on his forehead. By comparison with such figures, Christian is saved by his sense of terror and his modest incomprehension.

The inability to connect sign with sign coherently in the work, which begins as a source of alarm, ends as a release from signs altogether and an escape from allegory into a mood of trustful incertitude. In arguing for such a resolution I would disagree with Stanley Fish to whose account of the work I am otherwise deeply indebted.[18] Yet, if the work leads to the transcending of allegory, why, we may ask, does

Ignorance, a manifest allegory, loom so large at the close? Why, if the work celebrates a holy agnosticism, is the last temptation to be met called Ignorance? Why is Bunyan at such pains to insist on his damnation, so that at the end he becomes the summarizing anti-type to the triumphant pilgrims? To approach answers involves a journey back along the Way and even perhaps a digression.

The positive valuation of uncertainty is manifestly in line with Calvinist theories of election. In the great twenty-fourth chapter of Book III of the *Institutes*, those who would seek to comprehend the process of their own election receive a gruesome warning:

> Puny man endeavours to penetrate the hidden recesses of the divine wisdom, and goes back even to the remotest eternity, in order that he may understand what final determination God had made with regard to him. In this way he plunges headlong into an immense abyss, involves himself in numberless inextricable snares, and buries himself in the thickest darkness . . . And this temptation is the more fatal, that it is the temptation to which of all others almost all of us are prone. For there is scarcely a mind in which the thought does not sometimes rise, Whence your salvation but from the election of God? But what proof have you of your election? When once this thought has taken possession of any individual, it keeps him perpetually miserable, subjects him to dire torment, or throws him into a state of complete stupor.[19]

In *The Heavenly Footman*, Bunyan himself issues a similar caveat:

> If thou be prying overmuch into God's secret decrees, or let thy heart too much entertain questions about some nice foolish curiosities, thou mayest stumble and fall . . . to [thine] eternal overthrow . . . Take heed therefore, follow not that proud and lofty spirit, that, devil-like, cannot be content with his own station.[20]

The proper condition of the elect man is a state of confiding uncertainty.

Throughout *The Pilgrim's Progress* wayfaring is warfaring with imperious allegories. The apparent progress is a repeated *psychomachia* over an unchanging field of antithesis. Quite in line with this, Doubting Castle is presented as the answering term to the serenity of the Pilgrims beside the River of Life. Yet Doubting Castle differs from all the other catastrophes attending the hero and signals one of those transformations that all allegories tend to offer the reader. As usual, however, Bunyan first traps the unwitting reader into thinking that he knows how to interpret the situation. The folk-tale circumstantiality of Giant Despair's manners, his slightly submissive relations with his wife, the apparently irretrievable situation of the Pilgrims, the relish with which taunts and tortures are recounted, all persuade us that this captivity has the same objective authority as Vanity Fair. Yet Christian's recollection of the key leads us to recognize with surprise that this prison is self-imposed. Like the man in the iron-cage, Christian imprisons himself in guilt for a fault, temporarily leaving the Way, already forgiven to the Elect. This most outrageous of all the fractures of narrative proba-bility signalizes Christian's release from the authority of allegorical threat and is accompanied by an allusion to Christ's resurrection.[21] Giant Despair is overtaken by the physical decay he wished to impose on Christian; after his escape, Christian sets up a warning direction sign, the only occasion he does so, as though the castle were avoidable; in Part II the castle is levelled to the ground. As the climactic victory, it is followed by the visit to the Delectable Moun-tains. If this interpretation is correct, then the awakening and return to his sleep of the Dreamer at this point should not perplex criticism as it has done.[22] This is not an arbitrary break, let alone a covert reference to Bunyan's own release from gaol. It is a signal (not apparently altogether a successful signal) that Christian has been reborn and the Dreamer must formulate a new dream about his remaining journey.

What that change is we see most clearly in the strange episode of Flattery that follows the visit to the mountains. Once again the Pilgrims are misled, by a manifest cheat and one they have, moreover, been warned against. We seem back in the realm of fear and failure, with its attendant image of imprisonment, this time in a net. Yet when an angel comes to release them, they answer blithely that they are 'Poor pilgrims going to Sion'. No guilt affects them, despite his admonitions. Their punishment is merely external, and without a trace of irony they thank the angel who has just belaboured them and go on their way rejoicing (p. 173). The contrast with Doubting Castle is surely calculated. The anxiety to do the right thing, which produced the demons of allegory, has been replaced by an admission that error is inherent in the way and makes no difference to their status as pilgrims. What started out as combat with antithetical threats has now become the accepted pulse of error and insight which gives life to their inner experience. The allegories have lost their power over Christian's imagination.

Significantly this access of confidence to the pilgrims is accompanied by a loss of vitality in the book, as it was in *Grace Abounding*. The loss of terror is equivalent in Bunyan to a certain loss of identity. When the pilgrims enter the Celestial City they lose even their names and become simply, 'these two men'. Christian ends as a citizen of the unknowable, the very state which through his journey has filled him with such perplexity, and his journey is a preparation for a state of experience beyond all analysis. But Bunyan's imagination is most deeply stirred in the concluding passages except for the account of the River of Death, by the figure of Ignorance and his fate.

I now want to return to Ignorance. If we ask what he is ignorant of, then as usual we are slightly surprised by a paradox. He hails from the country of Conceit, which means, of course, knowledge as well as vanity, and he speaks with the certainty of inner light. Like the earlier allegories, he functions in relation to Christian's new condition as parody. Like Ignorance, Christian now enjoys the freedom of his interior world, released from the threats generated by his own desire for knowledge. But he differs from this parody by bearing upon him the scars of the battles he has fought in the search for holy ignorance. What the son of Conceit is ignorant of is just that—terror. Christian's new acceptance of the evil within experience approaches closely Ignorance's equally calm denial that it exists at all. Indeed Hopeful's criticism, at this point, of believers who are sustained principally by guilt and the fear of hell seems an implicit comment on the old Christian. The difference lies in the necessity for the trancendence of pain, in the discovery that guilt was not the foundation of the inner life but a dark passage that led there. Christian in his new state can recognize in Ignorance an object of pity (a feeling never granted to earlier threatening figures)—a figure who cannot grow beyond his youthful over-confidence into the related but oh-so-different confidence of spiritual maturity (p. 190).[23]

Bunyan uses allegory, then, to produce its own demise. Ignorance is a figure who interests the reader but who poses no allegorical problem at all to Christian, who has passed into a state beyond the claims of the earlier tumultous imagery. The weakness of this procedure is that, though Bunyan can affirm this condition theoretically, he can find no really satisfactory idiom to present it. Even the account of the Celestial City seems to me to involve an unspecific and clattering rhetoric, worlds away from the real strength of the style earlier on.[24] That strength had derived from his struggle to resist the usual assumptions of allegory, and it had expressed itself in paradox, antithesis, and calculated shock. Bunyan's persistently acknowledged, proudly paraded, ignorance almost compelled him to reverse traditional allegory's elevation of knowledge. So interiorized does he make his model of the religious life that it often seems close to those very Quakers and Ranters whom he controverted so strenuously in his youthful days.[25] His severity with Ignorance is a means of insisting on a distinction that otherwise might not have been wholly clear.

One result of this interiorizing is remarkable—the comparative absence of Christ from the immediate experience of the Pilgrim. In *Grace Abounding* He is everywhere acknowledged, but in *The Pilgrim's Progress* He is only occasionally in Christian's mind. If we ask what takes His place in the work, then the answer is, I would suggest, the Road itself. The Road functions not as a proposition but as the location of all the experiences Christian passes through. Its effects upon his personality are educative rather than instructional and Christian's relation to it, his regret at leaving it, his joy on finding it again, his total, unanalytical acceptance of it, is like a loving relation with a person. It works not like allegory but like Coleridge's symbol, an intimate apprehending of Christ's own words 'I am the *way*, the truth and the life' and 'No man *cometh* to the Father but by me'. To answer a question I raised earlier, it is the road that provides what external authorization there is for the allegory. However, in making a road the principal symbol for God, Bunyan renders Him inactive and attributes all activity instead to Christian's responses to the road. The inner experience of Christian takes precedence over even the sacred history of the Bible. So extreme is the individuality of this model of the religious life that even the Scriptures, that last public meeting-place of advanced Protestantism, yield their priority to a purely private history. God becomes the name for certain intimations in the devout man's experience of life. Bunyan's Christology was perfectly orthodox, yet the effect of the allegory is to turn Him into something approaching a symbol of the individual's deepest apprehensions. It is perhaps not so surprising a fact that one Dissenting group, the Presbyterians, should in the eighteenth century have become almost entirely Unitarian in their faith.[26]

Traditional allegory is by contrast with this, a social mode. Its images find their place within a structure of thought which the reader must be able to recognize and which has the authority of shared and public doctrine. Allegory is the least heretical of modes. *Piers Plowman* starts in an act of responsibility to the 'Fair field full of folk' and Dante rescues himself from exile by ideally reorganizing his city within the City of God. Even in its origins, the allegorizing of pagan mythology and the Christian Bible was undertaken to restore to the use of later societies writings addressed to earlier cultural assumptions. Bunyan's individualism and his elevation of private experience may seem to turn this process back to front. In another way, however, he continues the life of allegory. Allegory's claim on the reader is that it seeks to give the purest and amplest definition to representative modes of apprehension, by freeing us from the particularity of narrative. In *The Pilgrim's Progress* Bunyan preserves just this purity of allegory for the post-Renaissance individualist sensibility, even though in doing so he remodels it entirely.

NOTES

1. Modern critics of allegory have indicated a line of descent. See, for example, Angus Fletcher, *Allegory: The Theory of a Symbolic Mode* (Ithaca, 1964) and E. Honig, *Dark Conceit: The Making of Allegory* (London, 1959). Literary forms, like other parents, can be understood retrospectively through their progeny, but we still need to distinguish historically between primary and what is, in effect, secondary allegory.

2. *The Statesman's Manual: A Lay Sermon* (1816), in *Biographia Literaria* (Bohn's Library edn, London, 1885), p. 322.

3. A. Fletcher, op. cit., p. 35.

4. The largest collection of such images is Robert Cawdrey, *A Treasurie or Store-house of Similies* (London, 1600). For a later collection, see Thomas Shelton, *A Centuries of Similies* (London, 1640).

5. 1 Cor. 4:20. Christian has already identified Talkative without recourse to Scripture.

6. The Valley of the Shadow is clearly a place with resonances, but in comparison with, say, Orgoglio's Castle in *Faerie Queene* (I. viii. 30–41) it is unspecific in its associations. Spenser presents the Castle as Hell harrowed by Christ, the mind imprisoned by ignorance, a place of total sensory assault and deprivation, a pagan temple smeared with the blood of sacrifice, yet another image of Catholic imperialism, etc., etc. Such multiple associations would for Bunyan distract the reader's attention from the mind of Christian.

7. G. Offor (ed.), *The Works of John Bunyan* (1862), vol. i, title, paras. 2, 26, 31.

8. Ibid., p. 15, para. 82 and p. 18, para. 104; in para. 82, in two sentences, 'all' is used three times, in para. 44 four times, in 157 and 168 three times in each.

9. Ibid., p. 19, para. 113; p. 27, para. 174; p. 30, para. 187. The experience of estrangement finds perhaps its most striking analogy in the baby stolen by gypsies 'from friend and country' (p. 18, para. 102).

10. Ibid., p. 10, para. 37 and p. 12, para. 53.

11. Ibid., p. 29, para. 184.

12. He desires the texts of promise and damnation to come together in open combat in his mind (p. 33, para. 212).

13. On both occasions he is worried by their uncanonical nature; ibid., p. 13, paras. 62–5 and pp. 35–6, paras. 229–30.

14. Ibid., p. 36, para. 234. I can find no significant use of the word before this point.

15. Ibid., p. 29, para. 184.

16. See especially Mario Praz, *Studies in Seventeenth Century Imagery*, 2 vols (London, 1939–47).

17. 'Technical terms have been the light of science, but in many instances, the shades of religion', 'On the aversion of men of taste to evangelical religion', *Essays* (London, 1863), p. 228.

18. *Self-Consuming Artifacts* (Berkeley, 1972), pp. 224–64.

19. *Calvin's Institutes* (MacDonald Publishing Company, Florida, nd), pp. 515–16.

20. Offor, iii. 385. Cf. *The Jerusalem Sinner Saved*, Offor, i. 102.

21. Christian releases himself on the morning of the third day, Sunday, 'a little before it was day'; cf. Matt. 23:1.

22. See Offor, iii. 145–6. Offor himself sees it as the moment of Christian's entry into the ministry. Roger Sharrock submits John Brown's interpretation to a sane analysis; *John Bunyan* (London, 1968), p. 70.

23. Christian's conversation with Ignorance is not an attempt to free himself from false arguments, but to convert a misbeliever.

24. Even the syntax becomes unwontedly contorted: 'As they walked, ever and anon these trumpeters, even with joyful sound would, by mixing their music, with looks and gestures, still signify to Christian and his brother how welcome they were into their company and with what gladness they came to meet them' (p. 202).

25. Sharrock, op. cit., p. 30. Ranters and Quakers are singled out for attack in *The Heavenly Footman* (Offor, iii. 385).

26. See the article on Unitarianism in F. L. Cross (ed.), *The Oxford Dictionary of the Christian Church* (1957), p. 1391. In Liverpool both Gateacre and Toxteth Chapels were originally Presbyterian and became Unitarian places of worship.

The Dreams of Bunyan and Langland

DAVID MILLS

For a medievalist, the most obvious 'medieval' feature of *The Pilgrim's Progress* is its form, an allegorical action set in the framework of a dream. Paradoxically, this form embodies two contradictory impulses. Angus Fletcher has described the defining potential of allegory:

> Since allegorical works present an aesthetic surface which implies an authoritative, thematic, 'correct' reading, and which attempts to eliminate other possible readings, they deliberately restrict the freedom of the reader. . . . The mode appears not only to restrict the reader's freedom, but further to restrict itself, in scope of moral attitude and degree of enigma.[1]

This description (against which in fact Fletcher defends the mode) suggests that allegory affords the writer an escape from the intricacies of emotional, intellectual, personal, and social involvement into a simplified world—simplified in that each figure lacks internal complexity and also in that the values represented by the various figures are seen as mutually exclusive. Allegory thus denies the reader a range of response, directing him towards a system of unquestionable absolutes. It can become an artistic prison, inhibiting rather than aiding the creation of works of artistic insight.

The dream-form, on the other hand, has been characterized by A. C. Spearing as a form suggesting ambiguity and uncertainty. Of medieval dream-poems he writes:

> The dream-framework . . . explains the mere fact of the existence of a poem; it exists as an account of the narrator's dream. . . . This explanation is potentially highly ambiguous, since a dream may be considered as

the product of divine inspiration or as the expression of a merely human mood or fantasy. Secondly, the dream-framework inevitably brings the poet into his poem, not merely as the reteller of a story which has its origin elsewhere, but as the person who experiences the whole substance of the poem. . . . But this leads to further ambiguity, because though the poet can in this way discuss the problems of his art . . . he also, by appearing in his dream, disappears, since he becomes part of his own fiction.[2]

It is thus in the nature of the genre that the connection between the psychology of the author and that of the dreamer, and the connection of the dream to both, should be unspecified. And it is also characteristic of the genre that the attitude of the author and his narrator-persona towards the material related in the vision should not be clearly distinguished. By these means, the potential certainties of allegory are undercut by the vehicle of the dream form.

The present essay considers the use made of this contradictory form by two writers—the fourteenth-century alliterative poet William Langland, and the seventeenth-century preacher John Bunyan. Ostensibly, the two are separated by a divide deeper than that of time alone. Langland's faith is informed by medieval Catholicism; his writing is influenced by the allegorical techniques of medieval biblical exegesis; he is the heir to the traditions of Old and Middle English alliterative poetry. His poem, *Piers Plowman*, is an emotionally disturbing and structurally complex scrutiny of the implications of given theological truths for the fourteenth-century individual. Its title in Robert Crowley's 1550 printing of the B-text, *The Vision of Pierce Plowman*,[3] conveys no clear idea of the character of the work; probably no title could. Bunyan, on the other hand, holds the elective faith of a seventeeth-century Puritan; allegory is so far from an accepted mode of expression that he feels obliged to justify its use; the main influence upon his writing and theology is the Authorized Version of the Bible. *The Pilgrim's Progress* is on the face of it a simple assertion of Puritan faith, and no reader could doubt its content and intent from the extensively explicit title of Nathaniel Ponder's 1678 edition:

> *The Pilgrim's Progress from this world to that which is to come:*
> *Delivered under the similitude of a dream, wherein is discovered,*
> *the manner of his setting out, his dangerous journey; and safe*
> *arrival at the desired countrey.*

Despite these differences, however, both works have proved able to rise above the limitations of their given theologies and modes and to compel response from readers to whom both theologies and literary traditions are alien. Each of the writers seems to have originally envisaged a specialized and restricted audience. John Burrow has argued that Langland's poem was read by the clergy, but that even in the fourteenth century it reached the new audience of prosperous literate laymen;[4] by the sixteenth century it was accepted—for different reasons—by Protestant and Catholic alike. Similarly, Bunyan appears to have in mind an audience which shared his Puritan theology, but his work has also reached a wider lay audience, so that 'most of it has been read and re-read by those who were indifferent or hostile to its theology, and even by children who perhaps were hardly aware of it'.[5] Such breadth of appeal is gained not by sacrificing theological truism, but by complementing theological assertion with an allegorical exploration of the psychology of belief, so that the reader is involved in an unresolved debate about the nature and purpose of religious faith.

Langland's poem strikes the reader as being more naturalistically dreamlike than Bunyan's narrative. An explanation of this impression, and an illustration of Langland's general allegorical technique, may be gained from an examination of his account of the Tree of Charity (B 16/1–94),[6] where, by progressively overloading an image with allegorical significance and simultaneously moving rapidly between literal and allegorical levels, the 'observed object' seems to change and disintegrate before us. The tree is first presented as a picture with labels, a useful allegorical construct and mnemonic; for example,

> Mercy is þe more þerof; þe myddul stok is ruþe;
> The leues ben lele wordes, þe lawe of holy
> chirche. . .   (5–6)

As the dreamer, hearing Piers's name, falls into an ecstatic swoon, he sees the tree as a three-dimensional object, though still emblematic; it is supported by three props (the Trinity) against three wicked winds (the World, the Flesh, the Devil) and produces fruits of three kinds (Matrimony, Widowhood, Virginity). But the dreamer then seems to forget the allegorical import of the scene and treates the tree like a literal fruit tree, asking to be allowed to taste an apple. Piers, the fruit-farmer, tosses stones into the tree and shakes the branches, and the fruit, in defiance of its literal nature, begins to howl. As the individual apples fall, they are recognized as pre-Redemption prophets and patriarchs:

> Adam and Abraham and Ysaye þe prophete,
> Sampson and Samuel and Seint Iohan þe Baptist
> (81–2)

whom the devil, like an apple thief, gathers up to add to his store while Piers, the angry farmer, grabs a prop and hits out at him. The emblematic tree has become literal, a recognizable tree in an orchard, protected by the farmer from winds and pests, but dropping its windfalls and vulnerable to apple-scrumpers. As the description develops, the tree ceases to be important for itself and becomes the centre of an action for the ownership of the fruit. Simultaneously, its original function as an emblem of moral virtues in the individual Man yields to the fruits of those virtues in Mankind as a whole, and thence to the historical perspective of unredeemed Man stolen away to Hell by the devil, which institutes the historical action of the Incarnation in a new image that follows. The account oscillates challengingly between the literal and allegorical levels, sometimes signalling its incongruity by its comically unexpected collocations:

> And Piers caste to þe crop and þanne comsed it to
>   crye;
> And waggede widwehode and it wepte after;
> And whan he meued matrimoyne it made a foul noise.
> (75–7)

and sometimes subsuming one level beneath another, as in the final picture of the angry Piers, which is irresistibly literal. The effect of this imagistic allegory is emotionally and intellectually disturbing as the reader grapples with the shifting tones and significances of the observed image.

Bunyan's narrative seems less naturalistically dreamlike than Langland's because he affects greater modal simplicity. He gives the impression of holding the observed image constant and locating the differences in realization within the viewpoints of structurally separate observers.[7] The reader is invited to consider the central figure, Christian, for example, from two distinct viewpoints—as an emblematic figure exemplifying a particular thematic point, and as a human-being whose actions are attributable to his inner psychology and the pressures of his social circumstances. As emblem, Christian is objectified in the same way that the various sights in the House of the Interpreter are objectified. It is a function of the objectification that, in considering Christian, the reader is made aware of the presence of the narrator as detached observer, just as in the House of the Interpreter he is conscious of the emotionally detached Christian as observer, seeking the meaning of the sights but never empathizing with the figures that he sees. The figures in the Interpreter's scenes are regarded as counters; and logically they are merely automata,[8] without past or future, bound always to return to the start of their actions to perform for the next set of pilgrims, as they do later for Christiana and her company. So to the dreamer Christian is also a counter, a mechanical participant in a chain of exemplary actions which can be repeated for and by each reader. Each new reader is shown Christian's action as each new pilgrim is shown the Interpreter's sights, and through the narrator we can seek the meaning of Christian's actions without involvement at a human level.

The sense of the emblem is strongly evoked in the opening picture, where the narrator—like Christian, a wanderer in the world—is admitted to a sight which seems to have been awaiting his presence before it comes to life:

> I saw a man clothed with rags, standing in a certain place, with his face from his own house, a book in his hand, and a great burden upon his back. I looked, and saw him open the book, and read therein; and as he read, he wept and trembled.   (p. 39)

The insistence upon the observer's presence ('I saw,' 'I looked') correlates with the essentially visual nature of the account and the cumulation of isolated phrases suggestive of the deliberate selection of significant detail. The figure has no context in space (note the wilfully indefinite 'in a certain place') or time (we do not know the events preceding this scene), so that the picture becomes enigmatic and provoking; the reader asks 'why?' rather than 'who?' As the description anticipates the sights of the Interpreter's House in mode, so it also contains details echoed later in two figures there—the picture of Evangelist, Christian's mentor and pattern ('It had eyes lift up to Heaven, the best of books in its hand, the law of truth was written upon its lips, the world was behind its back' [p. 60]), and the man in the cage ('He sat with his eyes looking down to the ground, his hands folded together, and he sighed as if he would break his heart' [p. 65]). Sharing details of the emblems of the spiritually enlightened and the despairingly damned, the picture is not naturalistic—not, that is, the picture of a tramp or beggar setting out on a journey with his goods on his back. The rags, emblems of spiritual poverty, and the burden, emblem of sin, do not exist in 'reality' and are appropriately ignored by the neighbours who seek to help Christian. The house and book may be understood literally, but they are here used primarily for their emblematic force, as in the later picture of Evangelist, indicating Christian's desire to reject worldly ties and his reliance upon the Word of God for enlightenment and guidance. The reader interprets intellectually, but is not required to respond emotionally.

Immediately, however, the narrator recedes and the reader views Christian through the eyes of his colleagues in society; emblematic significance yields to human response and diagnosis, as Christian returns to his city home, to his wife and children, and time passes. The visible signs of his inner state vanish; Christian betrays no trace of his distress to his family. In him, concern for his family's safety and for their response to him stands beside his concern for his own safety. Christian can now appropriately be regarded as a neurotic, overwhelmed by some undefined and perhaps indefinable fear which has no apparent logical cause. The visible burden now

becomes a mere image, vaguely suggestive of some emotional pressure which cannot be defined ('I am myself
undone, by reason of a burden that lieth hard upon me') and
can therefore sustain the logical diagnosis of 'some frenzy
distemper'. Similarly, the warning of destruction is based on
'certain' information, but the source is unspecified, and
Christian's obviously distressed state calls even that warning
into question. The neighbours, in their terms, have no cause
to believe him, and seem justified in their mundane hope that
rest will restore his emotional balance and dispel his fears.

Here, and throughout the work, Bunyan's vision has a
simple, emblematic force. Over-all, it has a picaresque form,
being the emblematic journey of a central emblematic figure,
Christian. In so naming his hero, Bunyan signals that he is
destined for salvation—for if a Christian cannot attain it,
none can. And at the same time, the name defines the hero's
nature and effectively indicates that he cannot be other than a
Christian—cannot, that is, adopt the positions of others
whom he encounters. His path is clear and straight, and his
goal of the Celestial City is fixed and sure. Yet the same
allegorical determinism which conveniently by-passes
arguments of theological justification and programmes
Christian for Heaven can, if projected on to a naturalistic
level, produce the illusion of a figure whose psychological
complexity has been overridden by a single obsession—in
effect, a neurotic. Bunyan thus acknowledges the analogy
between the divinely inspired and the neurotically possessed,
recognizing that to the human eye the two may be indistin-
guishable, even though they demand the contradictory responses of admiration and scorn.[9]

Langland, in contrast, proposes no equivalent certainty, for
his goal is not fixed and sure, and his dreamer, even in
allegorical terms, is not so unequivocally defined as Bunyan's
Christian. At the centre of the poem is Piers Plowman, who
is assimilated into the pattern of recurring images of shifting
significance already noted. Piers enters as a literal ploughman
looking over a hedge in astonishment to hear that no one, not
even a palmer, knows where to find Truth (B 5/537–55). As
he attempts to guide the world to Truth, however, Piers
becomes a force for social order and moral leadership in

society, assuming kinglike and even Godlike powers as he tries to translate a personal faith into a workable social code. Then, as he recognizes the social and theological limits of his belief, he reverts to his literal level and the mentor becomes the searcher, vowing to change his own life:

> 'I shal cessen of my sowyng', quod Piers, '& swynke
>   no3t so harde,
> Ne aboute my bilyue so bisy be na moore;
> Of preieres and of penauance my plou3 shal ben
>   herafter.   (B7/122–4)

In succeeding passus, Piers is seen as ideal, possessing supra-human knowledge (B 13/124–30), tending the Tree of Charity in Man's heart, identifiable with St Peter as the founder of the Church (B 19/317–34) and with Christ Himself (B 15/209–12), whose very name fills Man with joy and hope. At the end of the poem he is sought by Conscience:

> 'By crist!' quod Conscience þo, 'I wol bicome
>   a pilgrym,
> And wenden as wide as þe world renneþ
> To seken Piers þe Plowman, þat pryde my3te
>   destruye. . .   (B20/380–2)

the only hope in a world dominated by Antichrist. Yet Piers remains fallible and human, capable of fits exasperated anger in the face of his limitations, as when he summons Hunger to punish idlers (B 6/171–73), tears up Truth's pardon (B 7/119) or hits out at the apple-stealing devil—actions which stand against his confident advice to the pilgrims, his exposition to the dreamer on the Tree of Charity, or his ploughing of the world under the mandate of God. Piers seems both searcher and sought simultaneously, a figure whose widening emblematic significance stands beside his recurring human responses. As object sought, his significance shifts as that of Bunyan's Celestial City does not.

Like Bunyan, Langland acknowledges the link between inspiration and obsession. He does so in the figure of his dreamer, who, in his waking moments, is regarded as mad

by his fellow-men in his single-minded quest for the means
of salvation:

> And I awaked þerwiþ, witlees nerhande,
> And as a freke þat fey were forþ gan I walke
> In manere of a mendynaunt many yer after.
>
> (B 13/1–3)

> Ac after my wakynge it was wonder longe
> Er I koude kyndely knowe what was dowel,
> And so my wit weex and wanyed til I a fool weere.
> And some lakkede my lif— allowed it fewe;— . . .
> That folk helden me a fool; and in þat folie I raued . . .
>
> (B 15/1–4, 10)

Yet the dreamer can retrospectively acknowledge the justice
of this judgement, and can view himself with detachment
and humour denied to Christian. Moreover, his obsessive
waking conduct matches his curiously argumentative manner as he enters his own dreams and interrogates the various
characters. Waking, he is a William; sleeping he is Will in all
its senses, including the power of choice, human desire, and
simple wilfulness. As an allegorical figure, he lacks the
unambiguous endorsement accorded to Christian, and he and
the reader must acknowledge the possibility that his visions
are merely deluding fantasies.

The sense of isolation, whether resulting from election or
obsession, is reflected in the image of the journey, which is
used by both writers. Paradoxically, the image implies a
desire for stasis, the yearning for a spiritual security, represented by Langland's Tower of Truth and Bunyan's Celestial
City. But at the same time it reflects upon the individual's
psychological insecurity and upon his sense of isolation from
his fellow-men in society. Both Langland and Bunyan face the
possibility of reconciling the desire for spiritual security with
that for social stability, and both finally reject the possibility
for similar reasons. In Langland, the world stands between
the Tower of Truth and the Dungeon of Wrong, to one of
which each individual will be assigned on death. Man does
not recognize this perspective, but Langland postulates a
spiritual pilgrimage in which men will repent of their sins,

will cease to move physically in search of worldly gain in order to progress spiritually. Piers proposes an allegorical journey inwards so that redeemed Man can see the castle of Truth established in his heart. Man thus becomes a microcosm; his inner pilgrimage in this life to inner truth mirrors and determines his temporal pilgrimage, through death, to the Tower of Truth, Heaven. In the process a society imitative of heavenly society in its charity and justice will result. Yet the postulate is made to be rejected, for the individual sustains inner truth only by moments, and a society of the redeemed alone is never possible. The good are exploited by the evil; no man can be established in truth by civil and moral law. Piers' utopian vision founders on an intractable legality expounded by a priest:

> 'I kan no pardon fynde
> But do wel and haue wel, and god shal haue þi soule,
> And do yuel and haue yuel, and hope þow noon ooþer
> That after þi deeþ day þe deuel shal haue þi soule.'
>   (B 7 /115–18)

This failure drives Piers to devote more time to prayer and meditation and to direct the poem towards a quest for inner certainty induced by self-examination and revelation.

Bunyan similarly proposes a unity of psychological, social and spiritual stability; it is the unity envisaged by Mr Worldly-Wiseman:

> Thou mayest be eased of thy burden, and . . . thou mayest send for thy wife and children to thee to this village, where there are houses now stand empty, one of which thou mayest have at reasonable rates; provision is there also cheap and good, and that which will make thy life the more happy, is, to be sure there thou shalt live by honest neighbours, in credit and good fashion.   (p. 50)

Home, wife, children, neighbours, worldly prosperity, and spiritual ease! Here, as in Langland, a unity of moral law ('The village is named Morality'), civil law ('A gentleman whose name is Legality') and the conventions of civilized conduct ('His son whose name is Civility') is envisaged. But Christian is overwhelmed by the awful vision of Mount Sinai and the threat of the Law, and is disabused by Evangelist as Piers is by the priest: 'Ye cannot be justified by the works of the law; for by the deeds of the law no man living can be rid of his burden' (p. 55).

The rejection of the philosophical postulate means, logically, that there can be no compromise of the world and the spirit. The elect are socially isolated in so far as they are spiritually enlightened, so that Christian's withdrawal into his spiritual obsession has its counterpart in his rejection by his fellows. Naturalistically a contributory factor in Christian's withdrawal into self-communion, this hostility is also emblematic of the hostility of world to spirit and becomes a necessary sign that the individual is in a state of grace. When Piers commits himself to his inner journey, Langland signals the transition by changing the meaning of his image: 'Of preieres and of penaunce my plouȝ shal ben herafter' (B 7/124). But for Bunyan there is no such break. The narrator intrudes as if signalling the return of the emblematic level as Evangelist appears ('I saw upon a time', 'I saw also', 'as I perceived', 'I looked then'), and Evangelist thus seems to personify the voice of the Holy Spirit within, directing Christian to follow his spiritual intimations, to seek something of whose existence he is uncertain ('Do you see yonder shining light?' He said, 'I think I do'). So Christian completes his rejection of the world in emblematic flight, closing his ears to its call. Evangelist later provides the text for the picture: 'He that comes after him, and hates not his father and mother, and wife, and children, and brethren, and sisters; yea, and his own life also, he cannot be my disciple' (p. 54). Charity will praise him for the act: 'If thy wife and children have been offended with thee for this they thereby show themselves to be implacable to good; and thou hast delivered thy soul from their blood' (p. 85). Such sentiments are appropriate not to the literal abandonment of family, but to the emblematic rejection of all worldly affections for spiritual aspirations.

However, Bunyan is reminiscent of Langland in his simultaneous insistence upon a literal level to the picture. The city, wife, children, and neighbours have already been realized at a literal level in the opening scene, and the great field across which Christian runs seems to be of the same order as the fields in which he earlier walked outside the city. The physical detail, 'The man put his fingers in his ears, and ran on crying "Life, life, eternal life"' (p. 41), seems comically inadequate to its emblematic function but suggests the literal action of the demented, to which the neighbours appropriately respond ('Some mocked, others threatened; and some cried after him to return'). The emblematic action is thus not absolutely separated from the literal action.[10]

The tension between the levels of meaning is important. The scene is primarily emblematic, the response of the neighbours in part indicating its distance from a reality in which there is no light or wicket gate. But the insistence upon a literal level allows Bunyan later to reassess Christian's separation from a human viewpoint. The neighbours' jeers may be inappropriate to the emblematic scene, but Charity's harsh theology is equally inappropriate to Christian's later account of the scene, with its movingly controlled under-statement of suppressed emotion: 'You must think that my wife and poor children were very dear unto me' (p. 84). Christian's emotional response here is not invalidated by an emblematic reading which denies particular emotion.[11] As elsewhere, an event first briefly sketched out as emblem can later be extended and revalued in human terms, changing and completing its significance, so that the event is viewed twice, rather as Langland can re-utilize an image with new signifi-cance. Thereafter, the event carries a force revived with later passing allusion, as when Christian comments to Ignorance: 'Leaving of all is an hard matter, yea, a harder matter than many are aware of' (p. 185).

Christian's progress is therefore in itself a development—a literal estrangement from his fellows reflecting his journey inwards towards an inner truth, beginning with the weaken-ing of worldly desires. As such, it also presupposes a correlation of progress with the passage of time. Bunyan observes Christian from the awakening of his spiritual con-sciousness to his death and entry into the Celestial City, just as Langland shows his dreamer progressively ageing until he awaits his particular judgement as the world around him, under Antichrist, awaits the Second Coming and the Last

Judgement. But at the same time the forces of Good and Evil
are not only represented objectively in Heaven and Hell,
Tower and Dungeon, Celestial City and City of Destruction.
They are also embodied within the individual, bearing upon
Man's inner nature. So Langland sees Wrong as a force active
in Man's carnal nature:

> Lef nauȝt þi licame for a liere hym techeþ,
> That is þe wrecched world wolde þee bitraye.
> For þe fend and þi flessh folwen togidere,
> And þat shendeþ þi soule.
>
> (B 1/38–41)

Wrong is opposed by Truth, who has given his precepts to
Man and provided Man with faculties to aid him—his senses,
reason, conscience, and above all his *kynde wit* or natural
understanding. Man can build his own tower of Truth in his
heart:

> Thanne shaltow come to a court, cler as þe sonne. . . .
> And if grace graunte þee to go in in þis wise
> Thow shalt see in þiselue truþe sitte in þyn herte.
>
> (B 5/585, 605–6)

Similarly, Bunyan's City of Destruction and the Celestial
City may be regarded as symbolizing forces of evil and good
operating within the individual. Christian moves from one to
the other, but theoretically could turn back as many others
do, deterred by the dangers ahead (Pliable, or Mistrust and
Timorous), or pulled back by disbelief and the attractions of
the world (Atheist). Many of the figures journeying along
the road seek the impossible, to reconcile the claims of the
world and the spirit, and give only an illusion of progression.
In fact, they do not change but continue to their death and
inevitable damnation at their particular points of equilibrium
between the two inner forces. By-Ends provides a clear
example. He projects his self-interest into religion and shuns
the worldly opprobrium visited upon the faithful:

> They are for holding their notions, though all other men

are against them, but I am for religion in what and so far
as the times and my safety will bear it.   (p.139)

As his name indicates, he cannot change his predetermined
nature and hence does not progress. He stops at Demas's
silver-mine, his own point of equilibrium, where he will die.
The destruction of such figures, the transport of others to
Heaven (Faithful) or Hell (Turn-away), the entrances to Hell
along the way all suggest that the road is also a line of spiritual
force operating within each man. As such, the sense of
development in time and understanding is not a necessary
consequence of the journey-image.

Moreover, for this reason, the balance of forces in Man is,
for Bunyan, as much psychological as spiritual. Christian is
between fear and hope as well as being between evil and good
and damnation and salvation. Hope, represented by the
Celestial City, is less immediate. Christian sets off unsure that
he can see his goal, and even when offered the sight of the
Celestial City from the Delectable Mountains, he cannot be
sure of his vision: 'They could not look steadily through the
glass; yet they *thought* they saw *something like* the Gate, and also
some of the glory of the place' (p. 161, my italics). Ignorance
provides a grim and memorable example of self-deluding
hope. Bunyan does not deny the force of hope, as embodied in
Hopeful who can translate his impression into firm fact ('Did
we not see from the Delectable Mountains the Gate of the
City?' [p. 175]) and whose hope sustains him throughout, as
Christian comments ('You have been Hopeful ever since I
knew you' [p. 199]). But the existence of Hopeful allegorically
locates hope outside Christian himself, who is most strongly
impelled by fear.

Bunyan's view of fear is complex. Christian's is a creative
spiritual fear, driving him away from the world into isolation.
Christian characterises it as the fear that 'driveth the soul to lay
fast hold of Christ for salvation' and that nourishes reverence
for God, His word and ways in the soul, 'making it afraid to
turn from them' (p. 191). Christian's journey becomes a flight
rather than a progress, for every step along the way from
emotional and social stability increases the difficulty of return;
he muses in the Valley of the Shadow:

> Sometimes he had half a thought to go back. Then again
> he thought he might be halfway through the Valley; he
> remembered also how he had already vanquished many
> a danger; and that the danger of going back might be
> much more than for to go forward: so he resolved to go
> on.   (p. 97)

This impelling fear contrasts with the fear of worldly ostrac-
ism which deters so many from progressing: 'They have
slavish fears that do overmaster them. I speak now of the
fears that they have of men' (p. 193). The desire to compromi-
ise with the world is, however, a mark of the weakness in
such men of true spiritual fear and presents less danger to the
committed Christian than the confining power of spiritual
despair, emblematized in the man in the cage in the House of
the Interpreter and seen in the episodes of the Slough of
Despond, Doubting Castle or the crossing of the River. If
Christian lacks the spiritual optimism of Hopeful, he also
lacks the martyr-faith of Faithful. His creative fear always
borders on a spiritual despair which threatens to drive him to
mental and emotional self-destruction as well as to spiritual
damnation, so that the City of Destruction assumes a psychological as well as a spiritual dimension. It is not surprising
that Christian can defend the actions of Little-faith against
the criticisms of Hopeful. *The Pilgrim's Progress* thus becomes
a study in Puritan consciousness as well as in Puritan
determinism, and its spiritual allegory of the progress of the
elect to Heaven is accompanied by recurring imagery of
coercion, violence and confinement indicative of the operation of fear within the individual.

The two viewpoints in the work can also correlate with
spiritual and psychological effects, as in the battle of Christian and Apollyon, where the scene is first shown as emblem,
diminishing its particular force, and then later, as Christian
talks to Faithful, seen in terms of the participant's response.

> In this combat no man can imagine, unless he had seen
> and heard as I did, what yelling, and hideous roaring
> Apollyon made all the time of the fight; he spake like a
> dragon: and on the other side, what sighs and groans
> brast from Christian's heart. I never saw him all the

while give so much as one pleasant look, till he perceived he had wounded Apollyon with his two-edged
sword.   (p. 94)

Yea, I thought verily he would have killed me;
especially when he got me down, and crushed me under
him as if he would have crushed me to pieces. For as he
threw me, my sword flew out of my hand; nay he told
me he was sure of me, but I cried to God, and he heard
me, and delivered me out of all my troubles.   (p. 110)

The first account not only stresses the dreamer's presence
('had seen and heard as I did', 'I never saw') but presents a
self-conscious organization of material ('on the other side').
The verbs—with the possible exception of *brast*—have no
concrete force, and the key words are all nouns ('yelling',
'roaring', 'sighs', 'groans'), contributing to the sense of a
static account. The image 'he spake like a dragon' frustrates
our expectation of 'roared' and actually prompts irrelevant
speculation on how a dragon does speak—a piece of ineffec-
tive overwriting which is balanced by the curious comment
that Christian did not give 'one pleasant look' in the battle.
The opening disclaimer of ability to communicate the
experience verbally completes the distancing effect of the
whole account.

In contrast, in the second account Christian focuses upon
himself and his responses. The passage is peppered with
first-person pronouns. Its organization is at once chronological, causal and climactic. Its syntax is verb-based, using
words with strongly physical and violent overtones ('got me
down', 'crushed', 'crushed to pieces', 'threw', 'flew', 'cried'),
and their force is strengthened by asseverations ('yea',
'verily', 'especially', 'nay') and by the almost breathless
continuity of the syntax; the punctuation is less a guide to
syntactically complete periods than an indication of breath-
ing-pauses in a continuous passage. The sense of emotional
calm after the energy, seen in the more formal and restrained
'delivered me out of all my troubles', correlates with the
return of spiritual assurance. Here the reader finds himself
engaged with Christian's predicament and response, revalu-
ing the scene and, in some measure, questioning the Narra-

tor's earlier detachment, for Christian's account achieves the
sense of tension which the Narrator claims to be unable to
convey.

Langland, who seeks the source of spiritual awareness in
human speculative curiosity, achieves a similar conflict of
emphasis. His emblematic allegory, however clear and logical, tends to lack emotional conviction. Piers's allegorical
journey with its mechanical labelling is a good example:

> Thanne shaltow come to a court, cler as þe sonne.
> The moot is of mercy þe Manoir aboute;
> And alle þe walles ben of wit to holden wil oute;
> The kerneles ben of cristendom þat kynde to saue,
> Botrased wiþ bileef-so-or-þow-beest-noȝt-saued . . .
>
> (B 5/585–9)

The castle is a construct of intellectual ingenuity but without
any exploration of the appropriateness of the image to the
theme. In contrast, Langland utilizes an image-pattern of
growth, cultivation, and harvest across a range of significances from the literal through the moral to the spiritual and
Biblical. The images aptly suggest the growth of spiritual
awareness and knowledge in Man, but also have a tensive
vitality lacking in purely expository allegory or in the logical
expositions of individual figures. An extract from Holy
Church's description of the plant of peace may serve as
illustration:

> For heuene myȝte nat holden it, so heuy it semed,
> Til it hadde of þe erþe yeten hitselue.
> And when it hadde of þis fold flessh and blood taken
> Was neuere leef vpon lynde lighter þerafter,
> And portatif and persaunt as þe point of a nedle
> That myȝte noon Armure it lette ne none heiȝ walles.
>
> (B 1/153–8)

The plant, growing in the 'pot' of heaven, is transplanted to
earth where it paradoxically becomes flesh and blood. Formerly too heavy for Heaven, it is now 'lighter' than a linden
leaf. It becomes sharp—like a needle; or like a lance for battle;
or, leaving the idea of sharpness behind and taking up the

martial associations, like a battering ram (*none hei3 walles*)—perhaps looking to the Harrowing of Hell. Theological paradox is here invested with the intensity of emotional experience as the image moves and leaps disturbingly in response to the attempts to realize simultaneously the virtue of charity and its historical expression in the Incarnation. The passage anticipates the large-scale episodes, such as the Tree of Charity, which punctuate the poem, providing the emotional affirmation of truths whose wholeness has been lost by intellectual dissection. Such passages of high poetic power have the force of spiritual revelation in Langland.

The insistence in both Langland and Bunyan upon the emotional experience of faith stands in some measure against their claim that good and evil have objective existence, in God and the Devil and their agents. In Langland, Conscience and Meed present to a king arguments for the government of the realm either by moral or by economic principles. Both figures are absolutes, simple in their nature and incapable of communicating directly to each other because their terms of reference are irreconcilable; Conscience can never encompass economic expediency, and Meed is incapable of moral self-examination. Yet the debate before the king merely externalizes an inner debate in which the individual balances the claims of conscience and economics in reaching an assessment. In the simple struggle of good and evil, Conscience is on the side of God and Meed on the side of the Devil—agents warring for control of Man; but within the individual they are simply functions of Man's consciousness, and can be balanced or reconciled. Langland's concern with human psychology is embodied not in a journey-image but in a series of inner debates which serve to realize the relative nature of Truth. The dreamer consults thought, wit, study, scripture, receiving from each a partial answer to his questions according to the terms of reference of that faculty; but it is his job as a complex human being to synthesize the different accounts. He can appropriately challenge any personification because its approach cannot comprehend the problems of a human being or convey the appropriate sense of emotional conviction. He rightly draws attention to Lady Holy Church's failure to convince him, a complaint which

she cannot understand and which therefore draws from her
an intemperate and unhelpful rebuke:

> 'Yet haue I no kynde knowyng', quod I, 'ye mote
>   kenne me bettre
> By what craft in my cors it comseþ, and where.'
> 'Thow doted daffe!' quod she, 'dulle are þi wittes.
> To litel latyn þow lernedest, leode, in þi youþe.'
>   (B 1/138–41)

The inner debates require resolution at a higher level of
intuitive recognition of the Truth:

> 'Piers þe Plowman!' quod I þo, and al for pure Ioye
> That I herde nempne his name anoon I swowned
>   after. . .   (B16/18–19)

Piers, like all other figures, is at once objective and
subjective—a force sent from God and active principle in
Man's heart which the individual can bring into being.
    Bunyan is similarly conscious of the ambiguous
'objective-subjective' existence of personifications. As Christian crosses the Valley of the Shadow he hears the blasphemous promptings of evil rising within himself:

> . . . many grievous blasphemies . . . which he verily
> thought had proceeded from his own mind. This put
> Christian more to it than anything that he met with
> before, even to think that he should now blaspheme him
> that he loved so much before; yet, could he have helped
> it, he would not have done it: but he had not the
> discretion neither to stop his ears, nor to know from
> whence those blasphemies came.   (p. 98)

Christian supposes the voices to be sinful impulses within
himself, presumably normally repressed but here released
under stress, and this possibility is not wholly negated by the
Narrator's insistence, from his emblematic viewpoint, on
their origin in objective evil:

> One thing I would not let slip, I took notice that now

poor Christian was so confounded that he did not
know his own voice, and thus I perceived it . . . one of
the wicked ones got behind him and stepped up softly to
him and whisperingly suggested many grievous
blasphemies to him. . .   (p. 98)

The allegory may be seen, according to viewpoint, as the
externalization of inner psychological forces and as the
dramatization of a universal struggle of good and evil for
the soul of man. This dichotomy is in fact latent in much of
the allegory, since figures such as Worldly-Wiseman,
By-Ends, and Ignorance, as well as Faithful and Hopeful, are
allegorically realized as objective and independent entities,
but have significance only in so far as their arguments
demand response from Christian and can therefore be seen as
representations of voices and impulses within him.

Although the emblematic struggle of good and evil demands resolution in terms of rational, theological responses,
the inner struggle is more emotional and less readily resolved. In a purely moral argument, Langland's Conscience
must easily defeat the corrupting Meed; but Meed's hold
upon worldly society demonstrates that Man does not make
decisions solely according to morality. In dramatizing the
debate of the two characters, Langland presents Conscience
as a sober and decorous lawyer, deferentially kneeling before
the king with an 'An't please your lordship':

> 'Nay', quod Conscience to þe kyng and kneled
>   to þe erþe.
> 'Ther are two manere of Medes, my lord, bi
>   youre leue.'   (B3/230–1)

His speech is reasoned, logical, structured; the two kinds of
Meed are discussed in turn, the argument is supported by
example and authority, and Conscience concludes with an
account of the just, Meedless society. But this logic is cold
and unappealing beside the lively duplicity of the corrupt
Lady Meed, cynically exploiting her feminine weakness with
a touching display of distress ('Thanne mournede Mede, and

mened hire to þe kynge', B 3/170) and emotionally represent-
ing herself as an innocent and wronged woman:

> And þow knowest, Conscience, I kam noȝt to chide,
> Ne to depraue þi persone wiþ a proud herte.
> Wel þow woost, Conscience, but if þow wolt lie,
> Thow hast hanged on myn half elleuene tymes . . .
>
> (B 3/178–81)

Her personalized attack, with its scornful singular address
and the spat-out vocatives *Conscience*, may lead the reader to
forget that she is the accused and that Conscience cannot by
nature *lie*. If he recalls that, moments before, he has seen her
corrupting lawyers and priests in the court, he will only
marvel admiringly at her audacity. Such fascinating and vital
evil can be countered not by logic alone but by a spiritual
truth apprehended with equal intensity—by Piers, who
seems to embody a semi-mystical spirituality which defies
reason but exerts an almost ecstatic influence upon Man. As
such, Piers is as much a poetic as a theological creation,
typifying Man's unconscious yearning for spiritual security.

There is a similar ambivalence in the reader's response to
Bunyan's Christian. Logically, we can endorse him as an
emblematic figure; but the neurotic aspect of his personfica-
tion, the unattractive contrast of his self-interested fears and
the biting contempt and ruthless rationality with which he
crushes those who do not hold his beliefs, make him an
unsympathetic figure. In him one sees the force of Aldous
Huxley's comment:

> A man may have (and will be suitably rewarded for the
> having) a certain kind of spiritual wealth and at the same
> time lack (and be punished for the lacking) certain other
> gifts and graces. Intellectually, for example, he may have
> and it will be given him; but emotionally and
> æsthetically, it may be taken away from him because he
> has not.[12]

Increasingly, as Christian withdraws from the world, he
sheds outgoing emotions, as if spiritual perfection demanded
the stultification of human love and compassion. He is
therefore judged in two ways—in relation to those whom he

condemns theologically, against whom he is judged emotionally deficient; and in relation to his own ignorance of this
limitation, as others are ignorant of their own limitations.
Both judgements may be seen in his dealings with the
question posed to him by Mr Hold-the-world. Mr
Money-love's original answer to By-Ends' question clearly
demonstrates for the reader a worldly self-interest in religious
matters of which the speaker and his hearers are comically
ignorant. The ironic suppression of any spiritual dimension
in the company's commendation of the reply as 'wholesome
and advantageous' is comic, and also a prelude to the
reassertion of that dimension by Christian and Hopeful
which the reader may gleefully anticipate. Yet at the same
time the reader recognizes the futility of rebuking the blind
for being blind and choice of the *old* Mr Hold-the-world to
pose the question suggests the appropriateness of a compass-
ionate response. Christian's response, though theologically
faultless, lacks any compassionately persuasive intent and
seems designed only to humiliate. There is a strong sense of
hysterical overstatement in the emotively climactic '[Such
answer] is both heathenish, hypocritical and devilish', and an
unattractive relish in 'and your reward will be according to
your works' (p. 143), which prompt an instinctive sympathy
in the reader for the silenced group, however erroneous their
views. The limits of the response are indicated by Hopeful's
commendation of 'the soundness of Christian's answer', for
Christian has responded to a proposition, not to a questioner.
His failure to see the deficiencies of his own response
suggests a lack of self-knowledge akin to that of his question-
ers, but without the comic overtones.[13]

Because both Langland and Bunyan invite an emotional
response from the reader which may run counter to an
emblematic or moralistic interpretation, their allegories are
not merely statements, even though at one level they can be
so read. But the awareness of oscillating viewpoints and
standards of assessment directs the reader towards the literary structure which generates these contradictory responses.
From our response to the narration of the dream, we are led
back inevitably to the Dreamer-Narrator; for the dream is
his, and may be seen as ambiguously offering him spiritual

consolation and also expressing his inner fears and aspirations. Langland's vision may be seen as the product of an aimless wanderer's idle curiosity:

> In a somer seson when softe was þe sonne
> I shoop me into a shroud as I a sheep weere;
> In habite as an heremite, vnholy of werkes,
> Wente wide in þis world wondres to here.
>
> (B Prol/1–4)

The journey is prompted by the warm sun, there is a conscious absence of spiritual concern, the quest is only for *wondres*. The dreamer's questions seem idle, speculative, and childlike, as when he asks Holy Church 'Who owns the money in the world?', 'How may I save my soul?', 'How can I recognise Falsehood?'; or responds to Conscience's identification of a figure as Christ with an apparent terminological quibble: 'Why calle ye hym crist, siþen Iewes called hym Iesus?' (B 19/15). Such tangential questions determine the course of the vision, making it at one level the reflection of an individual, argumentative mind. Yet what begins in idle curiosity becomes a serious, obsessive search for the meaning of existence—to recognize the False; to know Do-well, etc.; to find Piers Plowman who alone can give meaning to life. The vision thus comes to control and give purpose to the dreamer's life and values, giving him new spiritual insights. As expression of the psyche and as revelation, it is uniquely his.

Bunyan's vision also responds to a dreamer's need. At its start we see him as a man in an alien environment, for the world is a wilderness, connotative of formlessness and sterility. The dreamer finds refuge, and dreams of a world resembling ours, not formless but with landscape, towns and villages, roads and people. Yet this world is clear and simplified, unlike ours. A clear track leads from the City of Destruction to the Celestial City and Christian travels it with visible signs of his elect state—the lack of burden, his garment, his roll. In this monodimensional world issues are clearcut and certainty is possible. The figures move in predictable and repeatable patterns, trapped by the natures defined by their names, like the exemplary automata of the

Interpreter's House. Such a world seems like an escape from the complexities of waking existence and, in its certainties, threatens to become the literary prison of our opening thesis.

But this vision offers no consolation to the dreamer for his return to the wilderness of 'reality'. For him, it ends not with Christian's entry to Heaven, but with Ignorance's damnation at the very gates of the Celestial City, leaving us between hope and fear emblematically, like Christian in the Interpreter's House. And a further dimension is added to fear by the recognition that Christian, though he experiences terror and despair, even when crossing the river, is still emblematically destined to Heaven and cannot succumb as an ordinary human being can. Christian cannot retain his identity and accept the position of another— can only hope by becoming Hopeful, can only compromise with the world by becoming Worldly-Wiseman. But a human being can change. The figures may be seen as embodying the thoughts and desires of any man, and at a given moment any of them may dominate the personality; a human being, in his complexity, can be Christian and yet become Worldly-Wiseman. In this way the vision denies the possibility to the dreamer of the certainty which he witnesses. His concern is with priorities, not absolutes—not the hermit-ideal of withdrawal from home and society, but the balance of worldly and spiritual claims. Christian here serves not only as emblem but as warning of the psychological destructiveness inherent in obsessional withdrawal from the world—a warning surely not lost upon the many Puritans who enjoyed a happy domestic life and took an active part in worldly affairs.

The dreamer's dilemma seems at times signalled by the uncertainty of his own response to the vision. Sometimes he displays an almost comic indifference to the literal level of the events he narrates, as in the excessive itemizing of Faithful's emblematic death:

> And first they scourged him, then they buffeted him, then they lanced his flesh with knives; after that they stoned him with stones, they pricked him with their swords; and last of all they burned him to ashes at the stake. Thus came Faithful to his end.   (p. 134)

The mechanical accumulation of torment actually weakens the

sense of horror to the point at which it is comically undercut by a weary *last of all* and an anticlimatic and redundant final sentence. Sometimes his ironic vision destroys the emblematic force of events, as in his concentration upon the comically incompetent Giant Despair, unable at times to lift his hand or to run, still less to despatch his prisoners, and lectured in bed by his brusque, decisive wife. This domestic comedy detracts from the seriousness of Christian's contemplated suicide and, by demanding comic involvement, prevents the successful realization of an emblematic episode. Christian's sudden production of the key of promise completes the pointed tension between emblematic and literal levels. Such instances alert the reader to deficiences in the Narrator's response, and to wider issues of appropriate responses to the vision.

Finally, from a contemplation of the Narrator-persona, the reader is led out of the work through its final ambiguity, that of the connection between the fictitious Narrator and the author himself.[14] Langland's Narrator is a poet, uneasily aware that he is apparently like social parasites such as false minstrels, sturdy beggars, idle and feigned contemplatives, whom he condemns. Yet he defends his profession to Imaginative as an admissible adjunct to the holy life; agreeing that there are many books to tell him what Do-well and the rest are, he none the less urges the need for an answer to satisfy *him*:

> Ac if þer were any wight þat wolde me telle
> What were dowel and dobet and dobest at þe laste,
> Wolde I neuere do werk . . .
>
> (B 12/25–7)

This seems to mean that he requires an experience of Truth, such as Piers provides, rather than the stock intellectual and theological answers of his contemporary instructors. To that extent, he clings to the hope that his dream is a divine revelation, like those given to Daniel. The status of the dream—escape from responsibility for a wastrel, or divine revelation—determines the status of the poem—entertainment or edification; and both determine the dreamer's (and Langland's) identity—the poet as social drop-out or the poet as prophet. The issues are left unresolved.

Bunyan too, recognizes a link between artistic and divine inspiration. In his Apology he justifies the work as moral allegory, citing biblical precedent, but stresses that it began as a spontaneous and self-sustaining inspiration ('And they again began to multiply, / Like sparks that from the coals of fire do fly') which he cultivated ('For having now my method by the end, / Still as I pulled it came'). The work was initially for Bunyan's private satisfaction ('I did it mine own self to gratify') and not for publication. The possibility of literary inspiration is not accorded to the narrator as it is in Langland,[15] but an identification with Bunyan is suggested initially in the margin-gloss which identifies the *den* in which the dreamer seeks refuge with the *gaol* in which Bunyan was imprisoned. The reader is thus required to acknowledge consciously a link between the author's biographical experiences and the events narrated without being able sharply to distinguish biography from imaginative re-creation or invention. Hence, for example, identification of the fictitious *den* with the historical *gaol* significantly suggests the transformation of forceful imprisonment into voluntary retreat, which lends a further perspective to the issues discussed above—the concern with worldly rejection and spiritual election, the images of coercion and constraint, and the subjective and objective significations of the allegory.

The use of a dream-framework immediately suggests to a modern critic the possibility of a Jungian interpretation of the action as expression and therapy. But its conscious value to a pre-Jungian author may well be in its establishment of succeeding planes of reference whose connections are never made explicit. In both our works, a writer observes a narrator relating a vision. In Langland, the dreamer can observe himself within his own dream, and can further observe himself in his dream entering a further dream-dimension, as in the ecstatic swoon in which he sees the Tree of Charity. In Bunyan, the writer can see his Narrator dreaming of a figure who in turn observes other figures, as at the Interpreter's House, occupying a dimension from which he is excluded. Such structures are not primarily allegorical but ironic, suggesting connections between the levels by a range of analogies, but essentially frustrating conclusions and handing the resolution back to the reader without comment:

> And siþþe he [Conscience] gradde after Grace til
> I gam awake.   (B20/386)

> So I awoke, and behold it was a dream   (p. 205)

The structure becomes, in effect, the meaning. Although such a technique is not exclusively medieval, it is characteristic of the greatest fourteenth-century poems and Bunyan's use of the same technique may perhaps be considered a more important link with medieval literature than his occasional use of romance-motifs. Certainly, however, in arguing that Langland and Bunyan use such structures to frustrate the potential restrictions of the defining allegorical mode, I am urging also that both should be regarded primarily not as allegorists, but as ironists, who use the allegorical mode as the vehicle of their irony.

NOTES

1. Angus Fletcher, *Allegory: The Theory of a Symbolic Mode* (New York, 1964), p. 305.
2. A. C. Spearing, *Medieval Dream-Poetry* (Cambridge, 1976), p. 5.
3. Cited in the Kane-Donaldson edition of *Piers*, p. 6. The editors note that the first edition bears the erroneously transposed date 1505. This, the first printed text of the poem, was issued by a Puritan as an anti-Catholic piece.
4. See further, J. Burrow, 'The audience of *Piers Plowman*', *Anglia*, lxxv (1957), pp. 373–84.
5. C. S. Lewis, 'The vision of John Bunyan', *The Listener* (13 December 1962), p. 1006.
6. All references and quotations are from George Kane and E. Talbot Donaldson (eds), *Piers Plowman: The B Version* (London, 1975).
7. The polarity of presentation is one of many valuable insights in Wolfgang Iser, *The Implied Reader: Patterns of Communication in Prose Fiction from Bunyan to Beckett* (Baltimore and London, 1974), chap. 1.
8. See further, U. Milo Kaufmann, *The Pilgrim's Progress and Traditions in Puritan Meditation* (New Haven and London, 1966), chap. 4, esp. pp. 83–6.
9. The hint for this point comes from Fletcher, op. cit., p. 288: 'The well-known stubborness, conscientiousness, and idealism of the compulsive neurotic come through in fictional works as the undeviating, totally

committed, absolutist ethics of characters like . . . the Christians [*sic*] of Bunyan.'

10. For a somewhat different view, see Charles W. Baird, *John Bunyan: A Study in Narrative Technique* (Port Washington, 1977), p. 106: 'The very concrete particularity of some of this development endows the images and actions with moral and religious ambiguity and suggests imaginative expansions of meanings unrestricted by stipulatory devices. This mimetic fullness and concreteness also lend force and authority to additional, significant allegorical effects.'

11. See further, Elizabeth Adeney, 'Bunyan: a unified vision?', *Critical Review* xvii (1974), pp. 97–109, and esp. p. 99: 'As for Charity's speech, this kind of dismissiveness, which sums Christian's family up and puts them aside in one movement of the mind, betrays a glib and unthinking inhumanity to which Bunyan simply does not adhere'.

12. Aldous Huxley, 'On Grace', reprinted in *Music at Night and Other Essays* (1931; Penguin edn, 1950), p. 61.

13. Elizabeth Adeney, although responding in similar fashion, seems reluctant to attribute the tensions to any conscious design; op. cit., pp. 108–9: 'To relinquish this world for the next is one thing; but the idea implicit in much of the story, that it is a necessary part of the Christian's progress to give up even the ability to respond in an open and balanced way to the world and its inhabitants while still dwelling in it, is a rather different thing. The difference remains unresolved because . . . Bunyan appears to remain unaware of it.'

14. See further, G. Kane, *The Autobiographical Fallacy in Chaucer and Langland Studies* (Chambers Memorial Lecture, London, 1965).

15. The use of the dream-poem to define the status of poet and poetry is characteristic of the medieval genre. Spearing, op. cit., p. 5, sees this tendency as symptomatic of a new interest in the nature of literature in the fourteenth century. Perhaps for this reason, it is not part of Bunyan's concern.

The Problem of Misfortune in *The Pilgrim's Progress*

NICK DAVIS

Know ye not that they which run in a race run all, but one receiveth the prize? So run that ye may obtain (1 Corinthians 9: 24).

Bunyan seems to have been fascinated by this familiar Pauline image: the individual Christian must regard himself as a participant in a foot-race whose prize is the Kingdom of Heaven. It is in the first place a reassuring metaphor because it contains the suggestion that salvation is a reward for endeavour, and therefore serves somewhat to mitigate the harshness of the Calvinist doctrine of election. As Christopher Hill remarks, Bunyan's is 'a Calvinism with a difference'; whereas high, predestinarian Calvinism tended to view all human striving as an absurdity, on the grounds that the salvation of the elect and the damnation of the reprobate was a foregone conclusion, for Bunyan, as for some other later seventeenth-century thinkers of Calvinist formation, notions of 'desert' and 'works' had a way of returning by the back door.[1] But it is also a taxing metaphor, which, straightforward enough at first sight, becomes more complicated on inspection. Bunyan draws out some of the implications in *The Heavenly Footman*, an early work offering an extended commentary on Paul's statement.[2] He echoes his authority in emphasizing that, although a large number of contestants may take part, only one can gain 'the crown that standeth at the end of the race'.[3] It is manifestly necessary to run fast, and to persevere in the race, but speed and perseverance are not in themselves enough: the route of advance lies through Christ, and the erring can only recognize it through the inward promptings of the Spirit; those who appear to have outstripped the rest may in fact be running backwards.[4] The contestants are obliged to run not only because salvation beckons them, or appears to do so, but also because 'the devil, the law [i.e. the temptation to rely on works], sin, death, and hell, follow them'.[5] It would appear that a principle of pure malevolence also has a hand in the organization of the race, making appeals to 'fair play' rather inappropriate. As the metaphor is developed in Bunyan's tract, the assurance that it seemed at first to offer is relentlessly qualified and undercut, and the reader is finally left with the simple injunction to 'run': 'But be sure thou begin by times; get into the way; run apace and hold out to the end; and the Lord give thee a prosperous journey. Farewell.'[6]

Consideration of the metaphor of the 'unfair' contest may help to define a central problem of exposition in two works dealing more directly with Bunyan's own complex experience of conversion. The autobiographical *Grace Abounding to the Chief of Sinners* and *The Pilgrim's Progress* both have at their centre a protagonist who is a beneficiary of divine grace;[7] in this sense they rehearse a cumulative 'progress', from which the reader is invited to draw a heartening conclusion. But the experiential weight of the works tends to exert its force rather in the opposite direction. *Grace Abounding* is the writing up of a period of varied and seemingly endless mental torment, which can be surveyed only in retrospect as a graduated ascent to a plateau of equanimity—to the condition of relative assurance announced by the work's title. And Christian's pilgrimage is likewise represented as a fitful 'progress' from obstacle to obstacle, in which the surmounting of one trial does not necessarily augur success in the next, or next-but-one.[8] The most terrifying aspect of the trials undergone by Bunyan's protagonists is surely the radical absence of certainty attendant on the whole enterprise of the quest. It is as if Christian—like the infernally harassed Bunyan of *Grace Abounding*, forever catching glimpses of a salvation from which he feels himself to be excluded—is unwittingly caught up in a monstrous game of snakes-and-ladders, in which the pitfalls greatly outnumber the means of ascent. The most threatening snake of all makes its appearance, one notes, at the very pinnacle of attainment in *The Pilgrim's Progress*, in that passage where poor, conceited Ignorance is denied admission to the Celestial City and handed over directly to damnation: 'Then I saw that there was a way to Hell, even from the Gates of Heaven . . .' (p. 205). Ignorance has, perhaps, attempted to 'cheat' by joining the course at a late stage. Yet in at least one respect his condition disquietingly resembles that of the better-fated pilgrims: their apprehension of reality, like his, may turn out at any point to be absolutely erroneous; they are seldom in a position to know with any rational assurance whether their next forward movement will place them on an ascending ladder or a plunging snake.

In the course of their quests for certainty of personal salvation, *certitudo salutis*, Bunyan's central figures are exposed to an infinity of persecutions whose main effect seems to be the undermining of certainty; but at the same time this affliction is understood to be a trial imposed by Providence, the apparent randomness of whose operations is an illusion born of man's corrupt nature. It is characteristic of Calvinist thought that it should at once apprehend divine purposiveness everywhere, and declare its operations to be inscrutable. The tension between these two ideas frequently issues in an acquiescence to the Stoical vision of fatality as a storm which must somehow be weathered out:

> When thicke cloudes doo couer the heauen, and a violent tempest aryseth, then bycause bothe a heauysome mystynesse is caste before oure eyes, and the thunder troubleth oure eares, and all oure senses are amased with terrour, we thynke that all thynges are confounded and tombled togither: and yet all the whyle there remaineth in the heauen the same quietenesse and calmenesse, that was before. So muste we thynke that whyle the troublesome state of thinges in the world taketh from us abilitie to iudge, God by the pure lyghte of his ryghteousnesse and wysedome, dooth in well framed order gouerne and dispose even those very troublesome motions themselves to a ryght ende.[9]

Although Calvin speaks of a storm which masks an ultimate serenity, and in which serenity somehow inheres, it remains a storm none the less to those unfortunate enough to be caught in it; the idea of violent, arbitrary affliction cannot finally be exorcized within the scope of the storm image. This same image dominates the central section of *Grace Abounding*, where it is elaborated and integrated with the development of the narrative to a point where its status as metaphor is virtually hidden from view: no other language for the description of Bunyan's torments is made available to the reader, and so none is conceivable.[10] Similarly, in the first evocation of the Valley of the Shadow of Death this quasi-metaphor shows signs of coming to the fore:

> and over that Valley hangs the discouraging clouds of
> confusion; death also does always spread his wings over
> it: in a word, it is every whit dreadful, being utterly
> without order.   (p. 96)

But in the context of the narrative this is a misleading report, given with a view to dissuading Christian from the encounter; in the course of his successful negotiation of the Valley it becomes clear that the appearances of confusion and disorder are a fiendish device.[11] The storm image provides one possible way of imposing artistic order on an experience of chaos, but in *The Pilgrim's Progress* this strategy is rejected in favour of one that offers greater scope for narrative development. One of the difficulties of imaging fatality as a storm is that this comes near to depriving the afflicted protagonist of the status of an agent altogether. He and the reader have even lost the limited assurance embodied in the injunction, 'run!' In *The Pilgrim's Progress* as a whole Bunyan faces up once again to the intractability of fortune, but in such a way as to suggest that human agency has a place in a world controlled by an extra-human Providence, and that the providential order is not altogether masked from human experience. In order to show how Bunyan effect this imaginative reconciliation, it will be necessary to examine his work in its relation to a largely secular artistic tradition.

A number of critics have remarked on Bunyan's evident indebtedness, in both Parts of *The Pilgrim's Progress*, to the romances of adventure which must have formed the staple of his reading in his youth, prior to conversion.[12] Bunyan was a beneficiary of the literary development described by R. S. Crane as follows:

neglected or criticised by men of letters, they [medieval romances] came more and more to be the special property of the uneducated and old-fashioned. This evolution, which was well under way before the close of the sixteenth century, had by the middle of the seventeenth practically run its course. Henceforth, for over a hundred years, the admirers of the old stories . . . were to be found almost exclusively among the plebian and uncultivated classes.[13]

The tastes of the reading public in the mid seventeenth century can be gauged from a list of 'the Most Vendible Books in England' compiled in 1658: included are such titles as *Prince Arthur, Parismus, Ornatus and Artesia, Palmerin of England, Valentine and Orson* and *The Seven Champions of Christendom*.[14] It seems reasonable to accept Sir Charles Firth's judgement that *The Pilgrim's Progress* owed at least some of its immediate popular success to its partial colonization of the imaginative terrain of romance literature. The work's affinities with Richard Johnson's *Seven Champions*, familiarly known to Bunyan as 'George on horseback', are examined elsewhere in the present collection.[15] Modern criticism has also perceived that certain parts of Bunyan's classic bear a tantalizing resemblance to recorded folktales. It is, in the nature of things, impossible to identify specific sources, since the transcription of popular oral narrative did not begin in earnest until the Romantic era. Nevertheless, Harold Golder has argued convincingly for the general influence of folktale story-patterning in the treatment of the pilgrim's sojourn in Doubting Castle;[16] and certain elements of Bunyan's narrative—for example, the nocturnal terrors which haunt the Valley of the Shadow—have clear analogues in folktales collected in modern times.[17] It may, however, be argued that, in evaluating the debt of *The Pilgrim's Progress* to secular fables of adventure, the drawing of a line of demarcation between the influence of chivalric romance and the influence of demotic folktale is a more difficult and indeed a more nugatory task than it appears to be at first sight. Because of the change in the social composition of its audience, and through the recomposition and redaction of available narratives, romance literature in Bunyan's time was climbing steadily down its phylogenetic tree. It was coming once again to resemble the sort of folktale which had exerted a strong shaping influence on early chivalric romances.[18]

The most significant changes associated with the popularization of chivalric romance can be briefly set out as follows. (1) Wish-fulfilment assumes a greater prominence. In the first place, this simply takes the form of a different kind of reading: a readership which no longer has any practical or even theoretical concern with chivalry will naturally tend to approach chronicles of knightly adventure as a literature of 'escape'. And, given that the world of knighthood has become almost entirely foreign, those responsible for the production of new romances will be encouraged to play up the genre's inherent exoticism. (2) Popular romance, as represented by the works of Richard Johnson, or by late redactions of such medieval romances as Bevis of Hampton,[19] possesses what formalist critics would term a high 'functionality'. Gone is the interdependence of widely separated episodes which served, in principle, to unify the most sprawling of medieval romance-cycles; instead the reader is presented with a series of incidents which are, individually, realized with some imaginative force, but whose concatenation in a significant whole is largely allowed to take care of itself. (3) As a concomitant of this pursuit of a different kind of narrative economy, interest in the fate of a particular hero becomes the thread which guides the reader through the defiles of the narrative. Individually striking adventures are welded into a running story by the simple device of attaching them to a single figure—or in the case of *The Seven Champions*, a group of subsidiary heroes linked to the principal hero, St George, by an arbitrary turn of the plot. This use of the hero as a hook on which to hang a series of adventures tends to separate him still further from his fellow-men, who are condemned to a comparative stasis. (4) But at the same time the hero becomes a more homely figure, not so much in his prowess as in his needs. (This may appear to be at odds with (1), but there is no real contradiction.) (5) And, most germane to the present argument, external fate becomes a more pervasive force in the shaping of the hero's adventures than is generally the case in medieval romance. All these modifications give popular romance of the sort known to Bunyan and his audience a close affinity with folktale narrative, in which the same tendencies can be recognized. Circumstantial evidence for this interpretation of the genre's development appears to be furnished by the unusual shape of Richard Johnson's literary career: of his published prose romances, *The Seven Champions* (1596) is the closest to medieval analogues, *Tom a Lincolne* (two parts, 1599 and 1607) effects a domestication of the chivalric hero, and *The History of Tom Thumb* (1621, though there may have been earlier editions), which is probably Johnson's work, may be regarded as the first English 'fairy-tale' to circulate in printed form. It is easy to see how the traits of popular oral storytelling, partially submerged in popular heroic romance, are always ready to break surface in Johnson's narrative style. Before a return can be made to the treatment of misfortune in *The Pilgrim's Progress*, something more must be said of the last-mentioned traits, (4) and (5).

Knighthood itself is a major thematic concern of the classic medieval romances: the adventures of their heroes and heroines may be seen as a place of encounter between the complex ethic of chivalry and the reality which it seeks to accommodate. But the kind of narrative which was, in general, found to be best suited for this task of ideological exploration dealt more simply with the relations between an isolated human protagonist and a generalized, inscrutable Other, imposing trials but also conferring privileges for which man in his given social being is ineligible; this Other, of which chivalric romance can render no rational account, makes its presence felt in the strange fatality which pursues Malory's Round Table knights, both individually and as a body, or in the blatant magic which prizes the hero of *Sir Gawain and the Green Knight* away from the security of Camelot.[20] And it is this underlying narrative pattern which assumes *a priori* value with the popularization of chivalric romance, a shift of emphasis which is clearly registered in a work like Richard Johnson's *Tom a Lincolne*. The heroes of Johnson's late romance are not really engaged in any exploration, except in a rather trivial, geographical sense; they are seldom confronted with morally significant choices. Instead, their task is to come to terms with a destiny which has already singled them out: they are 'essentially' heroes. The story begins by placing Tom a Lincolne in a state of ignorance which interferes with his well-being. Born the natural son of King Arthur, he is brought up, unaware of his true parentage, as a burgher of Lincoln—to be precise, as the son and heir of a prosperous sheep-farmer. But Tom's inherent nobility, which is also a sort of waywardness, causes him to fall foul of his foster-parents. It sends him in pursuit of adventure in distant countries, whence he can return to enjoyment of the rightful privileges denied him by the odd circumstances of his birth. There is thus a temporary correspondence between Tom's essential nature and his outward mode of life. In the second part of the romance he is, however, deprived of his well-being once again through the chance revelation of his bastardy, and it falls to Tom's sons to refurbish the family honour by embarking on a similar career of triumphant adventure. Eventually they return to a prosperous old age as respected citizens of Lincoln, held up throughout as the goal of rational human endeavour. It is apparent that Tom and his progeny, unlike the heroes of courtly romance, are committed by their special destiny not so much to a process of self-discovery as to a process of self-vindication. No new, compelling object of desire emerges in the course of their adventures. Their greatest need, namely an honoured, comfortable existence, can be assumed from the outset; but they have to undergo an indefinitely protracted series of trials and persecutions before they can possess it undisturbed.

Johnson's imagination is of a thoroughly materialistic cast. In his interpretation the mysterious Fairy Land of Celtic fable becomes an island inhabited solely by women, which may be reached by sailing westwards across the Atlantic. Even the monstrous dragon fought by St George in *The Seven Champions* can be shrewdly sized up like a composite human artefact:

> the bignes of the Dragon was fearfull to behold, for betwixt his shoulders and his taile were fiftie foote in

distance, his scales glistered brighter than silver, but
farre more harder than brasse, his belly of the coloure of
gold, but more bigger than a Tun.[21]

While fighting the dragon, St George is sustained by the
revifying properties of 'orringes'. In spite of its penchant for
exotic settings and extravagant incident, romance in the
manner of Johnson does not issue any serious challenge to the
categories of ordinary experience: rather, it estranges the
familiar by reassembling it in novel patterns. (This is precisely where one would wish to locate its 'escapism'.) What
then is the role of Fate in a relatively disenchanted world,
where natural effects follow natural causes in a way that
appears to be entirely unproblematical? An idea of external
compulsion has to be retained, it would seem, in order to
account for the odd, skewed relationship obtaining between
the hero and his 'essence'. If the hero simply possessed his
essence he would be invulnerable, a sort of god; if on the
other hand he was without essence, which seems to be a
defining trait of the *picaro*, he would merely be involved in a
series of adventures shaped by pure contingency. In the
popular heroic romance, however, Fate steps in to prevent
the hero from being, simply and without more ado, what he
actually is. To this extent he is its victim. It intervenes again
and again in the narrative of *Tom a Lincolne*, driving forward
the cycle of loss and reparation on which the heroes involun-
tarily revolve. But at the same time this fatality is not
altogether a negative force because, even as it imposes
persecutions, it guarantees the link between the hero's
essence and his visible condition at any time. Whether he is
aware of it or not—a matter of relative unimportance—the
hero stands on peculiarly intimate terms with an Other
which ensures the ultimate coherence of his life and exploits;
this special intimacy allows him to move with somnambular
confidence towards the possession of what is rightfully his.[22]

The romances of Richard Johnson can be seen to effect a
somewhat uneasy compromise between the outward forms
of chivalric romance, which they continue to respect, and the
inward dynamic of folktale. And the artistic superiority of
The Pilgrim's Progress may be attributed in part to its fuller

absorption and integration of folktale influences. Bunyan may have derived a sympathetic understanding of folktale narrative in part from his youthful immersion in popular heroic romances like *The Seven Champions of Christendom*, where folktale formulae are present in numerous passages as sub-text. But folktale traits obscured in or absent from such romances are given full realization in Bunyan's narrative, arguing a close acquaintance with folktale in the flesh. Most strikingly, perhaps, Christian has lost virtually all the trappings of the martial hero, bar the armour which he receives at the Palace called Beautiful and which is forgotten by the time he overtakes Faithful; even the stirring fight with Apollyon is defined in Part II as an unfortunate accident, the result of Christian's failure to descend into the Valley of Humiliation without slipping on the way. Christian is conceived instead as an everyman-figure possessed of no extraordinary aptitude or capability. The popular *Märchen* ('fairy-tale') has, as Max Lüthi observes, 'a partiality for the negative hero: the insignificant, the neglected, the helpless. But he unexpectedly proves to be strong, noble and blessed.'[23] This is precisely the case of Bunyan's hero, who has a single-minded determination to complete his journey to the Celestial City where he will reap the rewards of service to a glorious Prince, and who in the course of his journey discovers the resources which enable him to attain his goal. But the *Märchen* also has its own way of accounting for the good fortune visited upon the hero, and for the misfortune which befalls other individuals whose desires are no less clearly delineated than his own. In a sense, all the human figures in *The Pilgrim's Progress* have their minds set on joys comparable to those promised by the Celestial City. Some are perverse enough to mislocate them, which prevents them from taking up the journey of discovery and turns them into antagonists of Christian and the other true pilgrims. Others, however, are actually seen to desire the same prize or reward as Christian but to fail grotesquely of their objective because they go about the quest in the wrong way. This returns us to the problem defined at the outset. Given that a number of pilgrims of similar capacities are presented with the opportunity of travelling towards the Celestial City, how is it possible to explain the 'rightness' of the course of action adopted by the few who make a successful journey? Theology can supply an external solution to the conundrum: Christian, Faithful, and Hopeful are sustained, unlike their less fortunate acquaintances, through the absolutely unconditioned bestowal of divine grace. Yet this is not the interpretation which the patterning of the narrative keeps uppermost in the reader's mind. As U. M. Kaufmann has pointed out, 'prevenient grace, like prevenient knowledge, if too evident in the springs of narrative, is likely to destroy the illusion of a dynamic career . . . Christian and the other pilgrims of the first and second parts spend no time worrying about the illusoriness of their freedom'.[24] Nor is it possible to accept Stanley Fish's argument that Bunyan does everything in his power to subvert the metaphor of 'progress' which informs the entire work. By cleaving quite openly to the patterns of folktale, Bunyan is able to displace the crucial issue of unequal fortune from a position where it blocks the development of narrative; while it remains, implicitly, a theological problem, it also becomes a problem to be mediated through recourse to an artistic strategy with which Bunyan and his audience would have been familiar.

In order to begin his journey, or 'progress', Christian has to isolate himself from his fellow-men in the most radical way. He rushes from the City of Destruction amidst the derision of his neighbours and the entreaties of his bewildered family. Bunyan plays up the disquieting qualities of the episode:

> So I saw in my dream that the man began to run. Now he had not run far from his own door, but his wife and children perceiving it began to cry after him to return: but the man put his fingers in his ears, and ran on crying, 'Life, life, eternal life.' So he looked not behind him, but fled towards the middle of the plain.   (p. 41)

In the course of the journey Christian sheds, perforce, more acquaintances than he keeps. It is characteristic of his bearing that he should hurry past the stalls of Vanity Fair with his ears plugged and his eyes cast up towards Heaven (p. 127). But Christian's social isolation is a dramatic as well as a moral necessity because it enables him to form the more important relationship which assures the success of his journey;[25] that is, a relationship with the providential order underlying the apparent chaos of the world, and introducing a sense of pattern—of which the pilgrims themselves are only fleetingly aware—into the adventures which make up their journey. The genuine travellers appear to enjoy a bond of instinctive sympathy with the world in which they undergo their testing; but they find it difficult to make this bond a property of conscious knowledge, and indeed a great deal of their experience goes flatly against it. Christian, for example, seems to possess a spontaneous knowledge of the topography of the route which is, however, most readily available when least needed.[26] It does not prevent him going astray at By-path Meadow. Nevertheless, Bunyan manages to suggest throughout that Christian and his friends do actually have the wherewithal to overcome the obstacles which block their path, if only they can rediscover their affinity with the world's inherent order.

The pilgrims are placed in communion with this hidden order primarily through the mysterious powers latent in language. One notes first of all that the Bunyan of *The Pilgrim's Progress* is not much given to puns. It would be against Bunyan's purposes to capitalize on the ambiguities latent in speech, because the work rests rather on an implicit theory of language which accords every word a single, true meaning. The correct naming of persons and things takes on, it need hardly be said, major significance throughout. For the most part names are simply supplied by the dreamer as objective onlooker, but sometimes the attribution of a name is built into the dynamic of the narrative: 'is not your name Mr By-Ends of Fair-speech?' asks Christian (p. 137) when he has listened for a while to the conversation of his new companion, showing that he has got the measure of him. The judgements delivered on Faithful by the jurors of Vanity Fair merely give dramatic expression to the proclivities already revealed in the juror's names:

. . . 'Hang him, hang him,' said Mr Heady. 'A sorry scrub,' said Mr High-mind. 'My heart rises against him,'

said Mr Enmity. 'He is a rogue,' said Mr Liar. 'Hanging
is too good for him,' said Mr Cruelty. . .   (p. 134)

What is in effect the jurors' own self-condemnation is given
by this means a quite unanswerable finality. Their names
crystallize their essential natures, leaving no more to be said.
Since the verses of *The Pilgrim's Progress* offer to encapsulate
the significance of fresh occurrences in memorial form, they
also place a considerable emphasis on naming. An instance of
this is the initial evaluation of Master Ignorance:

> Let Ignorance a little while now muse
> On what is said, and let him not refuse
> Good counsel to embrace, lest he remain
> Still ignorant of what's the chiefest gain . . .
>   (p. 163)

Language, and especially the lexical part of language,
therefore assumes something of the status of an imperative in
the narrative of *The Pilgrim's Progress*, rather as individual
heroism does in the romances of Johnson. It represents what
is (though it may not at first sight appear to be so) and what
must be (when deceptive appearances have been set aside).
But the emitter of this definitive language is not necessarily
or even primarily the pilgrims themselves; it is a language
already implanted in the world, and accessible to them only
in piecemeal form. The touchstone of truth all through
Christian's journey is of course the Book written by the
Prince to whose court he is proceeding, which sets him on his
way, admonishes him in the person of Evangelist, provides
the substance of his conversation and sometimes intervenes
directly to facilitate his journey, as when a biblical phrase
providentially comes to mind in the Valley of the Shadow
(p. 97). And *The Pilgrim's Progress* is unlike a folktale in so far
as it offers to supply a final interpretation of the events which
compose it by reference to this external authority. But it is
folktale-like, on the other hand, in so far as it hints at the
existence of a general 'interpretability' which just eludes the
human agents involved. This is the delicate balance which
Bunyan sustains, by and large, in his account of Christian's
journey, but which tips somewhat in the direction of overt

commentary when he comes to deal with the journey of Christiana. It is characteristic that in Part I Christian should fight Apollyon, but that in Part II we should be told precisely *why* Christian was obliged to fight Apollyon (p. 288).

The existence of a domain of order and sense lying just beyond the reach of ordinary discourse is suggested in Part I of *The Pilgrim's Progress* through the frequence of the pilgrims' encounters with riddles. Riddles frequently crop up as part of the plot-machinery of folktale: a hero may be required to solve a verbal riddle in order to demonstrate his fortunate condition, and so attain good fortune. But the form of the *Märchen* also has a strong affinity with the form of a riddle. (Max Lüthi points out that in some European dialect-areas the same word is used for 'riddle' and 'fairy-tale'.) It could be said that the 'coming right' of a *Märchen*, which usually produces some inherently unlikely shift in relations between characters, violating the norms of social dealing—the tailor finds himself married to a princess, the hag is transformed into a beautiful and high-born lady—is strictly comparable in its mode of procedure to the solution of a riddle posed in speech. In both cases we are dealing with the establishment of a new and unexpected link between the ostensibly incompatible, and with the drawing out of possibilities hidden in and thwarted by the given, normative organization of society and language. In *The Pilgrim's Progress*, then, as in the *Märchen* to which it is indebted, riddles are more than a device of the plot. In a sense they *are* the plot, because the unfettering and transformation of language—which involves the release of its truth-bearing properties—takes place by the same title as the unfettering and transformation of Christian, culminating in his entry to the Celestial City. Riddles distributed along Christian's path, whether they be embodied in words or objects, are placed there not so much to mark his progress, in the sense of developing awareness or growing sanctity, as to signify the possibility of progress, a transformation that cannot be explained in incremental terms.

Riddling as pressed into the service of Bunyan's narrative might be regarded as the antithesis of punning: instead of making play with language's multiplicity of meaning, it points to the presence of a single, true meaning partly obscured by language in its familiar forms and habitual associations. The vanquisher of a riddle gives the impression of having released a truth previously hidden from common awareness, and of having reaffirmed the power of language to ideal directly with what is enigmatic in human experience. Christian and his fellows demonstrate their affinity with the underlying order of things in the first place by accepting that truth announces itself in a riddling form. This is a theoretical lesson imparted near the very beginning of the journey at the House of Interpreter, the taking to heart of which distinguishes Christian from those, like Talkative, who are disinclined to penetrate beneath language's surface. The oddest encounters of the journey, like that with 'a man black of flesh, but covered with a very light robe', can be correctly interpreted and so overcome, provided that the pilgrims can find the right key: once entangled in the black man's net, Christian comments,

> Now do I see myself in an error; did not the shepherds bid us beware of the flatterers? As is the saying of the wise man, so we have found it this day: A man that flattereth his neighbour, spreadeth a net for his feet.   (p. 172)

The reference is to the Book of Proverbs: Christian's adversary can in the event be identified as a flatterer, not because of anything he has said, but because his action is seen to conform to a pattern laid down in a scriptural text.

In the second place, the pilgrims are able to solve the verbal riddles which confront them in the journey by ascending to the higher level of discourse represented by 'Scripture language'.[27] At one point Mr By-Ends and his companions pose the question of whether it is possible to cultivate religion out of considerations of worldly advantage 'and yet be a right honest man' (p. 140). They have a number of arguments to buttress their affirmative answer (see pp. 140–2), but Christian quickly disperses the cloud of sophistry by assigning By-Ends' contention to its correct biblical category:

> Then said Christian, Even a babe in religion may answer ten thousand such questions. For if it be unlawful to

follow Christ for loaves, as it is, how much more abominable is it to make of him and religion a stalking horse to get and enjoy the world. Nor do we find any other than heathens, hypocrites, devils and witches that are of this opinion.   (p. 142)

Christian goes on to cite a series of scriptural examples, reducing his antagonists to a nonplussed silence. In encounters of this kind the divine Word is used rather like a magic sword to cut through the equivocations whose element is ordinary speech (and its correlative, ordinary consciousness). But at the same time the frequent intrusion of biblical language imposes a certain fragmentation on language in general. There is an additional suggestion that the *ratio* of the providentially ordered world and the *ratio* of human discourse do not quite correspond. Those who know most, like the Shepherds of the Delectable Mountains, tend to speak most laconically, as in this notorious conversation:

> *Christian.* Is this the way to the Celestial City?
> *Shepherds.* You are just in your way.
> *Christian.* How far is it thither?
> *Shepherds.* Too far for any but those shall get thither indeed.
> *Christian.* Is the way safe or dangerous?
> *Shepherds.* Safe for those for whom it is to be safe, *but transgressors shall fall therein.*
> *Christian.* Is there in this place any relief for pilgrims that are weary and faint in the way?
> *Shepherds.* The Lord of the Mountains hath given us a charge *Not to be forgetful to entertain strangers*: therefore the good of the place is before you.   (p. 158)

The Shepherds, who bear the promising names of Knowledge, Experience, Watchful, and Sincere, are not really in a position to tell the pilgrims more than they already know—that they are in the Delectable Mountains, that they are on their way to the Celestial City, and that their journey is incomplete. Like the Scriptures, the shepherds offer succour, and bear witness to 'the things of God', but again like the Scriptures, they only speak in so far as they are spoken to. On leaving the Delectable Mountains the pilgrims will still be surrounded by the old uncertainties. It seems that the halting, interrogative discourse of Christian and his fellow, a necessary adjunct to their quest, cannot be fully accommodated within 'Scripture language'.

The pilgrims' encounters with 'Scripture language' and its riddles are, however, an augury of hope, a sign that language participates in the providential ordering of things. As if to confirm this a still higher level of articulacy, to which Bunyan's narrator cannot begin to do justice in his own language, opens before those who are approaching the presence of the King. The dreamer observes that once Christian and Hopeful, now approaching the end of their travels, had refreshed themselves in the King's garden and vineyards, 'they talked more in their sleep at this time, than ever they did in all their journey':

> . . . and being in a muse thereabout, the gardener said even to me, 'Wherefore musest thou at the matter? It is the nature of the fruit of the grapes of these vineyards to go down so sweetly as to cause the lips of them that are asleep to speak.'   (p. 197)

At the summoning of the pilgrims across the River of Death which ends Part II of *The Pilgrim's Progress*, Mr Despondency's daughter, says the dreamer, 'went through the River singing, but none could understand what she said' (p. 370). The hierarchical arrangement of languages might be regarded as establishing the necessary conditions for the accomplishment of the journey by those who accept it, and are accepted by it: it is a feature of that larger world which is understood to enfold the human world, and by fully entrusting themselves to the order which it adumbrates, the pilgrim-heroes ensure—or perhaps one should say, make plausible—the eventual success of their quest.

The doctrine of election, which has such a central place in Bunyan's theological writings, is virtually elided from *The Pilgrim's Progress*. This has to do with Bunyan's deliberate adoption of a human rather than a divine perspective in his presentation of Christian's struggle: election *qua* property of the divine will cannot be a part of human experience.[28] But this is not to deny that Christian and the other successful pilgrims are decisively set apart from the doomed would-be pilgrims who, as was noted above, have their minds fixed on the same rewards. Although the perversity of Master Ignorance, which issues in self-conceit and lack of willingness to pursue an argument, does not seem sufficient *per se* to account for his horrendous punishment, in this most difficult of cases Bunyan contrives to suggest that the gross discrepancy between his fate and that of Christian and Hopeful is somehow a manifestation of justice. In order to describe the special quality of the apartness enjoyed by Christian and his fellows, it would appear to be necessary to invoke another familiar attribute of the *Märchen* hero. He is the recipient of supernatural gifts showered on him largely by accident, because he has adventitiously done 'the right thing'. If oneness with the world defines his general condition, his gifts provide him with the actual means to vanquish his enemies and outdo his rivals.[29] For example, in a tale from the collection of the Brothers Grimm a boy happens to eat the flesh of a white snake, and this enables him to understand the language of animals; the animals subsequently furnish the help needed for the accomplishment of his quest. This folktale concept of 'giftedness' is a particularly suggestive one for Bunyan, because the state of being gifted, like the state of belonging to the elect, has in strict terms nothing to do with deserts. The realm of 'faerie', or the Other World which is in folktale narrative the immediate source of the hero's gifts, is as radically incommensurable with human categories of moral awareness as the inscrutable divine will postulated by Calvinist throught. And it could be said that, in the narrative of *The Pilgrim's Progress*, the giftedness of the successful pilgrims occupies a place corresponding to that of the formal concept of election in Bunyan's more theoretical accounts of 'the way / And race of saints' (p. 31).

The most conspicuous gifts that Christian receives along the way are tokens of salvation, among them a roll which will secure his admission to the Celestial City, bestowed without warning by 'three Shining Ones' (p. 70). He accepts them as a piece of absolutely gratuitous good fortune granted

him by the Prince whom he serves, and the tenor of
Bunyan's narrative does not oblige him to furnish any
further explanation for the singling out of Christian. The
incident is immediately set off by an encounter with Simple,
Sloth, and Presumption who, bound in fetters as they are,
foolishly or churlishly refuse Christian's own unconditioned
offer of aid:

> With that they looked upon him, and began to reply in
> this sort: Simple said, 'I see no danger'; Sloth said, 'Yet a
> little more sleep'; and Presumption said, 'Every fat must
> stand upon his own bottom, what is the answer else that
> I should give thee?' And so they lay down to sleep again,
> and Christian went on his way.   (p. 71)

This seems to be what finally separates the true pilgrims of
Part I from those who literally fall by the wayside. The
latter refuse to isolate themselves sufficiently from human
society, and from the opinions bred of ordinary social
dealings—an outlook fully imaged in the squat complacency
of Presumption's proverb. More critically, they fail to place
themselves in a position to receive the aids essential to the
accomplishment of their quest. If one seeks for explanations
of individual misfortunes in narratives of the *Märchen* type,
moral responsibility ultimately yields place to sheer mis-
chance. And a similar modulation occurs in Bunyan's treatment of the downfall of Ignorance: he is bested in argument
with Christian and Hopeful, but in the end it is his lack of a
roll to present at the gate of the Celestial City which
excludes him once and for all from salvation. By placing his
actors in a folktale setting, Bunyan limits the resemblance of
the Ignorance episode to an insane cautionary tale, like that
of the boy who had his arms cut off for asking too many
questions. At more than one point along the way it is hinted
that Ignorance is a reprobate, one pre-destined for damnation.[30] But the account of Ignorance's fate finally rendered
by the narrative is a more simple one, invested with the
unarguable imaginative authority of the *Märchen*. He is
ungifted.

APPENDIX

The Crows and the Soldier
(Die Krähen)

For a characteristic folktale treatment of fortune and misfortune, the reader is referred to the following *Märchen* from the Grimms' collection. Here recourse to the same sources of aid by different parties produces strangely contrasting results. A sort of moral justice is seen to be dealt out by totally amoral agents.

A soldier who has, by honest means, saved a good deal of money, is led out into the wilds by two supposed comrades. Here they pick a quarrel with the unsuspecting man, and rob him of his money; having blinded him they leave him bound to the foot of a gallows-tree. He optimistically takes this to be a wayside cross, and prays to Heaven for protection. At nightfall he overhears the conversation of three crows who come to perch in the tree: discussing their latest discoveries, they observe that the king's daughter is ill, and can only be cured by consuming the ashes of a particular flower growing nearby; that the night's dewfall has, 'if only men knew it', the power to restore sight; and that a drought in the town can be ended by the removal of a particular stone from the market-place. Taking advantage of this information, the soldier regains his sight, cures the king's daughter, ends the drought, and is rewarded with the princess's hand in marriage. His erstwhile comrades are impressed by his sudden good fortune, and beg forgiveness. When they have heard the soldier's story, they naturally set out for the gallows-tree in search of similar luck. The same crows appear, and are heard to lament the revelation of their secrets; they conclude that someone must have been eavesdropping. Before the two men can escape, the enraged crows fly at them and peck their eyes out.[31]

NOTES

1. See *The World Turned Upside Down* (London, 1972), pp. 329–30.

2. G. Offor (ed.), *The Works of John Bunyan* (1862), iii. 378–94. The arguments of *The Heavenly Footman* are briefly recapitulated by Evangelist in *The Pilgrim's Progress* (p. 123), at that point where Christian and Faithful are about to enter Vanity Fair.

3. *Works*, iii. 381–2.

4. *Works*, iii. 384, 392.

5. *Works*, iii. 382.

6. *Works*, iii. 394.

7. Christian says to the Porter of the Palace Beautiful, 'My name is, now, Christian; but my name at first was Graceless' (p. 79).

8. The anti-progressive aspects of this nominal 'Progress' are underlined in Stanley Fish, *Self-Consuming Artifacts* (Berkeley and Los Angeles, 1972), pp. 224–64. I wish to register my debt to Fish's account, though my reading of the work ultimately differs from his.

9. John Calvin, *The Institution of Christian Religion*, trans. T. Norton (London, 1561), S.T.C. 4415, f. 61v (i. xviii. 1).

10. For the treatment of the storm image in this work, see Owen C. Watkins, *The Puritan Experience* (London, 1972), pp. 114–16.

11. Bunyan is, however, careful to preserve a distinction here between the consciousness of Christian and the somewhat privileged consciousness of the dreamer, looking on. Christian is half aware that his antagonists are devils, against whom he has the means to protect himself, whereas the dreamer is fully aware of this.

12. See in particular Sir Charles Firth, Introduction to the Methuen edition of *The Pilgrim's Progress* (London, 1898), reprinted in R. Sharrock (ed.), *The Pilgrim's Progress: a Casebook* (London, 1976), pp. 81–103, and Harold Golder, 'John Bunyan's hypocrisy', *The North American Review* (June 1926), pp. 323–32 and 'Bunyan's Valley of the Shadow', *Modern Philology*, xxvii (1929), pp. 55–72.

13. 'The Vogue of *Guy of Warwick* from the close of the Middle Ages to the Romantic revival', *Publications of the Modern Language Association*, xxx (1915), pp. 166–7. It may also be noted that, as an itinerant tinker, Bunyan would have been expected to carry about with him a repertoire of stories—though in the event preaching took the place of storytelling.

14. Cited in Golder (1929), op. cit., p. 57, n. 3.

15. See below, pp. 212ff.

16. See 'Bunyan's Giant Despair', *Journal of English and Germanic Philology*, xxx (1931), pp. 361–78.

17. See in particular the striking story of 'The Dead Moon', recorded in the Lincolnshire fenlands in the mid nineteenth century. Here the 'Bogles and Dead Things and crawling horrors' are held at bay through good luck, the advice of a Wise Woman, and the sovereign power of the Moon and her light. The story appears in *Folk-Lore*, ii (1891), pp. 157–64. and with

dialect partially standardized in K. M. Briggs (ed.), *A Dictionary of British Folk-Tales* (London, 1970), i. 206–8.

18. Some medieval English traditions of romance storytelling never in fact moved far away from folktale. They are usefully discussed in Kathryn Hume, '*Amis and Amiloun* and the aesthetics of Middle English romance', *Studies in Philology*, lxx (1973), pp. 19–41. But these are not the direct begetters of the popular romances of the Renaissance period, whose antecedents are in general more literary.

19. Mentioned by Bunyan in the same context as *The Seven Champions*—that is, as the sort of literature which the worldly man prefers to the Scriptures; see *Works*, ed. Offor, iii. 711.

20. For the exploitation of 'faerie' in chivalric romance, see T. McAlindon, 'Magic, fate and providence in medieval narrative and *Sir Gawain and the Green Knight*', *Review of English Studies*, xvi (1965), pp. 121–39.

21. Edition of 1596 (S.T.C. 14677), p. 15. These same terms of description are woven into the account of a dragon fight in later versions of Bevis of Hampton; see edition of *c.* 1639 (S.T.C. 1996), f. F1r.

22. Leo Salingar suggests that a certain reading of Boethius provided a rationale, if one were needed, for the cyclical, providential pattern characteristic of the European *Märchen*, and frequently encountered in medieval romance narratives. According to this pattern, 'Fortune, seemingly hostile and capricious, acts at the end in concert with the latent powers of Nature and obeys a hidden providence'; *Shakespeare and the Traditions of Comedy* (Cambridge, 1974), p. 30.

23. *Once Upon a Time: On the Nature of Fairy Tales* (Bloomington and London, 1976), p. 145. A specimen *Märchen* is given in an appendix to this article.

24. *The Pilgrim's Progress and Traditions in Puritan Meditation* (New Haven and London, 1966), pp. 116–17.

25. Cf. Lüthi, op. cit., p. 68: 'This is *the* image of man which somehow shines forth in every fairy-tale: outwardly isolated, but just for this reason free to establish essential contacts.'

26. As an instance of this, see the exchange which punctuates the final dialogue between Christian and Hopeful (p. 191).

27. An experience which had a catalytic role in precipitating Bunyan's conversion, as described in *Grace Abounding*, was a chance encounter with a group of poor women whom Bunyan overheard discussing 'the things of God' (*Works*, ed. Offor, i. 10): 'And methought they spake as if joy did make them speak; they spake with such pleasantness of Scripture language, and with such appearance of grace in all they said, that they were to me, as if they had found a new world, as if they were people that dwelt alone, and were not to be reckoned among their neighbours.'

28. See below, p. 257.

29. Cf. Lüthi, op. cit., p. 142: 'the fairy tale . . . presents its hero as one who, though not comprehending ultimate relationships, is led safely through the dangerous, unfamiliar world. The fairy-tale hero is gifted, in the literal sense of the word. Supernatural beings lavish their gifts on him and help him through battles and perils.'

30. See the comments of Christian and Hopeful at pp. 190 and 192 respectively.

31. Abridged from Edgar Taylor (ed. and trans.), *German Popular Stories . . . collected by M. M. Grimm, from Oral Tradition* (London, 1823 and 1826), ii. 67–73.

Bunyan's Military Metaphor

NICK SHRIMPTON

For followers of a God of Love Bunyan's pilgrims are remarkably pugnacious. Christian, like his successors in Part II of *The Pilgrim's Progress*, goes about his business 'with his sword drawn in his hand' and puts up a plucky defence when Apollyon blocks his way. Mr Great-heart's companions go so far as to volunteer for unprovoked conflicts. Giant Slay-good lives a good mile from the highway, yet a group of pilgrims set out after breakfast, 'with spears and staves', to conduct what has plausibly been described as 'a giant-hunt'.[1] In the next twenty pages Mr Great-heart both joins a skirmishing party for a detached operation against 'the Monster' of Rome and leads his own party out of the once sacrosanct 'way' for a full-scale attack on Giant Despair. They linger for seven days destroying the Giant's castle, and 'when Diffidence, the Giantess, came up to help him, old Mr Honest cut her down at one blow' (p. 339).

The bloodshed is, of course, allegorical. Great-heart represents the Christian pastor whose duty it is to remove such obstacles as Romanism and despair from the paths of his congregation. Honesty should overcome religious diffidence. The fight with Apollyon is the image of a spiritual conflict. But the violence will not entirely vanish into rhetorical smoke. Allegory has a surface as well as a significance, and that surface is the primary experience of the reader.

We are reminded of this primacy shortly before the end of Part II of *The Pilgrim's Progress* when that soldierly 'man of his hands' Mr Valiant-for-Truth explains how his family tried to dissuade him from pilgrimage. He gives us their catalogue of the deceivers with whom he would have to argue. But his first list is, revealingly, one of physical dangers. The speech is an accurate summary of the most immediate way in which *The Pilgrim's Progress* acts upon our imagination:

They told me of the Slough of Despond, where Christian was well nigh smothered. They told me that there
were archers standing ready in Beelzebub Castle, to
shoot them that should knock at the Wicket Gate for
entrance. They told me also of the wood, and dark
Mountains, of the Hill Difficulty, of the lions, and also
of the three giants, Bloodyman, Maul and Slay-good.
They said moreover, that there was a foul fiend haunting
the Valley of Humiliation, and that Christian was, by
him, almost bereft of life. 'Besides,' said they, 'you must
go over the Valley of the Shadow of Death, where the
hobgoblins are, where the light is darkness, where the
way is full of snares, pits, traps and gins.' They told me
also of Giant Despair, of Doubting-Castle, and of the
ruins that the pilgrims met with there. Further, they said
I must go over the Enchanted Ground, which was
dangerous. And that after all this I should find a River
over which I should find no bridge, and that that River
did lie betwixt me and the Celestial Country.

(pp. 352–3)

A wish to know why so violent a medium was chosen, and a
desire to explore its effects upon our reading, need involve no
diminution of our willingness to interpret Bunyan's allegorical reference.

These questions are made more urgent by the fact that
Bunyan's allegory is notoriously inconsistent. In any allegory
the surface action has a certain life of its own. In a work in
which allegory is intermittent that independent surface life
becomes more pronounced. *The Pilgrim's Progress* is several
other things as well as allegory. The consequence is that we
do not automatically or immediately assign action to an
allegorical pigeon-hole. A giant fight is a giant-fight, as well
as a struggle between faith and despair.

This multiplicity of literary modes (of which the allegorical and the literal-didactic are the most obvious) is, of course,
only one source of the confusion which this supposedly
simple book can generate. In the last two decades critics have
become increasingly preoccupied with the question of
whether or not *The Pilgrim's Progress* is in fact a progress.

Does the pilgrimage metaphor work? U. M. Kaufmann argued in 1966 that the book presented 'a conspicuous superimposition of stasis and linear movement'.[2] The truth, embodied in God's word, was established (and known to Christian) before the pilgrimage began. There could therefore be no question of the progressive discovery habitual in journey narratives. What is more, the Calvinist doctrine of prevenient grace means that even Christian's personal fate is predetermined. Prevenient grace and prevenient knowledge tend, in Kaufmann's words, 'to destroy the illusion of a dynamic career'.[3] Stanley E. Fish gave a further twist to this argument in 1972. For him the clash between the static and the dynamic is intentional. The journey metaphor is deliberately subverted. We are first tempted to believe in a literal progress, then chastised by the discovery that it is an illusion. 'For the reader as well as for the pilgrim,' Fish writes, 'to believe in the metaphor of the journey and in the *pilgrim's* progress, is to believe in himself, to prefer the operations of his discursive intellect to the revealed word of God'.[4] Ignorance completes his pilgrimage—but is damned, none the less, at the very gates of heaven.

Kaufmann claims that Bunyan's beliefs are fundamentally incompatible with his choice, as an artist, of the pilgrimage metaphor. Fish argues for a highly sophisticated Bunyan who recognizes and consciously exploits this discrepancy. What neither of these critics does is pause to consider the relationship between the untrustworthy metaphor of pilgrimage and the book's other predominant image, warfare. The fighting, interesting in itself, is all the more interesting for the light which it can cast on this important debate.

The first question must, however, be a simple one. Why is the book so bellicose? Bunyan grew up amidst a civil war and spent three impressionable years in the militia. Though he did not, as far as we know, have any experience of combat as a member of the important but untroubled Newport Pagnell garrison, the military language of the book does have a professional ring to it and Bunyan certainly knew enough about siege warfare to publish *The Holy War* in 1682. But the military imagery of *The Pilgrim's Progress* owes less to personal experience than it does to spiritual and literary tradition. The use of armed combat as a religious metaphor is an ancient one. Job sees human life as a relentless battle, and it is Job's imagery that is quoted when Christian discusses military courage with Hopeful, after the robbery of Little-faith (pp. 168–71). It is, however, in the supposedly pacific New Testament that warfare takes on its real importance. For St Paul the image is indispensable. His repeated use, and memorable formulation, of it ('Put on the whole armour of God') set it at the heart of Christian thought.

In the sixteenth century the well-worn image takes on a new lease of life. Erasmus's *Enchiridion*, first published in 1503, suggests the rich possibilities of military metaphor to a new generation of religious writers. The *Enchiridion Militis Christiani* (a Greek pun) is both the hand-dagger and the handbook of the Christian soldier. A 'compendious guide for living' is written under the thin disguise of a soldier's manual. Erasmus begins with a necessary homage to Job, 'that veteran, undefeated soldier',[5] and rapidly proceeds to an elaborate account of Christian life as a constant state of war. Most men, he claims, are unconscious of their danger:

> These folk, as if the war were already brought to an end, celebrate unseasonable holidays, when nothing could be so unlike real peace. It is wonderful in how much security they live, and in what a leisurely manner they go to sleep in both ears, while we are endlessly attacked by so many iron-clad troops of vices, are laid hold of by so many artifices, and are fallen upon by so many stratagems. Behold, in your last going forth they keep watch upon you with the highest vigilance, these most worthless demons, armed against us with a thousand deceits, a thousand noxious arts, who strive with fiery darts and poison arrows to pierce our minds from above; no javelin of Hercules or Cephalus was ever more certain than these weapons, unless they be fended off by the impenetrable shield of faith.[6]

The second chapter of the *Enchiridion* explains the weapons of the Christian knight (prayer and a knowledge of scripture) and collects the scattered military imagery of St Paul's epistles. Erasmus then supplies a 'manual of arms' in the form of twenty-two rules of conduct, and promises that 'if you exercise yourself diligently in it, our sovereign Christ will transfer you, rejoicing and victorious, from this garrison to the city of Jerusalem'.[7]

This procedure is echoed repeatedly in the Puritan literature of sixteenth and seventeenth century England. John Downame's enormous treatise *The Christian Warfare*, first published in 1604, for example, begins with a text from Ephesians ('Put on the whole armour of God, that ye may be able to stand against the wiles of the devil') and sets out to show '. . . the Malice, Power and the Politicke Stratagems of the spirituall Enemies of our salvation, Satan and his Assistants, the World and the Flesh; with the meanes also whereby the Christian may withstand and defeat them'.[8] We are, Downame argues, in one of his occasional flashes of vivid imagery, 'but fresh-water-souldiers and of small experience'.[9] His corrective training commences with the customary itemization of the Pauline armour of God, reserving for an equally lengthy Second Part the detailed description of our principal enemies, 'Security and Presumption, and on the other side . . . Doubting and Desperation'.[10]

William Haller published, in 1938, an extensive survey of such Puritan literature. His analysis identified, not one, but two central images:

> The Puritan imagination saw the life of the spirit as pilgrimage and battle. The images of wayfaring and warfaring which fill the Old Testament had been exploited by that fighting itinerant, Paul, and by generations upon generations of subsequent evangelists. Reaching the pulpits of the seventeenth century by a hundred channels, they there underwent new and peculiarly vigorous development. The occupants of many of these pulpits . . . had to dwell upon the responsibility of the individual . . . They told him that his soul was a traveler through a strange country and a soldier in battle.[11]

Wayfaring and warfaring are found in book after book. Bunyan has an equally concise phrase for this double interest. 'I have heard much of your husband,' Honest tells Christiana in Part II of *The Pilgrim's Progress*, 'and of his travels and wars which he underwent in his days' (p. 301).

Travels and wars, pilgrimage and battle are thus the dominant metaphors of the religious literature by which Bunyan is formed. He is working with a traditional imagery. Thomas Taylor, for example, had severally exploited the two images in *The Pilgrim's Profession* (1622) and *Christ's Combate* (1618). Bunyan's distinctive contribution to the tradition is twofold. He uses both images in the same book and, partly as a consequence of this, he invents a new kind of literary context for them.

Erasmus and Downame and Taylor had all attempted, with differing degrees of success, to disguise their essentially homiletic procedure. The *Enchiridion* and *The Christian Warfare* made gestures towards the military manual. *The Pilgrim's Profession* bore a flimsy resemblance to a set of instructions to travellers. Bunyan needs a similarly established form, but one which can embrace a simultaneous interest in warfaring and wayfaring. He finds it, of course, in the popular romance, the seventeenth-century equivalent of the thriller. Mr Valiant-for-Truth's list of dangers is little more, and certainly nothing less, than a good romance scenario. Worldly-Wiseman summarizes it still more tersely. He speaks of 'swords, lions, dragons, darkness' and excites the reader's interest in the very words with which he discourages Christian. The original audience of *The Pilgrim's Progress* was in no doubt about what it was encountering. The fourth 'objection' mentioned in the verse preface to Part II is to the 'method' of the book. 'Romance they count it, throw't away as dust' (p. 215). Bunyan does not bother to deny the charge. The conventional soldier becomes a questing knight, a traveller as well as a warrior. Bunyan has found a fertile medium for the two great Puritan metaphors.

Naturally enough, so important a topic has attracted a good deal of critical attention. One of the most incisive treatments of the relationship between the realistic and the romantic elements in *The Pilgrim's Progress* was supplied by Sir Charles Firth as long ago as 1898. He draws our attention to Bunyan's confession of a weakness, in his unregenerate youth, for ballads and 'old fables'. And the more specific reference, by an unfortunate soul in Bunyan's sermon *A Few Sighs From Hell*, to the particular old fables of 'George on horseback, or Bevis of Southampton'[12] leads Firth to a valuable comparison between *The Pilgrim's Progress* and the book in which 'George' is featured, Richard Johnson's romance *The Seven Champions of Christendom*. 'George' is, of course, St George, the leader of Johnson's magnificent seven. His fight with the Egyptian dragon proves to have close parallels with Christian's tussle with Apollyon. The giants encountered by St George and his comrade St Anthony are first cousins of Great-heart's victims. Bunyan's Enchanted Ground resembles the Enchanted Garden in which St David falls asleep. Firth's conclusions are cautious but, none the less, positive. 'One must not,' he writes, 'exaggerate these resemblances between Bunyan's story and the stories in which he had once delighted, but it is plain that he was not uninfluenced by them.'[13]

Thirty years later Harold Golder published a series of articles exploring these resemblances in much greater detail. To the giant and dragon fights, and the Enchanted Ground, Golder adds the motifs of the dark valley and the sword-bridge. Christian proceeds through the Valley of the Shadow of Death on an 'exceeding narrow' pathway between a ditch and a quagmire. The references are biblical. But, as Golder points out, 'they are nowhere associated in the Bible with an adventure like Christian's . . . Without the romances, the mire of David and the ditch of Job could never have made a sword-bridge'.[14] Nor is this all. Golder also identifies as conventional features of romance the unheeded warning (p. 95), the resisted temptation to return (p. 97), the useless sword (p. 97), the glimpse of a fair country or city from a distance (pp. 88 and 161), the arming of the hero (pp. 88–9), and the whole process of imprisonment in Doubting Castle. These parallels are drawn from a very extensive reading of medieval and Elizabethan romance. But, with the help of a specialist study like Mary Patchell's *The Palmerin Romances in Elizabethan Prose Fiction*, one can enlarge even this list of resemblances. Patchell mentions the encounter with lions and the safety of the innocent in their presence. This is something which Bunyan uses (rather uncertainly at times) in both Parts of *The Pilgrim's Progress* (pp. 78, 267–8). The unwitting failure of loyalty (a lapse often caused by a magic drink) is another set motif, echoed by Bunyan in Christian's careless loss of his roll while asleep in the Arbour, as is the dream which supplies the outermost framework of the book.

Perhaps most interesting of all, given the theological bias of *The Pilgrim's Progress*, is the importance of destiny in the Palmerin romances:

> Much of the action of the romance is governed by supernatural agencies, against which it is useless for our invincible knights to contend, or by an over-ruling Destiny, which determines the trend of the plot. Love, marriage, and death, fights with giants, animals, and monsters, and the overcoming of enchantments—all are predestined. In fact, the power of Destiny is so great that a knight can succeed in an undertaking only if it is preordained. Strength is not sufficient to insure success unless the adventure has been *reserved* for him.[15]

One begins here, I think, to realize how much more appropriate to Bunyan's determinist argument the military image (in its romance-knight form) can be than the pilgrimage or journey metaphor with which he commenced his book.

Bunyan's knowledge of such romance was clearly derived from a wide range of casual reading. The most instructive single comparison, however, is still that, first suggested by Sir Charles Firth, with Johnson's *The Seven Champions of Christendom*. For the parallels are not simply a matter of the folk-tale motifs to which he and Golder refer. Johnson's narrative form, a mixture of plot with discussions, set speeches and poems, is precisely that used by Bunyan. The frequent use of verse in *The Pilgrim's Progress*, for example, closely resembles Johnson's practice. Kalyb, the Witch of the Woods, gives her advice to St George's father in verse. Princess Sabra's dream vision of St George, on the eve of her forcible marriage to Almidor, is described in a poem, and it is a verse inscription (not unlike the one placed by Mr Great-heart under the severed head of Giant Maul) that St Anthony finds on the gate of Giant Blanderon's castle:

Within this Castle lives the scourge of Kings,
A furious Gyant, whose unconquered power,
The Thracian Monarch in subjection brings,
And keeps his Daughters Prisoners in his power:
Seven Damsels fair this monstrous Gyant keeps,
That sings him Musick while he nightly sleeps.[16]

The Seven Champions of Christendom might also have supplied
the Arcadian or pastoral note heard in *The Pilgrim's Progress*.
Mary Patchell has commented on the way in which pastoralism slowly becomes 'an invariable feature of the *novella
caballeresca*, both in Spain and in England'.[17] The balance
between chivalry and pastoralism is roughly the same in the
two books. Confined in *The Pilgrim's Progress* to the
Shepherds of the Delectable Mountains, it occurs in *The
Seven Champions of Christendom* in such details as Rossalinde's
lament over the supposedly dead St Anthony:

I'le lay my breast upon a silver stream,
And swim in Elisium's Lilly Fields,
There in Ambrosian Trees I'le write a theam
Of all the wofull sighs my sorrow yields.[18]

Even Johnson's decision to write a 'Second Part' about 'the
strange Fortunes of Saint GEORGE's three sons . . . Also the
manner and places of the honourable Deaths of the Seven
Champions'[19] reminds us of Bunyan's sequel. Part II of *The
Pilgrim's Progress* is similarly concerned with the adventures
of the hero's wife and children, and similarly culminates in an
impressive series of death scenes.

Perhaps most interesting of all, however, is something
which has been ignored in most comparisons between *The
Pilgrim's Progress* and popular romance. *The Seven Champions
of Christendom* is full of love, magic, and adventure. It is, none
the less, a highly religious work. Mary Patchell, discussing it
in the context of other Elizabethan romances, rather than in
the course of a comparison with Bunyan, remarks that, 'In an
amazing way Johnson has mingled enchantment and piety,
emphasizing the fact that each champion succeeds through
divine help'.[20] This book, in other words, is an extreme
example of that romantic reliance on destiny to which she has

previously drawn attention. And its conspicuous piety casts new light upon our habitual assumption that Bunyan must be struggling to bend a deplorably irreligious medium to his sacred purposes.

Certainly both Bunyan and his fellow Puritans disapproved of ballads and romances as distractions from the reading of the Bible. John Smyth, the spiritual father of the English Baptists, decided to publish his sermons because 'every bald tale, vaine enterlude, and pelting ballad, hath the priviledge of the Presse'. Why, he asked, should the stationers' shops contain nothing but 'Guy of Warwicke, William of Cloudeslee, Skeggins and Wolners jests, and writings of like qualitie'?[21] But *The Seven Champions of Christendom* is something of an exception. Its heroes are saints as well as knights. Johnson's collective term for them is frequently 'the Christians', just as Bunyan's hero is called 'Christian'. And the romantic action of the book is often religious even before Bunyan allegorizes it. St George's fight with the Egyptian dragon, for example, has been likened to the Apollyon episode for its description of the monster, and for its healing of the wounded hero with the fruit of a magic tree (Christian is healed with leaves from the Tree of Life). Yet in the end it is less magic which saves St George than prayer:

> So it was the noble champion's good and happy fortune a little to recover through the vertue of the tree, and to espy an Orange which a little before had dropped down, wherewith he so refreshed himself, that he was in short time as sound as when he began the Encounter. Then kneeled he down, and made his Divine supplication to Heaven, that God would send him (for his dear Sons sake) such strength and agility of body as to slay the furious and terrible Monster: which being done, with a bold couragious heart, he smote the Dragon under the wing, where it was tender without scale, whereby his good sword Ascalon, with an easie passage, went to the very hilt through both the Dragon's Heart, Liver, Bone and Blood . . .[22]

Christian makes similar use of the weapon of 'All-prayer' in the Valley of the Shadow of Death (p. 97). Equally striking is the parallel between the death scenes with which the second Parts of both books conclude. Not all of Johnson's champions get the chance to make a speech, and even those that do cannot, of course, rise to the sublime heights of Mr Valiant-for-Truth's farewell to the world. But St Denis's remarks, as he awaits execution at the hands of the pagan king of France, sound remarkably like a sketch for what Bunyan will one day achieve:

> . . . I take it with much joy, in that I die for him whose Colours I have worn from mine Infancy, and this my death seals up the obligation of all my comforts.[23]

The Seven Champions of Christendom, in fact, is pious as well as popular—and it is worth noting that here, as in Mr Valiant-for-Truth's speech, it is a military vocabulary which lends the rhetoric its peculiar dignity.

In all respects but one, indeed, the central lines of Johnson's prefatory poem ('The Author's Muse Upon the History') could accurately be applied to *The Pilgrim's Progress:*

> Such Ladies saved, such Monsters made to fall,
> Such Gyants slain, such Hellish Furies queld.[24]

The exception is, of course, the first of these topics. Bunyan offers us a version of romance from which sexual love has been removed. Interestingly, it would appear that it was precisely the bawdy that he most disliked about romances. In *The Holy War* Diabolus at one point causes:

> . . . by the hand of one Mr Filth, an odious, nasty, lascivious piece of beastliness to be drawn up in writing, and to be set upon the Castle Gates: whereby he granted, and gave licence to all his true and trusty sons in Mansoul, to do whatsoever their lustful appetites prompted them to do . . .[25]

The marginal gloss reads, 'Odious Atheistical Pamphlets and filthy Ballads & Romances full of baldry'. Sex is not entirely excluded from *The Pilgrim's Progress*. Faithful gives a brief account of his encounter with Wanton (p. 103), Mr Stand-fast's escape from the witch Madam Bubble (p. 361) is reminiscent of St George's youthful experience with Kalyb, and Christiana and Mercy are at one point rescued ('Such Ladies saved') from what is clearly meant to be a rape (pp. 241–2). But human love is never a dominant motive, and the treatment of Mercy's marriage is perfunctory.

Once its erotic content has been thus removed, however, romance proves to be an extraordinarily effective vehicle for Bunyan's argument. The romance-knight is a traveller as well as a warrior. Though he may travel with companions he characteristically fights alone, and single combat is a better metaphor for spiritual struggle than the manoeuvring of battalions. Above all, the magically assisted conflict of romance is almost always more appropriate to the expression of Bunyan's beliefs than conventional warfare. The escape from Doubting Castle is an interesting example of this peculiar aptness. Bunyan is often criticized for the weakness of his plotting at this point. Roger Sharrock, for instance, comments that 'Bunyan makes his theological point, though with some detriment to the effect of the adventure story' (p. 376). Certainly, as one reads the passage it is tempting to presume that the author is sacrificing the romance surface to the religious content:

> Now a little before it was day, good Christian, as one half amazed, brake out in this passionate speech, 'What a fool,' quoth he, 'am I, thus to lie in a stinking dungeon, when I may as well walk at liberty. I have a key in my bosom, called promise, that will (I am persuaded) open any lock in Doubting-Castle.'   (p. 156)

In fact Bunyan is offering an exact echo of his adventure story model. St. George's escape from the Sultan of Persia's prison is not meant to represent a sudden remembrance of God's promise of salvation. Yet it is effected in much the same manner. With one bound he too is free:

> . . . a thousand times a year he wisht an end of his life . . . many times making his humble supplications to the heavens, to redeem him from the vale of misery and many times seeking occasion, desperately to abridge his days and to triumph in his own tragedy.
>
> But at last, when seven years were fully ended, it was

the Champions lucky fortune to find in a secret corner
of the Dungeon a certain Iron Engin, which time has
almost consumed with Rust, wherewith, with long
labour he digged himself a passage through the ground,
til he ascended just in the middle of the Souldans Court,
which was at that time of the night when all things were
silent . . .[26]

The arduous process of excavation is dismissed in twelve
words. The focus is on the arbitrary discovery of a long
neglected 'Engin'. One remembers Mary Patchell's point
that a knight in the Palmerin romances 'can succeed in an
undertaking only if it is preordained'.[27] The theological
objections to the journey image quite clearly do not apply to
the particular version of the military metaphor that Bunyan
has chosen.

What is interesting, however, is less the ease with which
romance, as Johnson had practised it, could be turned to
Bunyan's ends than the effect of its conspicuous metaphorical
fitness upon the meaning of the book. The romance surface is
not just the sugar on a doctrinal pill. Like the surface of any
successful allegory, it contributes to rather than disguises
statement. The relationship between Bunyan's two central
images, and their relative success, help to determine our
understanding of The Pilgrim's Progress.

One must not, of course, exaggerate the gap between the
two metaphors of pilgrimage and war. Travel was a dangerous business in the seventeenth century, and for a pilgrim to
carry a sword was held to be normal enough. Thomas
Taylor, in The Pilgrim's Profession, dramatizes texts not only
as maps, guides, provisions, and companions, but also as 'a
weapon':

. . . a traveller hath need of a weapon to defend himselfe,
and to wound or keepe off his enemies. The same word
of God is a special part of our spiritual armour; it is the
sword of the Spirit.[28]

John Downame introduces a corresponding hint of the
pilgrimage into his exposition of the military metaphor, The
Christian Warfare:

> . . . if once we enrich our selves with the unvaluable treasures of Gods spiritual graces, and make the World a passage or place of pilgrimage, and desire to saile through this dangerous Sea into our owne heavenly Countrie; then this Arch-pyrate Satan will set upon us . . .[29]

But, though the two images may thus overlap, they do in the end serve different purposes. Pilgrimage, as William Haller has pointed out, was characteristically used in the important Puritan genre of spiritual biography. *The Pilgrim's Profession* was, in the words of its subtitle, 'A Sermon Preached at the Funerall of Mrs Mary Gunter', and was printed with an account of her edifying life attached. Mary Gunter's progress to sainthood, from a papist upbringing and an early career of petty theft, was particularly striking. But it was this process of conversion and confirmation in the faith to which the metaphor of pilgrimage was habitually applied.

Warfare, by contrast, was used to depict the state of life which succeeded conversion. John Downame makes this point very clearly at the beginning of his book:

> . . . Gods children . . . although they lived in peace and securitie before they were intertained into Gods family, yet no sooner were they admitted to be of Gods household servants but Satan and the world have raged against them, labouring both by inward temptations and outward furie, either to withdraw them from Gods service by flattering inticements, or utterly to destroy and overthrow them by open violence.[3]

More specifically, the battle was seen as a contest between the New Adam of the spirit and the Old Adam of the flesh. Erasmus, in the *Enchiridion*, speaks of the enemy as 'that old earthly Adam, in habit more than a citizen, in zeal more than an enemy, whom it is not permitted to enclose with an entrenchment, nor possible to drive out with an army'.[31] The body survives conversion, with its weaknesses intact.

William Haller has explained the practical implications of this concept particularly well:

> The manifestation of grace in the elect was faith. Those

destined to be saved in Christ believed in his power and willingness to redeem. Those who believed evinced to themselves their faith and their redemption by making incessant war on sin in their own members. It was not that they could do no evil. They sinned again and again. But the evil which they did they hated.[32]

Bunyan's *Grace Abounding* provides ample illustration of this struggle. The process of the author's conversion, which occupies the first third of the book, is described in the imagery of a progress or journey. 'But, oh!' now,' he writes, 'how was my Soul led from truth to truth by God!'[33] Thereafter, however, it is the imagery and the experience of combat which predominate. Bunyan's life becomes one of 'conflict' and 'Combate with the Devil'.[34] Until death intervenes, the battle will go on without cease.

Such an understanding of the two central metaphors of *The Pilgrim's Progress* can help, I think, to clarify that problem of whether or not the book does depict a progress, with which U. M. Kaufmann and Stanley E. Fish are properly so concerned. The essential point is that, even more clearly than in *Grace Abounding*, the dominant image of the book changes. Up to the moment of conversion, the shedding of the burden of sin at the foot of the Cross (pp. 69–70), Christian is indeed a pilgrim and his experiences can correctly be understood as a progressive linear sequence. 'God did,' as Bunyan writes in *Grace Abounding*, 'lead me into his words . . . he was pleased to take this course with me, first, to suffer me to be afflicted with temptation concerning them, and then reveal them to me.'[35] Almost immediately after the conversion, however, Christian becomes something else. In the House Beautiful he is armed. Henceforth he will be the Christian warrior, whose unprogressive and incessant struggles will be symbolized by the unpredictable wanderings of the questing knight. In *The Seven Champions of Christendom* St George warns Princess Sabra, who has fallen in love with him, that as a knight he is 'a wanderer from place to place'.[36] He's sworn 'to search the world, so far as ever the lamp of Heaven doth lend his light'.[37] But his

searchings do not have a fixed end towards which he steadily
advances. They are simply a perpetual duty which only death
will interrupt.

Once this change of image is understood, we need not be
surprised to find, for example, Ignorance further advanced
on the road than Faithful. Before the scene at the foot of the
Cross the journey is indeed progressive. Thereafter, perhaps
confusingly, it becomes a perambulation in which the sequence of events is not in itself significant. Experiences are,
accordingly, different in kind before and after the scene in the
armoury of the House Beautiful. Everybody who wishes to
be saved has to go through the Slough of Despond. The
conviction of sin is an indispensable part of the linear process
of conversion. But everybody does not have to experience
Doubting Castle or the Delectable Mountains. One may
reach heaven by a martyr's death in Vanity Fair as easily as
one may by a natural death in the River. From the House
Beautiful onwards the journey records endurance rather than
advance.

This double understanding of the journey metaphor can be
found elsewhere in Bunyan's work. In *Grace Abounding* we
encounter the two conceptions, and the potential confusion
between them, in embryonic form:

> Now had I an evidence, as I thought, of my salvation
> from Heaven, with many golden Seals thereon, all
> hanging in my sight; now could I remember this
> manifestation, and the other discovery of grace with
> comfort; and should often long and desire that the last
> day were come, that I might for ever be inflamed with
> the sight and joy, and communion with him, whose
> Head was crowned with Thorns, whose Face was spit
> on, and Body broken, and Soul made an offering for my
> sins: for whereas before, I lay continually trembling at
> the mouth of Hell; now me thought I was got so far
> therefrom, that I could not, when I looked back, scarce
> discern it; and, O thought I, that I were fourscore years
> old now, that I might die quickly, that my soul might be
> gone to rest.[38]

Bunyan is here lamenting the discrepancy between the

process of religious enlightenment and redemption (which is progressive) and the simpler process of human life from birth to death (which is not). In terms of the first he has gone as far as he can ever go. In terms of the other he has decades of struggle and temptation still to endure. It is the latter, comparatively static, experience which the military imagery and romance action of *The Pilgrim's Progress* depict.

The changed nature of the way is made apparent as soon as Christian has passed the Cross. On the stretch of road between the Wicket Gate and the Cross no unworthy characters could be encountered. Moral drama had to be presented through the emblems of the Interpreter's House. After the Cross, however, we suddenly find Simple, Sloth, and Presumption sleeping by the wayside, and Formalist and Hypocrisy tumbling over the wall into the road. The way is no longer an exclusive place, to which admission must painfully be won. Instead it is simply the world, understood as a dangerous wilderness. Formalist marches off into 'a great wood', Hypocrisy into 'a wide field full of dark mountains' (p. 74). The converted Christian shares this perilous world with the unconverted. His wanderings through it differ from theirs only in his militant willingness to resist temptation and his greater liability to violent assault.

It is, therefore, no accident that romance action should cluster particularly thickly after the arming of Christian. Bunyan wishes to emphasize his hero's change of status. The Hill, merely difficult coming up, is 'dangerous going down' (p. 89). At the bottom of it Christian fights Apollyon and walks the sword-bridge through the Valley of the Shadow of Death. At the end of the Valley he sees his first giants, and his first conversation with Faithful contains the latter's recollection of that very combat between the Old and the New Adam which Erasmus had described in the *Enchiridion*. Even Vanity Fair, normally seen as part of the realistic rather than the romantic side of the book, proves to have a military dimension. 'You must,' says Evangelist, 'through many tribulations enter into the Kingdom of Heaven . . . in that town you will be hardly beset with enemies who will strain hard but they will kill you' (p. 124).

Pilgrimage could itself, of course, sometimes be used as an

image of such unprogressive endurance. Thomas Taylor begins *The Pilgrim's Profession* with the text 'I am a stranger with thee, and a sojourner, as all my Fathers' (Psalms 39: 12) and seems initially to depict the pilgrim, in terms drawn from Exodus, as an outcast or stranger in the world. But it is hard to suppress the dynamic implications of pilgrimage for very long. Though the Israelites may have wandered in the wilderness, they were in fact, as Taylor recognizes, on their way to the promised land:

> . . . as for the world, it is but a way to their Country, & as a wildernesse thorow which the Israel of God passe towards their Canaan.[39]

Bunyan finds it necessary to replace his initial image with another. Progress gives way to knight-errancy, to a military perambulation.

Fish and Kaufmann might very reasonably object that this replacement is too inconspicuous to be successful. The book continues, after all, to be called *The Pilgrim's Progress* and we are nowhere explicitly instructed to abandon our first impressions. The answer (unless one is to argue that the 'progress' in question is the very transition from pilgrim to warrior that I have been discussing) is that we must be prepared to allow at least as much weight to the imagery of a book as to its title. The arming of Christian by the servants of the Lord of the Hill (himself Christ seen as the knight-errant) is to be taken seriously. The armour is not mere costume, not even a set of merely local allegorical references. It is the manifestation of a change of role.

Our sense of the growing importance of the fights, struggles and escapes in *The Pilgrim's Progress*, in other words, is not a superficial or irrelevant response. Mr Valiant-for-Truth's catalogue of dangers is a serious reminder of the meaning of the work. And the military imagery is not only important for the contribution which it makes to the book's internal coherence. It is also a reason for the paradoxical popularity of Bunyan's doctrinaire fiction. The process of conversion, which pilgrimage depicts, is a highly specialized business. But the ethical struggle between the Old Adam and the New is only an extreme version of a universal experience. Bunyan's military metaphor reflects the moral life of every reader. It is not just on the surface that Mr Worldly-Wiseman's 'swords, lions, dragons, darkness, and in a word, death' attracts us. The things which he mentions are central to the most enduring significances of the book.

NOTES

1. R. Sharrock, *John Bunyan: The Pilgrim's Progress* (London, 1966), p. 49.

2. U. M. Kaufmann, *The Pilgrim's Progress and Traditions in Puritan Meditation* (New Haven, 1966), p. 106.

3. Ibid., p. 117.

4. S. E. Fish, *Self-Consuming Artifacts* (Berkeley, 1972), p. 237.

5. Desiderius Erasmus, *Enchiridion Militis Christiani*, trans. F. P. Battles, in M. Spinka (ed.), *Advocates of Reform from Wyclif to Erasmus* (London, 1953), (hereafter Erasmus), p. 296.

6. Erasmus, p. 296.

7. Erasmus, p. 308.

8. John Downame, *The Christian Warfare* (London, 1634) (hereafter Downame), The First Part, title-page.

9. Downame, The First Part, p. 19.

10. Downame, The Second Part, title-page.

11. W. Haller, *The Rise of Puritanism* (New York, 1938) (hereafter Haller), p. 142.

12. G. Offor (ed.), *The Works of John Bunyan* (1862), iii. 711.

13. Sir Charles Firth, Introduction to *The Pilgrim's Progress* (London, 1898), reprinted in R. Sharrock (ed.), *The Pilgrim's Progress: A Casebook* (London, 1976), p. 91.

14. H. Golder, 'Bunyan's Valley of the Shadow', *Modern Philology*, xxvii, (1929–30), p. 66. Golder's other articles on this topic are 'Bunyan and Spenser', *Publications of the Modern Language Association*, xlv (1930) and 'Bunyan's Giant Despair', *Journal of English and Germanic Philology*, xxx (1931).

15. M. Patchell, *The Palmerin Romances in Elizabethan Prose Fiction* (New York, 1947) (hereafter Patchell), p. 39.

16. Richard Johnson, *The Famous History of the Seven Champions of Christendom* (London, 1670) (hereafter *Seven Champions*), The First Part, chap. 6 (unnumbered pages).

17. Patchell, p. 89.

18. *Seven Champions*, The First Part, chap. 6 (unnumbered pages).

19. *Seven Champions*, The Second Part, title-page.

20. Patchell, pp. 110–11.

21. See Haller, p. 183.

22. *Seven Champions*, The First Part, chap. 3 (unnumbered pages).

23. *Seven Champions*, The Second Part, chap. 19 (unnumbered pages).

24. *Seven Champions*, Prefatory Poem (unnumbered pages).

25. J. Brown (ed.), John Bunyan, *The Holy War* (Cambridge, 1905), p. 213.

26. *Seven Champions*, The First Part, chap. 10 (unnumbered pages).

27. Patchell, p. 39.

28. Thomas Taylor, *The Pilgrim's Profession* (London, 1633) (hereafter Taylor), p. 149.

29. Downame, The First Part, p. 3.

30. Downame, The First Part, p. 1.

31. Erasmus, p. 297.

32. Haller, p. 88.

33. R. Sharrock (ed.), John Bunyan, *Grace Abounding to the Chief of Sinners* (Oxford, 1966) (hereafter *Grace Abounding*), p. 39.

34. *Grace Abounding*, pp. 57 and 62.

35. *Grace Abounding*, pp. 41–2.

36. *Seven Champions*, The First Part, chap. 3 (unnumbered pages).

37. *Seven Champions*, The First Part, chap. 3 (unnumbered pages).

38. *Grace Abounding*, p. 42.

39. Taylor, p. 113.

Bunyan's Solidness

S. J. NEWMAN

I

'But must I needs want solidness, because / By metaphors I speak . . .?' Obviously not. Orwell says any strongly individual piece of writing gives one the impression of seeing a face somewhere behind the page. Bunyan's writing gives the impression of a whole body, legs astride, arms akimbo. One of his nineteenth-century readers testified that 'Not as a dream or allegory, but as solid literal history did it present itself to my boyish mind'.[1] There are, as in all allegories, moments when fable and moral get separated, but on the whole Bunyan's allegory is probably the most obviously compacted example of the mode. In comparison with Langland and Spenser we always know where we are in *The Pilgrim's Progress*.

It is just this fact that constitutes the problem for the modern reader, who on the whole does not know where he is and prefers a like-minded literature. Bunyan can, as Macaulay puts it, 'make a simile go on all fours'.[2] What it would seem he cannot do is make it take the wings of the morning and dwell in the uttermost parts of the sea—or even that ocean where each kind does straight its own resemblance find: Bunyan's monsters are negligible compared with Spenser's; his best abstractions are always obstinately anthropomorphic. This down-to-earthness in relation to ultimate questions of faith and doubt is likely to seem at best paradoxical and at worst jejune to the contemporary consciousness. Rebecca West is perhaps speaking for a majority of readers when she calls *The Pilgrim's Progress* an allegory for the world's childhood, *The Brothers Karamazov* an allegory for the world's maturity.[3] As the faith on which it floated recedes it is likely to seem increasingly stranded like a quaint Noah's ark, an outstanding example of what Arnold called 'an *Aberglaube*, or extra belief and fairy-tale, produced by

taking certain great names and promises too literally and
materially'.[4]

There is point in quoting Arnold because he was excep-
tionally quick to discern the effects of scepticism on the
literature of faith and adroit in devising a defence which
admitted scepticism without discrediting the literature. The
language of the Bible, for instance, is not literal language but
literary—'that is, the language of poetry and emotion, approximative language, thrown out, as it were, at certain great
objects which the human mind augurs and feels after'. The
idea of approximative language has proved seminal; most
twentieth-century criticism is literary precisely in its agnostic
conversion of the art of belief into the art of rhetoric.
Bunyan's solidness resists this conversion. He refuses to be
our contemporary and—to judge by the scarcity of recent
concern with his art—is in danger of being abandoned as an
anachronism. This is not a plea for a Bunyan industry.
Bunyan's first value for us is to focus the fact that critical
neglect is more than a literary matter, a fact which could be
blurred by sheer academic output. His second value is to
make us hesitate to bring the mass-produced tools, termino-
logies, and assumptions of contemporary critical rhetoric to
bear on such an obviously home-made artefact as *The
Pilgrim's Progress*. We have to initiate a more historical
endeavour in which criticism acknowledges the same sort of
bondage to time and circumstances as the object to which it
addresses itself.

II

The Pilgrim's Progress has the following claims on our attention: it is the last significant product of English religious folk
vision, it is the most important focus of English folk life
between Shakespeare and Dickens, and it is an outstanding
symptom of that life in process of disintegration. The *Shorter
Oxford English Dictionary* gives as its first definition of 'folk',
'A people, nation, race, tribe. Now *arch.*' And to revive our
experience of the word we need to go back to the fourteenth
century and a faire felde ful of folke: i.e. to a literature in
which 'folk' is a central national concept. In the masterpieces

of medieval superhumanism—*Piers Plowman* and the Mystery Plays—Catholic religious faith and English society generate a language which is partly the product of that collaboration and partly the substantiation of its ideals. The heart of Langland's vision is the sacramental vision of God incarnate in man; Piers Plowman but also *Petrus id est christus*. The stratifying tendencies of society are rebutted by an insistence on the sovereignty of the common. The vulgar and the visionary are equipresent; the poem is simultaneously a parable and a panorama. Scenes of everyday life are suddenly transformed by prophetic and apocalyptic images in a way that superficially resembles Blake's techniques in *Jerusalem*; but the resemblance is superficial precisely because Langland does not have to resort like Blake to a language dark with private significance. Langland's language puts to poetic work the verbal register of a society whose belief in miracle and revelation is part of the currency of its normal existence. Holy Church's speech in Passus I is an accurate sample of his art: with equal ease it moves from ceremony to colloquial bluntness ("'þow doted daffe," quod she, "dulle arne þi wittes'"), to proverbial wisdom and to the extraordinary fusion of mystery with solidity of specification in the account of God's love becoming flesh ('For heuene myʒte nouʒte holden it; it was so heuy of hymself, / Tyl it hadde of þe erthe yeten his fylle'). *Verbum caro factum est*. This is not approximative but incarnative language.

An even more impressive testimony to the range and centrality of the folk imagination is to be found in the Mystery Plays: more impressive because while it has been suggested that Langland's poem was written not for a popular audience but for an informed nucleus of well-to-do laymen[5] the audience of the Mystery Plays could range from king to peasant. And for all its accessibility the language of the best of these plays is no less richly co-ordinate than Langland's. The imaginative life of the plays is suffused with the idea of incarnation. God is literally down-to-earth in man and simultaneously transforms him. It is an intrinsically poetic notion—'Nothyng is inpossybyll, / Sothly, that God wyll'—and one that needs and finds a remarkable language to articulate it. Just as the act of a tradesman playing Christ

becomes more than merely the illusion of a relationship
between God and man, so does the substantiating power of the
language. In the York *Harrowing of Hell* Christ talks to the
devil in plain English ('Thou wikid feende, latte be thy
dynne!'), and in the greatest Crucifixion play his real presence
is mercilessly emphasized by the technical jargon of the York
pinners; but equally there can be a purity of plainness that
testifies to the immanence of the divine in the human. Mostly,
the colloquial and exalted cannot be isolated from one another.
The final feature of the language is its alliterative fusion of
these opposing qualities. Both here and in Langland one needs
something like a theosophy of alliteration to account for its
power to integrate sound, sense, and substance. It is an art of
the word which is creatively true to the vision it expresses.
When in the Towneley *Second Shepherd's Play* Gib says at the
nativity,

> Hayll, lytyll tyne mop!
> Of oure crede thou art crop,[6]

the words themselves are another nativity making flesh the
unified, non-Pascalian, greatness and littleness of man.

To consider these things is to approach something primary
in the genius of the English language; a quality that criticism
during the 1920s and 1930s sensed but, in its preoccupation
with the early seventeenth century, discovered in already too
late and fragmented a condition to be formulated as a
principle. Thus we get Leavis for instance gesturing rather
helplessly in a comparison between Donne and Milton to 'the
English use' of English; a principle he comes closest to
expressing in *New Bearings in English Poetry* where he applauds
Hopkins for making 'current idiom . . . the presiding spirit in
his dialect'. Christopher Ricks attacked the unexamined
assumptions of this kind of criticism when he called the
invocation of 'colloquial ease' in the language of poetry 'an
extraordinary critical shibboleth'.[7] Yet this sense of the
colloquial, of the current idiom, is more than a historical fad; it
is an awareness of something vital to the language, found at its
purest in this literature where God's English can be the King's
English, and the King's English the English of the folk.

The effect of the Renaissance on this culture was drastic. As

I. A. Gordon says, on the whole 'authorship in the English renaissance is to become the preserve of the gentleman and the scholar'.[8] The most brilliant and total—one almost wants to say totalitarian—instance of this development is *Arcadia*, a work as defiant of 'the English use' in its way as *Paradise Lost*, and one which epitomizes the new relationship between these scholars and gentlemen and the language of common life in the riot scene, where Sidney describes with Monday Club facetiousness the courtiers' dismemberment of 'an unruly sort of clownes, and other rebels'. There are two outstanding areas of resistance to this trend. The first is Hugh Latimer, whose sermons are the most vital English vernacular art between the fourteenth century and Shakespeare. Like Langland, Latimer's sense of the spiritual is inseparable from his sense of the corporeal. The word of God is naturally incarnate; even Christ's parables 'are so wrapped in wrinkles, that yet they seem to have a face and a similitude of a thing done indeed'. The century's supremacies—papal, royal, genteel—are rebuked in the name of a spiritual commonwealth. Papist Latin is attacked as esoteric ('God's word', he says ironically, 'may in no wise be translated into English'). He roundly tells Edward VI that 'the king's honour . . . standeth in the great multitude of people'; and he insists on his own folk heritage: 'My father was a yeoman . . . by yeoman's sons the faith of Christ is and hath been maintained chiefly.' Out of context that last statement may sound vainglorious, but Latimer's language is the proof of his convictions. At every turn it humanizes and, so to speak, earths doctrine and theory. The Bible is rendered into English that makes even Tyndale read like translatorese by comparison and makes one speculate on the condition of English society if there had been a Latimer Bible instead of the Authorized Version. Anecdote and proverb are essential components of his vision. If, as he says, Christ 'blessed our nature with taking upon him the shape of man' and 'The poorest ploughman is in Christ equal with the greatest prince that is', these are not pious or strident assertions but beliefs arrived at out of an imaginatively apprehended and loved sense of common life and the language of its lore and characters—the woman who went to the sermon at St

Thomas of Acres after a sleepless night because she 'never failed of a good nap there', the old man of Kent who thought 'Tenterton steeple' was the cause of the Goodwin sands.

According to G. K. Chesterton there are 'two spiritual realities out of which grow all kinds of democratic conception or sentiment of human equality . . . all men are tragic. And . . . all men are comic'.[10] Latimer's vision was of the second kind, and it was a comic vision he thought worth going to the stake for. His successor in defending the common language combined both spiritual realities to produce the most extensive, substantial, and integrated verbal identification of humanity in our literature. Tawney says that from 'the twelfth century to the sixteenth . . . the analogy by which society is described . . . is that of the human body'.[11] If we substitute 'being' for body (since from Langland to Shakespeare the spirit is a vital ingredient of the flesh) we can regard Shakespeare's achievement as the final statement of that analogy. Not only did he lead a life of allegory, he made an allegory of life. The Elizabethans have been called 'avid for words';[12] Shakespeare's selection of language really used by men images a society which is not static or stratified but dynamic, creative, and appetent, its word-hunger the sign of a vital and complex identity. Latimer's sense of the colloquial is stoutly egalitarian, Shakespeare's is 'apprehensive, quick, forgetive, full of nimble, fiery and delectable shapes'. Between them a national culture not only survives but triumphs.

But its tenure is threatened because both Latimer and Shakespeare are creatures of the Reformation. To argue the effects of a lost belief in an item of church ritual—transubstantiation of the host—on imaginative literature may seem to be making much of little, but the reverse is probably true. Latimer's scepticism about the real presence is not central to his own sermons but is immensely influential on Bishop John Jewel, whose plain speaking is the first major evidence of a rift between the solid and the visionary in English culture. In the *Sermon Preached at Paul's Cross* he declares his intention 'to rip up and to open unto you the high mysteries and secrets' of Catholic doctrine; and this ecclesiastical Jack the Ripper wreaks brilliant carnage on the

mass until what had seemed its properties in a miraculous
sense now seem properties in the stage sense merely. Indeed,
in his *Apology of the Church of England* he claims that the
Popes 'have brought the sacraments of Christ to be used now
as a stage play'.[13] In his later plays Shakespeare inverts this
identification by making theatre the refuge of sacred mysteries. The whole art of his romances is outlined in Lafeu's
repudiation of the Reformation:

> They say miracles are past, and we have our philosophi-
> cal persons, to make modern and familiar things super-
> natural and causeless. Hence is it, that we make trifles of
> terrors, ensconcing our selves into seeming knowledge,
> when we should submit our selves to an unknown
> fear.   (*All's Well that Ends Well*, ii. iii)

But perhaps because of the very audacity of his claims for the
theatrical imagination, Shakespeare's art is continually seen
to turn on itself and endorse the scepticism of the age. As
Philip Edwards shows,[14] his language is both forgetive and a
forgery; against Falstaff's ontological imagination we have to
set Theseus's scepticism—'How easy is a bush supposed a
bear'. And Anne Righter demonstrates that whereas the
Mystery Plays embodied 'the reaccomplishment rather than
the imitation of action',[15] Shakespeare's drama continually
questions its validity so that at one moment we are presented
with the full kingdom of man, at the next the king's a beggar
or a poor player. The medieval solidness is disrupted, flesh
and spirit begin to disjoin.

Between Elizabethan and Augustan humanism—the one
heuristic, creative, and vulgar, the other hieratic, critical, and
genteel—seems to lie a difference of centuries, yet fewer
years separate them than separate us from the Edwardians.
As the one civilization reached its epitome in Shakespeare the
forces that dispelled it were active in theology and science;
and in the opening of the seventeenth century can be
discerned a more drastic dissociation of sensibility than that
which Eliot predicated between thinking and feeling in
mid-century. The theological outcome of the Reformation in
England was the erastianism of Hooker and the Authorized
Version. Hooker's art consists in converting religious

thought into moderate, rational and, in all senses of the word, *civil* discourse. The divine and the natural are segregated: 'All things are in such sort divided into finite and infinite, that no one substance, nature or quality, can be possibly capable of both'. God is no longer immanent but transcendent; he is 'immaterial, pure, and of us in the world . . . incomprehensible'. He is politely kicked upstairs with all his mysterious ways. Theoretically, as his most recent editor argues, 'Hooker had grounded the religious authority of royal and episcopal commands in the all-inclusive character of human association; the sacral or potentially sacral character of the community was basic'. But as the immanent miraculous deity recedes, life is sketched in terms which are abstract and coercive rather than substantive. Perhaps for the first time in our literature the art of language becomes an entirely rhetorical procedure. This is most apparent in arguments which are contiguous to medieval theories. Brian Vickers has ably analysed the way in which Hooker uses the rhetorical figure *commutatio* in the following sentence: 'A kind of mutual commutation there is whereby those concrete names, *God* and *Man*, when we speak of *Christ*, do take interchangeably one another's room.' But the point is that we register Hooker's activity precisely as one of rhetoric and approximation, not of apprehension and incarnation ('concrete' is only prescriptive). And when Hooker says 'the weight of such sentences speak of the mystery of our coherence . . . with Jesus Christ', 'weight' is understood abstractly as 'persuasive or convincing power' (a meaning that entered English during the Reformation), not as the 'heaviness' expressed in *Piers Plowman*. The truth of poetry has dwindled into poetic truth. Life which medieval and sixteenth-century literature had imaged as potential, creative, and spiritually egalitarian is now framed as the moral precursor of the Newtonian physical universe—hierarchical and subject to immutable laws which however are enjoined and administered by Church and State. Hooker's 'Law of a Commonweal' is very different from Langland's or Latimer's conception of the commonwealth.[16]

The word of God also underwent a change in the Authorized Version. The word was God but in 1611 it turned into a solemn ritual, a language which is distanced and elevated,

sublimation rather than incarnation. Lawrence brushed away
three centuries of its tyranny when he remarked, in 'Introduction to Pansies', 'if you suggest that the word arse was in
the beginning and was God and was with God, you will just
be put in prison at once'; pre-Reformation literature had no
such difficulty in reconciling the soul with the sphincter. It is
a language which contributes magnificently in Scott, Dickens, and Lawrence himself towards lifting the novel out of
the rut of quotidian realism, but it had already played its part
earlier in polarizing matter and spirit, religion and folk.

Hooker and the Bible reject the particularizing power of
language. Bacon, the third great influence on the seventeenth
century, rejects its spiritual dimension, and with it the
collective genius of a people. Words, he says, 'are but the
current tokens or marks of popular notions of things'. The
popular mind is too unreliable, too anthropomorphic, too
infected by faith and creativity to perceive things as they
really are. Miracles are 'old wives fables, impostures of the
clergy, illusions of spirits'; 'it is not creditable, till it be
opened, what a number of fictions and fancies the similitude
of human actions and arts, together with the making of man
communis mensura, have brought into natural philosophy'.
Proverbs and popular wisdom likewise receive their death
sentence: '. . . I advise . . . a Kalendar of popular errors: I
mean chiefly in natural history, such as pass in speech and
conceit.'

Before his advent, says Bacon, the mind of man was 'like
an enchanted glass, full of superstition and imposture'.[17] In
order to clarify that glass, all commonplaces, all beliefs and
assumptions, all man's social and spiritual heritage must be
questioned. 'And new philosophy calls all in doubt': with
orthodox religion entrenched in Church and State, dissent of
all kinds proliferates in paradoxes, anatomies, essays, and
conceits, in which wit is no longer at play as in the sixteenth
century but put to work in an experimental analysis of the
human, the physical and the metaphysical. Shakespeare's
kingdom of man flies into particles. The very fact and nature
of identity becomes a dark mystery. There is 'all Africa and
her prodigies in us . . . we are all monsters', says Sir Thomas
Browne. The classic Puritan crisis of faith is also an identity

crisis—a discovery of the violence and ugliness within. As certainties recede, language seismographically records earthquake. In prose the Senecan style, 'turbid, inconstant and full of revolutions', is dominant; and after the Restoration criticism is quick to argue that eloquence—'this vicious abundance of *Phrase*, this trick of *Metaphors*, this volubility of *Tongue*'—should be 'banish'd out of all *civil Societies*, as a thing fatal to Peace and good Manners'.[18]

In fact the Restoration began with a call for a return to 'primitive purity'. The Royal Society exacted from its members 'a close, naked, natural way of speaking . . . preferring the language of Artizans, Countrymen, and Merchants, before that, of Wits, or Scholars'. But the precepts were inoperative. Between Restoration culture and popular language an impassible rift opened. Despite the oppression of Church and State and the ridicule of the new philosophy, the status and language of the populace was kept artificially alive during the Civil War by the hopes and promises of Puritan leaders. As Christopher Hill points out, 'The battles of the Civil War were prefigured in a rivalry of sermon styles', and the Puritans 'demanded plain sermons, addressed to the understanding not of scholars but of ordinary men'. Artisans and countrymen were told that 'God intends to make use of the common people in the great work of proclaiming the kingdom of his son'.[19] But God changed his mind and the legacy of Puritanism to the populace was not a kingdom but a wilderness of sects, a loss of common rights and a diminished status. With the Restoration language becomes inveterately a class issue. Scientists condemn the 'false *Chimeras*' of the popular imagination as primitive ignorance; statesmen affect a lucid elegance quite different from popular plainness; preachers are encouraged to avoid 'the use of vulgar Proverbs and homely similitudes, and rude and clownish phrases'.[20] The gentleman dictates the language of God and King and rejects the language of the folk.

The place of the poet in this climate was crucial, since it is the poet who will give final shape and distinction to the possibilities of language in any culture. And here too English folk culture was routed. With Milton deliberately constructing a linguistic fortress between his religion and a profane society the way was clear for Dryden's precedence. And in Dryden's hands the simple class distinction between the genteel and the popular changes into something more complex and unassailable. He is the first poet in our literature deliberately and systematically to purify the dialect of the tribe. And purification in Dryden's hands is a chemical rather than a social process. His passionate, evolving concern for the language subdues and renovates the nature of what it works in, sometimes even to his own disquiet. It is impossible to read the Dedication to the *Aeneis* without recognizing a language sense more delicate and exacting than any in English literature previous to it. And only a nation as tone deaf as England in the nineteenth century could have failed to notice that the application of that language sense in Dryden's couplets was not just or even chiefly an expression of rational or satirical clarity, but was the most intense distillation of sound and sense—married and mutually liberating—in English so far. Both in verse and in the other harmony of prose Dryden did for the language what Purcell was doing for its music; and if Dryden didn't, for various reasons, attain Purcell's 'clarity, brilliance, tenderness and strangeness' he made Pope's attainment of those qualities certain. But it is a language whose excellence derives from assumptions which are both capitalist and absolute:

> I trade both with the living and the dead, for the enrichment of our native language. We have enough in England to supply our necessity; but if we will have things of magnificence and splendour, we must get them by commerce. Poetry requires ornament; and that is not to be had from our old Teuton monosyllables . . .[21]

In language as in society the peasants are excluded or enslaved. For more than a century the poetic commonwealth of Langland and Shakespeare is replaced by the 'poetic city'.[22]

III

Far from being then what a student once, with refreshing candour, called a simple story dealing with simple people in a

simple way, *The Pilgrim's Progress* begins to emerge as a work
of peculiar significance. The significance is not simply that
Bunyan produced a piece of folk art in an age contemptuous
of the low in society and art, but that the nature of his art
testifies to a radical historical artistic consciousness in the
writer. For, as we can see from his autobiography, Bunyan
the man was at some remove from Bunyan the artist. *Grace
Abounding* is virtually a case history. From childhood Bunyan
is tormented by fearful dreams and 'apprehensions of devils
and wicked spirits'. In despair he grotesquely blesses 'the
condition of the dog and toad'. Even after his conversion,
when a respectable preacher, he has to fight down the
temptation to blaspheme before the congregation. The horror is countered by equally extreme reverence. He expresses
his attitude to the ministry by saying, 'I could have lain down
at their feet, and have been trampled upon by them; their
name, their garb, and work, did so intoxicate and bewitch
me'. Of course this sort of chiaroscuro would be expected of
a Puritan testament but Bunyan's language is a guarantee of
the authenticity of his torment. Despite his determination to
be 'plain and simple, and lay down the thing as it was', his
style is helplessly responsive to experience. Syntax blurs
under pressure ('I was driven as with a Tempest, my heart
would be unclean, the Canaanites would dwell in the land');
half-molten images are flung up ('By these things my mind
was now so turned, that it lay like a horse leech at the vein
still crying out, Give, give'); aphorisms are not distilled by
experience but smelted by frenzy ('Great sins do draw out
great grace', 'Live I must not, Die I dare not'). Above all
there is a rage for truth that rejects artifice. He even doubts
'whether the holy Scriptures were not rather a fable, and
cunning story, than the holy and pure Word of God'. This is
not the author of *The Pilgrim's Progress* but a character whose
'longings and breakings in his soul' anticipate the most
penetrating modern pathology of the religious temperament,
in William Golding's *The Spire*.[23]

The difference between *Grace Abounding* and *The Pilgrim's
Progress* is not only in the mastery Bunyan exerts over his
material in the latter, turning the light and darkness of
revelation into a fable and cunning story, but in the way Part

I (for we must now distinguish between the two parts) generalizes the psychosis of an individual into the crisis of a people.

The life of the folk is shown to be disinherited socially, divinely and linguistically. The only common land in the book, Christian is told at the House Beautiful, is Immanuel's Land; but that is at a great distance, in sight of the Celestial City. God has left the world. Hopeful tells Ignorance that 'Christ is. . . hid in God from the natural apprehensions of all flesh' (p. 189). The pilgrim belongs to neither kingdom. He has been 'driven out of his native country' (p. 80) and tells the citizens of Vanity Fair that he and his like are 'pilgrims and strangers in the world'. The earthly commonwealth—the faire felde ful of folke—shrinks to a cold catalogue of 'jugglings, cheats, games, plays, fools, apes, knaves, and rogues' (p. 125). The spiritual commonwealth is equally exclusive. All except Christian who wander from the straight and narrow meet horrible deaths; Ignorance is dispatched to Hell from the gates of the Celestial City itself. Langland's vision is far more generous. When the pardoner and 'a comune womman' go off together instead of following Piers, he simply comments 'I ne wot where þei bicome'; those who disobey God's laws '"ben ascaped good auenture; now God hem amende!"'[24] The language itself is denuded. Almost every commentator on *The Pilgrim's Progress* praises its colloquial vigour—yet compared with the fertile language of his predecessors, or even the sweltering slang of *Mr Badman*, Bunyan's prose here is often plain to the point of baldness. What is striking, coming to the work after Latimer for instance, is not the presence of colloquialisms but their scarcity. 'His home is as empty of religion, as the white of an egg is of savour' (p. 114) is cited time and again for want of alternatives. T. S. Eliot's comment on Hardy in *After Strange Gods*, that 'at times his style touches sublimity without ever having passed through the stage of being good', is more applicable to Bunyan. Much of the language in Part I is aggressively unliterary; there are no concessions to the graces. Fair-speech is a place of corruption. The life of the folk is a lenten survival through plainness, necessity, hardship, endurance and solitude, kindled only by signs of grace from another world.

Yet it would be a distortion of the book's quality not to notice that this record of disinheritance is tonic in its isolate energies. Neither genteel nor numinous, Bunyan's homely concreteness achieves its own victory. 'The soul of religion is the practic part' (p. 115); Part I justifies itself as applied rather than pure literature, in which the poetic capacity of language to focus and intensify experience is rejected for the more pragmatic function of reducing spiritual apprehensions to manageable proportions. We can see this if we compare Bunyan's depiction of Giant Despair with Spenser's Despayre in *The Faerie Queene* (I. ix. 53–4). Spenser's is obviously the more subtle and potent evocation of despair ('"Death is the end of woes: die soone, O faeries sonne!"') but it has the disadvantage of making you want to die. Doubting Castle is actually the most nearly comic episode in Part I, with its conversations between Mr and Mrs Giant, Mr Giant's convenient fits whereby he loses (for a time) the use of his hand, and Christian's absent-mindedness ('"What a fool," quoth he, "am I, thus to lie in a stinking dungeon, when I may as well walk at liberty"'). The unspiritual clarity of it all lodges the idea of despair in your head like a joke: it makes you want to live.

A similar point can be made about the depiction of pilgrimage. What does it mean, to be a pilgrim? It means to be a lowest common denominator. The first, enduring image of the pilgrim is the 'man clothed in rags . . . with his face from his house . . . and a great burden upon his back'. He is devoid of worldly wealth and worldly knowledge. Shame objects to 'the base and low estate and condition of those that were chiefly the pilgrims; also their ignorance of the times in which they lived, and want of understanding in all natural science' (p. 107). He is a 'labouring man'. At the outset Christian describes his course in terms which are virtually the English birthright: 'I have laid my hand to the plough' (p. 42). But unlike Langland's and Chaucer's ploughmen Christian has no birthright. He is not only a labouring man but a 'wayfaring man', a 'footman', a stranger and sojourner. 'I must venture,' he says: 'to go back is nothing but death, to go forward is fear of death, and life everlasting beyond it. I will yet go forward' (p. 75). Progress is not a matter of spiritual or psychological evolution but of survival through action. As

Mr Great-heart says, '"the way is the way, and there's an end"' (p. 289). The progress is not dramatic but arduous, pedestrian, felt along the narrative. There is no room for Dowel, Dobet or Dobest; only Do—or be damned. To venture and to adventure are always read in their root sense of putting at risk, making a trial of one's chance.

It is Bunyan's triumph to make this enduring of hazard seem attractive. The idea of adventure is perfectly balanced between the root sense and the later sense of exciting events. The adventures are representations of the psychological, moral and social pressures which induce men not to endure, but representations whose clarity and concreteness are a triumph over those pressures. The abstract unknown is caught, held and revealed as physical and particular: a giant, a monster, a gentleman.

This is one kind of solidity of specification; in Part II, where Bunyan's relation to his inherited culture is more genial, another more ambitious kind emerges. In Part I 'progress' signifies an expedition, in Part II it signifies improvement and cultivation. The wilderness of the world is reinvested with the properties of human society. Pilgrims cease to be lonely adventurers and become a community of strong and weak alike. 'Bowels becometh pilgrims,' says Christiana (p. 232), suggesting how the isolate 'masculine' Part I is replaced by the visceral 'feminine' Part II. All 'carnal and fleshly content' is eschewed in Part I; no sex and very little eating and drinking are allowed. In Part II carnal appetites are reinstated. Sleep for instance: no discredit is implied when Honest is found asleep under an oak, and Christiana doesn't betray her faith when she wishes 'for an inn for herself and her children, because they were weary' (p. 313). There is hospitality all along the route and plenty to eat and drink. All Christian is given to help him on his way is a roll (of paper). Christiana is given 'a piece of pomegranate . . . a piece of honeycomb, and a little bottle of spirits' (p. 266), and as an antidote to spiritual indigestion she is prescribed 'an universal pill . . . good against all the diseases that pilgrims are incident to' (p. 281). Sex is no longer the danger of Part I but the erotic accessibility of a more temperate zone. Christiana is charmingly conscious of and even obliquely receptive to the suggestions of the Ill-favoured ones: 'Now Christiana, imagining what they should mean, made answer . . . We are in haste, cannot stay . . . we will die rather upon the spot than suffer ourselves to be brought into such snares as shall hazard our well being hereafter' (p. 242). Mercy is described as 'alluring' and the tenderness in the Interpreter's question, ' "And what moved thee to come hither, sweetheart?" ' is helplessly converted into sexuality by her when, for answer, she 'blushed and trembled, and for a while continued silent' (p. 254). Gaius redresses the bias of Part I by saying, ' "as death and the curse came into the world by a woman, so also did life and health" ' (p. 316). Fertility and procreation are now signs of grace. Mercy, as well as being alluring, is 'a young and breeding woman'; the female pilgrims are complacently described as 'all of them very fruitful'.

Similar tolerance extends to behaviour. Manners are more humorously observed and delicately recorded than in Part I. Bunyan's use of names is a good index to this. In the account of Christiana's neighbours (pp. 230–1) his inventiveness answers to Dryden's standards of fine raillery. Mrs Bat's-eyes, Mrs Light-mind, Mrs Love-the-flesh, Mrs Filth: the names come trippingly off the tongue, the wit of their conception at once embodying and delighting in their naughtiness. The difference between these names and those of the jury in Part I is the difference between Horace and Juvenal. These malefactors die sweetly. Indeed foibles and elegancies are no longer necessarily a hanging matter. One of the Interpreter's Proverbs of Heaven is that there 'is a desire in women to go neat and fine' (p. 251). The most delicate comic moment in all Bunyan comes when Christiana, standing outside the Interpreter's House and overhearing her praises sung by those within, 'At last . . . knocked' (p. 245). And it is no longer a crime to be a gentleman. The word was almost irredeemable in Part I; here it is applied to Mr Honest and the male pilgrims generally.

The problem Bunyan faces in this approach to his subject is that of secularizing to the same degree that he humanizes. It is easy to see why some of the down-to-earth social portraiture should have led literary historians to claim the book as

an immediate antecedent to the novel, whose besetting
temptation is life for life's sake. But such solidness is not the
book's main characteristic. If Part I represents English folk
culture in a crisis of survival, Part II renews the spirit as well
as the body of that culture.

This is evident from the replacement of the isolated
'original' status of Christian in Part I by the spiritual community of Part II. Christian is 'the old pilgrim' (p. 314); the
novelty of his pilgrimage is rescinded to orthodoxy amidst
the communion of saints, and his family, descendents and
successors are portrayed not as beleagured members of a sect
but as the inheritors of primitive Christianity. And this is
both the symptom and stimulus of an imaginative revitaliza-
tion of the English common tongue. In Part I Bunyan was so
concerned to solidify his metaphors that the numinousness of
language was excluded. In Part II Bunyan's confidence in his
community is reflected in a different attitude to language.
The concrete causeway through difficulty pioneered by
Christian is deliberately shown up as a metaphor, a linguistic
construct. Great-heart, after describing Fearing's escape from
the Slough of Despond, says, 'He had, I think, a Slough of
Despond in his mind, a slough that he carried everywhere
with him' (p. 303). The slaying of Giant Despair and
demolition of Doubting Castle shows Bunyan expediently
dismantling his myth. In place of Part I's functional art, the
art of Part II is imaged in the man on Mount-Marvel 'that
tumbled the hills about with words' (p. 343). Language is
once again miraculous, poetic and potential. The 'enchanted
glass' is reinstated. The power of language to embrace the
corporeal and spiritual is intimated by Mercy's looking-glass
which 'would present a man, one way, with his own feature
exactly, and turn it but another way, and it would show one
the very face and similitude of the Prince of pilgrims himself'
(p. 345). Bunyan makes it possible for our old Teuton
monosyllables to participate again in the Kingdom of Heaven
and for the common people to be touched with divinity.

But Part II is not, for all that, a return to the medieval
condition of language and society. We do not, as in the
Mystery Plays, see man steadily within the dual aspect of
time and eternity. God remains aloof; harmony between God

and man is wholly dependant on man's rare and rarefied
capacity to transcend this world. Music is the crucial image
by which Bunyan expresses this capacity. 'Dust as we are, the
immortal spirit grows Like harmony in music.' Awkwardly
and rather prosaically Bunyan at one point breaks off from
his story to expatiate on this matter. The ground is 'heaviness
of mind' and over it are evolved the melody and harmony
which link man with God (p. 307). But the preacher's homily
is elsewhere incorporated in the text. 'Wonderful!' exclaims
Mercy, 'Music in the house, music in the heart, and music
also in heaven' (p. 272). As the book progresses, music in
heaven makes its presence increasingly felt. The way is sweet
with intimations of immortality, from the trumpet that
welcomes Christiana through the Gate (p. 236) to the 'most
curious melodious note' of birdsong beyond the House of
Beauty (p. 287). In the last pages time is gradually displaced
by eternity and men and women are transposed into un-
worldly harmony. On the Delectable Mountains the pilgrims
have 'their ears . . . filled with heavenly noises, and their eyes
delighted with celestial visions' (p. 364). The exalted mysteries of the Authorized Version dominate the book's diction
for the first time, and ultimately language itself is transcended: 'The last words of Mr Despondency were, "Farewell
night, welcome day." His daughter went through the River
singing, but none could understand what she said' (pp.
369–70).

IV

According to Northrop Frye English literature is most
popular—in the folk sense—when it is Protestant, radical,
and   Romantic.[25]   But   Protestantism   is   elective,
anti-egalitarian and potentially hostile to the catholic, collective representation of man through allegory. As a Protestant
allegory *The Pilgrim's Progress* is something of a contradiction
in terms. That Bunyan should have renewed and
incorporated, especially in Part II, a sacramental image of
society out of this implicit contradiction is his greatest
achievement, and one which might have led to a further
evolution of the allegoric tradition. In practice Bunyan's

influence on succeeding literature is more as a visionary than as an allegorist. Great though they are, the final pages of *The Pilgrim's Progress* come dangerously near to rendering inoperative the idea of the 'common'. Salvation, which until that moment had seemed near at hand—had even seemed achieved—is removed to another dimension. With Christiana and her companions sublimed out of sight and sound, the middle way between damnation and exaltation, which had seemed open, closes again. We cannot say, as Dryden did of Chaucer, 'here is God's plenty'. Bunyan's community of pilgrims, we are reminded, is not a commonwealth. Neither is the new English social nexus represented, except as the City of Destruction or the Town of Vanity. In the eighteenth century, the most vigorous treatment of common people is in secular city literature which depicts them as colourful pariahs—either as in Defoe's aggressively 'low' *Moll Flanders* or as in *The Beggar's Opera* and *Jonathan Wild* where low life images moral and political realities beneath the civil skin.

When a sacramental sense of life returns to literature in the Romantic age allegory is displaced as an imaginative mode by symbolism. Theoretically symbol should, as Coleridge says, partake 'of the Reality which it renders intelligible'; in practice it tends to substitute for the Catholic *microtheos* of allegory a Protestant elective portentousness. The relationship between Protestant inspiration and poetic vision at this time is multiple and complex but its outstanding exemplification in the poetry of Wordsworth shows how much the Romantics derived from the spirit of Bunyan and how little from the 'vegetated body' of his allegory. Clough was quick to spot Wordsworth's 'spiritual descent from the Puritans': 'a certain withdrawal and separation; a moral and almost religious selectiveness, a rigid refusal and a nice picking and choosing, are essential to Wordsworth's being'.[26] There's such divinity doth hedge a leech-gatherer that all sense of his commonness is excluded. For all its outward concern with low and rustic life and language the predominant impression from Wordsworth's poetry is of a depopulated and depopularized territory,

> With all the numberless goings-on of life,
> Inaudible as dreams!

Wordsworth's chief influence on our language was not to

enlarge and revalue the vernacular but to increase the tenure of 'genteel' English. When he became popular in the 1830s his main influence was on the educated gentry, to whose discourse he added a tone which deepened and solemnized its civility. Perplexity, which had been excluded from the polite register after the Restoration, was finally institutionalized in the Victorian period. The tone of the centre was established—in the narrative voices of Thackeray and George Eliot, in the prose of Newman and Arnold—as 'educated, reserved, subtle, sad, differing'.[27]

Where Bunyan's influence is at first sight more rewarding in terms of folk art is among Victorian city-dwellers and parvenus—who, Samuel Smiles reminds us, 'are of the people, belong to them, and spring from them'.[28] *The Pilgrim's Progress* becomes invested with new secular urgency at this time. As a child Alton Locke, for instance, identifies London as the City of Destruction, 'the turnpike at Battersea-bridge end' as the Gate, 'and the rising grounds of Mortlake and Wimbledon' as the land of Beulah. But the greatest representative of these classes, Dickens, encountered the paradox that his main source of imaginative material lay in the city of destruction. In order to continue the folk tradition he had to depict it under the condition of its second disinheritance, by the Industrial Revolution; a condition for which Bunyan made no provision except escape, and which had to be related to Bunyan mainly in terms of fracture, distortion and parody. Mrs Gamp's phrase 'this Piljian's Projiss of a mortal wale' is indicative of the way in which 'common' speech is grotesquely disjointed from its heritage. Unlike Ruskin who saw in this distortion only a 'Corrupt language . . . gathered by ignorance, invented by vice, misused by insensibility'[29]—the damnable outcome of the city of destruction—Dickens found it full of fabulous and visionary potential, so that for the last time in our literature the language of common life interacts unselfconsciously with the mind of the artist until it is impossible to draw a line between the creations of art and the creativity of life. But Dickens's apprehension of the spirit of a people inheres, with purer and more peculiar intensity than that of his predecessors, in his creative faculties alone. He cannot rest or sustain his vision on a collective social or religious culture, so that it is always on the verge of hallucination: of becoming a psychic allegory in place of Shakespeare's allegory of man. And after Dickens the most potent expression of English city life reinvents the city of destruction as a shadowy reduction of Dickensian psychomachy: Milly Theale's vision of 'grey immensity' in *The Wings of the Dove*, Conrad's heart of darkness, Eliot's 'Unreal City'; a place of disaffection. These have to be compared with what Joyce's Catholic imagination was making of Dublin during the same period.

Among these forces the old English common language is reduced from vernacular to dialect. There is symbolic aptness in the fact that the nineteenth century's major folk artist, Clare, should end his life in an asylum ('I am—yet what I am, none cares or knows'). What was once the culture of the people becomes a backwater depicted variously as stagnant, picturesque, or primitive; linguistically, it is always subordinate to, and sometimes morally recessive from, a normative, educated, and genteel narrative register. Even in Hardy folk life is undercut by a sense of its impending extinction or betrayed by a tendency to quaintness. By the end of the century folklore has on the whole either become something of archaeological concern or frankly peripheral to modern interests. Bunyan himself has been digested by the historical processes he intervened in and inaugurated. Robert Bridges is making more than a literary judgement, he is summing up the victory of one culture over another, when he calls *The Pilgrim's Progress the* 'language of life . . . translated into a dialect'.[30]

The late Victorian rediscovery of folk-song played a decisive part in reviving English music. In Vaughan Williams, the crucial figure of this revival, music became a distinctively national language, binding together earthy and visionary impulses and renewing the creative bond between folk consciousness and the originating mind of the artist (significantly, the most vital relationship between Bunyan and twentieth-century culture is to be found in this music). But in our literature folk art had no such reviving influence. Its collective culture remains, as one nineteenth-century archaeologist called it, a 'lower culture'. The greatest English

religious writers of the twentieth century, Lawrence and
Eliot, on the contrary pursue to its limits the evolutionary
and isolating tendencies of the protestant ethos. Eliot's words
at the end of *East Coker*—

> We must be still and still moving
> Into another intensity
> For a further union, a deeper communion—

could stand as an epigraph on the imaginative dynamic of
both writers, even though one which needs to be pursued
through paradox. Lawrence after all had the acutest sense of
vernacular since Dickens. Throughout his life he remained
suspicious of the moral and social confines of King's English.
Both writers were influenced by depth studies of folk
culture. Eliot's sense of history in *Little Gidding* expressed the
idea of a communal reconciliation through and beyond time.
But Lawrence's most significant art struck away from the
corporate implications of the vernacular towards 'the
tremendous *non-human* quality of life'; he also rejected the
generalizing potential of allegory as an evasion of this
intrinsic quality. Dostoyevsky, he complained, described
people 'as theological or religious units, they are all terms of
divinity, like Christ's "Sower went forth to sow," and
Bunyan's *Pilgrim's Progress*'.[31] Eliot's anthropological myths
in *The Waste Land* are broken images, folk fragments. The
questing, infinitely subtle tone of *Four Quartets* lends a certain
factitiousness to Eliot's resolving 'symbol perfected in death'.
As Lawrence remarks, 'we know these new English
Catholics. . . . They are Protestants protesting against
Protestantism.' Each writer depicts a life which is experimental, originating, divisive of flesh and spirit, its 'communion'
transcendent. At crucial moments each also appeals to the old
Catholic sense of life as a sign of unattainable homogeneity of
experience. Eliot's quotation from Thomas Elyot in *East
Coker* invokes a lost language to embody a lost harmony:

> daunsinge, signifying matrimonie—
> A dignified and commodiois sacrament.

And in *A Propos of Lady Chatterley's Lover* Lawrence argues
that the 'Christian religion lost, in Protestantism finally, the

togetherness with the universe, the togetherness of the body, the sex, the emotions, the passions, with the earth and sun and stars'.

The interaction between language and life is subtle, and the force of suggestion required, within a short essay, to blaze a trail through a literature as vast as ours is necessarily crude. All the preceding argument can hope to present is a conviction that somewhere in that literature are to be found clues—imperfect and sometimes too perfect—of one such mode of interaction. There are obviously other modes which if considered would redress the rather deteriationist bias of this thesis. Even within the thesis no irreversible pessimism is intended. There have been recent signs of renewed interest in our folk heritage. Richard Dorson has championed English folk studies in America. John Holloway in a recent article deplores the absence of folklore studies from the university scene.[32] But the real need is not for academic or institutional approval but for creative literary concern, and here the signs are less promising. Ronald Blythe and Melvyn Bragg have published reminders and memorials of collective rural life; Philip Larkin in 'The Whitsun Weddings' and 'Show Saturday' beautifully defeats the nostalgia and scepticism elsewhere prominent in his poetry; William Golding's *The Inheritors* manages magnificently to enforce against the tragic irony of its conclusion a realized innocence that revives a sense of original creativity like a race memory. But as John Holloway says, 'To think that folk life and the folk artefact belong only to the rural and archaic becomes a sentimentalized and atavistic myth'. Most modern English studies of urban life have tended—as in John Braine, Alan Sillitoe, Stan Barstow, David Storey—to express an attitude which is defensive, sceptical, often hostile to the idea of imagination and creativity as a popular attribute; Richard Hoggart describes the urban majority's 'acceptance . . . of a flat, tough and tasteless world'.[33]

In chapter 2 of *English Folk-Song* Cecil Sharp distinguishes between art music 'which is the work of the individual, and expresses his own personal ideals and aspirations only' and folk music which 'is the product of a race, and reflects feelings and tastes that are communal rather than personal'.

Perhaps our most characteristic literature has arisen as a reciprocation of those kinds of making in a collaborative relationship between artist and folk. The creative power of such a writer is not his private 'property' but is intrinsic to the life he portrays; his imagination is not fictive but onto-logical. I have suggested that the related growths of Protestantism, scepticism, and gentility disintegrated that relationship. But English culture has reached a condition in which those forces are no longer vital but exhausted. Not long ago, in a series of interviews with novelists, Frank Kermode said, 'if I had to decide what this section of good English novelists had most obviously in common I should say it was a kind of modesty. Not only do they emphasize their own limitations; for the most part they're happy to ignore all the larger claims that can be made for their craft.'[34] The burden of creativity laid on the writer by the substitution of art for religion has eventually grown too heavy and must be shrugged off. A. Alvarez describes the attempts of the Movement poets 'to show that the poet is not a strange creature inspired; on the contrary, he is just like the man next door—in fact he probably *is* the man next door'.[35]

This kind of egalitarian modesty (I'm as dull as the next man) is at the furthest remove from the creative apprehen-sions of the folk imagination and seems to mark the moment in our literary civilization when scepticism declines into pyrrhonism. It has been succeeded by a strange cultural interregnum in which the writer's relation to his material can no longer be openly acknowledged as creative. The death of God and the death of the novel have happened concurrently, leaving imagination a curious anomaly, either to be killed off in documentary realism or driven to play with itself in ultimately sterile preoccupations with the fictiveness of fiction. Between the reporter and the fictional-ist, between realism and fabulation no obvious middle way presents itself. There is need for renewed non-academic consideration of ways in which the English allegorical tradi-tion projected a catholic sense of life, deriving imaginative sustenance from a spiritual insight into the language and values of the people. Because Bunyan stands at the end of that tradition and because his 'solidness' at once incorporated and incarcerated it, his present neglect is of peculiar significance.

NOTES

1. R. D. Altick, *The English Common Reader* (Chicago, 1957), pp. 255–6.

2. 'Southey's edition of *The Pilgrim's Progress*', *Critical and Historical Essays* (London, 1848), i. 415.

3. G. Ford, *Dickens and his Readers* (Princeton, 1955; 1965 edn), p. 190.

4. R. H. Super (ed.), *The Complete Prose Works of Matthew Arnold* (Michigan, 1968), vi. 358; subsequent quotation, ibid., p. 243.

5. J. Burrow, 'The audience of *Piers Plowman*', *Anglia* (1957), pp. 373–84.

6. Quotations from P. Happé (ed.), *English Mystery Plays* (London, 1975), pp. 259, 560, 293.

7. *Milton's Grand Style* (London, 1963; 1967 edn), p. 75.

8. *The Movement of English Prose* (London, 1966), p. 74.

9. Quotations from *Sermons* (Everyman Library edn, London, 1906), pp. 31, 65, 84, 85–6, 184, 215, 174, 217.

10. *Charles Dickens* (London, 1906; 1927 edn), p. 175.

11. *Religion and the Rise of Capitalism* (London, 1926; 1966 edn), p. 35.

12. G. Willcock, 'Shakespeare and Elizabethan English', *Shakespeare Survey* (1954), p. 24.

13. John Ayres (ed.), *Works* (Cambridge, 1845), i. 14, iii. 64.

14. *Shakespeare and the Confines of Art* (London, 1968), *passim*.

15. *Shakespeare and the Idea of the Play* (London, 1962; 1967 edn), p. 18.

16. Quotations from A. S. McGrade and Brian Vickers (eds), *Laws of the Ecclesiastical Polity* (London, 1975), pp. 273, 274, 36, 51, 281, 136.

17. Quotations from *The Advancement of Learning* (Everyman Library edn, London n.d.), pp. 126, 28, 133, 103, 132.

18. Quotations from Browne, *Religio Medici* (Everyman Library edn, London, 1906), pp. 17, 61; Dryden, *Of Dramatic Poesy and other Critical Essays* (Everyman Library edn, London, 1962), ii. 13; Sprat, *The History of the Royal Society* (London, 1667), pp. 111–12; subsequent quotation, ibid., p. 113.

19. *The Century of Revolution* (London, 1961; 1969 edn), p. 161; *God's Englishman* (London, 1970; 1972 edn), p. 253.

20. J. Glanvill, *An Essay Concerning Preaching* (London, 1678), p. 73.

21. Dryden, ed. cit. ii. 252.

22. See W. H. Auden, *The Dyer's Hand* (London, 1963; 1975 edn), p. 85: 'the rules which produce aesthetically perfect poetry would produce a totalitarian nightmare in society'.

23. Quotations from *Grace Abounding* (Everyman Library edn, London, 1928), pp. 34, 89, 11, 5, 27, 17, 78, 80, 32, 25.

250 BUNYAN'S SOLIDNESS

24. J. Bennett (ed.), *Piers Plowman; Prologue and Passus I–VII* (London, 1972), pp. 56, 59.

25. M. Bottrall (ed.), *William Blake: Songs of Innocence and Experience* (London, 1970), p. 173.

26. G. McMaster (ed.), *William Wordsworth: A Critical Anthology* (London, 1972), p. 184.

27. Hardy, *Tess of the D'Urbervilles* (Macmillan Pocket Edition, 1957), p. 146.

28. *Life and Labour* (London, 1905), p. 283.

29. E. T. Cook and A. Wedderburn (eds), *Works* (London, 1908), xxxiv. 294.

30. R. Sharrock (ed.), *Bunyan: The Pilgrim's Progress* (London, 1976), p. 110.

31. H. T. Moore (ed.), *The Collected Letters of D. H. Lawrence* (London, 1962), i. 291, 432; subsequent quotation from E. D. McDonald (ed.), *Phoenix* (London, 1936), p. 394.

32. 'Folklore, fakelore, literature', *The Cambridge Review* (26 November 1976), p. 54; subsequent quotation, ibid., p. 55.

33. *The Uses of Literacy* (London, 1957; 1969 edn), p. 290.

34. M. Bradbury (ed.), *The Novel Today* (London, 1977), p. 111.

35. *The New Poetry* (London, 1962), pp. 20–1.

The Theology of *The Pilgrim's Progress*

GORDON CAMPBELL

The Church Book of Bunyan Meeting records in the minutes of September 1660 a decision to appoint three brethren to seek 'a convenient place for our meeting so soone as they can (we being now deprived of our former place)'.[1] The loss of St John's Church to the Bedford congregation signified their separation from the new Stuart church. Henceforth they can legitimately be called sectarians, a term which distinguishes them from those who wished to reform the state church. This latter group may, with all due caution, be described as Puritans.[2] Bunyan was a sectarian rather than a Puritan. He did not advocate the purification of the state church, but separation from that church.

Bunyan's doctrine of the separated church appears in *The Pilgrim's Progress* in the episode in which Christian visits the Palace Beautiful, the house 'built by the Lord of the Hill . . . for the relief and security of pilgrims' (p. 78). We should note that Christian does not enter the Palace Beautiful until he has left his burden at the cross. As he explains to the porter of the palace, 'My name is, now, Christian; but my name at the first was Graceless' (p. 79). The church, in Bunyan's view, could not admit unredeemed sinners; he records in *Grace Abounding to the Chief of Sinners* that in the church there was 'room for body and soul, but not for body and soul, and sin'.[3] Even Christian's profession of faith does not gain him immediate access to the palace. The porter explains the procedure:

> 'I will call out one of the virgins of the place, who will, if she likes your talk, bring you in to the rest of the family, according to the rules of the House.'　　　　　　　(p. 79)

An examination of *The Church Book of Bunyan Meeting* shows that Bunyan drew the house rules of the Palace Beautiful from his own church, for it appears that those who desired to

join the Bedford church had to wait outside till they were
called in. The congregation decided

> that such persons as desire to joyne in fellowship, if
> upon the conference of our friends with them . . . our
> saide friends be satisfyed of the truth of the worke of
> grace in their heartes . . . they shall desire them to come
> to the next church-meeting, and to waite neare the place
> assigned for the meeting, that they may be called
> in.   (folio17)

Bunyan himself was admitted to Gifford's church by such a
process: 'I . . . propounded to the church that my desire was
to walk in the order and ordinances of Christ with them, and
was . . . admitted by them' (*Grace Abounding*, i. 39). Candi-
dates who wished for membership of the Bedford church
were required to describe the 'worke of Grace' to the family
of believers, and this is precisely what Christian does on
being accepted into the Palace Beautiful. This ritual of public
profession could, Bunyan thought, be abused by 'false brethren'. He explains in *The Barren Fig-Tree* that the church is
not at fault if some 'creep in unawares' by 'a show of
repentance and regeneration', and observes that 'it is one
thing to be in the church, or in a profession; and another to be
of the church, and to belong to that kingdom that is prepared
for the saint' (iii. 563).

Several features of Bunyan's allegorical church commend
themselves to our attention. It is noticeable that the palace is
not part of 'the way', but rather stands 'just by the highway
side'. In Bunyan's opinion church membership was not
essential to salvation, though he thought it important for
spiritual growth. Indeed, it is significant that Faithful's
account of his journey from the City of Destruction does not
record a visit to the Palace Beautiful at all. We should also
note that Christian is not baptized on entering the church. In
A Confession of My Faith, and a Reason of My Practice Bunyan
states that it is a mistake 'to think that because in past time
baptism was administered upon conversion, that therefore it
is the initiating and entering ordinance into church communion' (ii. 605).[4] Baptism was not a means of grace, and was
thus a matter for individual conscience. In Part II of *The*

Pilgrim's Progress Christiana and her children do profess their faith at the House of the Interpreter and then enter 'The Bath Sanctification', as Bunyan calls it in his marginal note (p. 255); but the fact that this bath is enjoined by Christ ('for so her Master would have the women to do') suggests that Bunyan may have in mind the baptism of the Holy Spirit. And since the bath is set in the context of an allegorical narrative, the extent to which it should be translated into a symbol or into a symbolic act is in fact not clear. The same can be said of communion, to which Bunyan may be alluding in the description of Christian's meal in the Palace Beautiful: 'Now the table was furnished with fat things and with wine that was well refined, and all their talk at the table was about the Lord of the Hill' (p. 85). Is this merely a description of Christian fellowship, or does it constitute an unritualistic Lord's supper, with the 'fat things' of Isaiah 25: 6 standing in for the more usual bread? Baptism and the Lord's Supper were, Bunyan said, 'shadowish, or figurative ordinances' (*A Confession of my Faith*, ii. 604).[5] The allegorical depiction of ordinances that are in themselves shadowish and figurative is not conducive to precise interpretation.

The doctrinal obscurity of *The Pilgrim's Progress* on these points suggests that Bunyan's doctrine has not been transported intact into the imaginative work. A similar phenomenon is observable in Milton, for many of the statements in his *De Doctrina Christiana* appear to be contradicted in *Paradise Lost*. The discrepancies proceed at least in part from the fact that both *The Pilgrim's Progress* and *Paradise Lost* avail themselves of the doctrine of accommodation, according to which, in the words of Milton's Raphael,

> what surmounts the reach
> Of human sense, I shall delineate so,
> By lik'ning spiritual to corporeal forms,
> As may express them best.
> (*Paradise Lost*, v. 571–4)

This idea of an explanation of divine things accommodated to the limited understanding of man was justified by reference to what William Perkins called 'sacred Metaphor'[6]—a commonplace of Renaissance thought clearly articulated by

Bunyan in the doggerel that prefaces *The Pilgrim's Progress*, where he acknowledges that his story 'is feigned' but insists that 'Some men, by feigning words as dark as mine, / Make truth to spangle, and its rays to shine' (pp. 33–34).[7] (The concept that truth may inhere in fiction is not of course restricted to theological writing; George Chapman, for example, introducing his *Whole Works of Homer* [c. 1616], notes the paradox that there is not 'such reality of wisedomes truth in all humane excellence as in Poets fictions', and a century earlier Stephen Hawes had expressed his admiration for poets who were 'clokynge a trouthe wyth colour tenebrous'.)[8] At the same time Bunyan notes that 'My dark and cloudy words they do but hold / The truth, as cabinets enclose the gold' (p. 34). That the words of a fiction represent a truth that is somehow distinct from the words is yet another common-place: 'Language', said William Alexander, 'is but the Apparel of Poesy'[9] and most of his contemporaries would have agreed. Admitting that 'solidity' is essential in one who 'writeth things divine to men' (the words echo Milton's), Bunyan claims emphatically that 'solidity' does not preclude the use of metaphors:

> Was not God's laws
> His Gospel-laws in olden time held forth
> By types, shadows and metaphors?   (p. 34)

The Bible is his final precedent for his method. And his epigraph from Hosea touches on the same point—'I have used Similitudes'.

The central similitude of *The Pilgrim's Progress* is Christian's soterial journey. On his back Christian has a burden. The meaning of this burden is not precisely defined by Bunyan, and if one looks elsewhere in his writings one will see that it may be associated with a cluster of meanings. The scriptural basis of the metaphor, the source which any seventeenth-century reader would have recognized, is explained by Bunyan in *Come and Welcome to Jesus Christ:*

> He that is come to Christ . . . has cast his burden upon the Lord. By faith he hath seen himself released thereof; but he that is but coming hath it yet, as to sense and

feeling, upon his own shoulders. 'Come unto me, all ye that labour and are heavy laden,' implies, that their burden, though they are coming, is yet upon them, and so will be till indeed they are come to him.   (i. 264)

But what is the burden? Is it the sin described in *The Doctrine of the Law and Grace Unfolded* that hangs on the soul 'like so many blocks, at its heels, ready to sink it into the fire of hell' (i. 546)? Or is it that which is described in *Christ a Complete Saviour*, the 'guilt that breaks the heart with its burden' (i. 210)? If the burden is guilt, is it the burden of guilt that motivates Christian's journey? Bunyan stresses in *Come and Welcome* that 'it is not the overheavy load of sin, but the discovery of mercy; not the roaring of the devil, but the drawing of the Father, that makes a man come to Jesus Christ' (i. 286). Is Christian in *The Pilgrim's Progress* drawn to Christ by the Father? Certainly Hopeful maintains that Christianity should not be grasped as an insurance policy against hell-fire. Speaking of backsliders, he says

> being hot for Heaven, by virtue only of the sense and fear of the torments of Hell, as their sense of Hell, and the fears of damnation chills and cools, so their desires for Heaven and salvation cool also. So then it comes to pass, that when their guilt and fear is gone, their desires for Heaven and happiness die.   (p. 193)

Here, then, is the theological position of the book. But is it true of Christian's experience? I think not. In the opening pages of *The Pilgrim's Progress* Christian suggests that the reason for his journey is two-fold. First, 'by reason of a burden that lieth hard upon me'; and second, a 'way of escape' from the fate of a city which 'will be burned with fire from Heaven' (p. 39). The two motives are related, for Christian expresses the 'fear that this burden that is upon my back will sink me lower than the grave; and I shall fall into Tophet' (p. 40).[10] Evangelist responds with a parchment saying '*fly from the wrath to come*', and Christian does so. Speaking as a theologian, therefore, Bunyan insists that escape from the fires of hell is not a proper or sufficient motive for a man to come to Christ; writing an imaginative tale, he portrays quite the opposite. Bunyan's imaginative depiction of Christian's experience has created a theology of human experience that is at odds with Bunyan's theoretical views on the subject. And as Christian's experience changes, so does the theology by which he lives: the final episodes of Part I of *The Pilgrim's Progress* show that the fear of hell has been almost completely obliterated by the prospect of the delights of heaven.

Bunyan's emphasis in *The Pilgrim's Progress* on a theology accommodated to human experience results in the suppression of one of his central beliefs—election to salvation and reprobation. In 1663 Bunyan published *A Map, shewing the order and causes of salvation & damnation*. No copy of this edition survives, but a version was printed in the 1692 collection of this works. At the top of the page is a symbol of the Trinity. Two lines proceed from the Son. The line on the left begins with election and proceeds by many steps to heaven; the line on the right begins with reprobation and leads eventually to hell. Some of the steps on the chart recall incidents in *The Pilgrim's Progress*. On the 'election' line, for example, conviction of sin is followed by a temptation to despair. And in *The Pilgrim's Progress* Help explains that the 'miry Slough' into which Christian falls is 'the descent whither the scum and filth that attends conviction for sin doth continually run, and therefore it is called the Slough of Despond' (p. 46). Parallels such as this might lead one to think that *The Pilgrim's Progress* is true to the theology of the *Map of Salvation*, yet such a conclusion would have to be modified in the light of that which precedes conviction of sin on the *Map*. Between the Son and this 'conviction' are election, the covenant of grace, and effectual calling, three of the basic doctrines in Bunyan's theology.[11] Why are these doctrines not incorporated into the fiction of *The Pilgrim's Progress?* The problem is exacerbated by the fact that in Bunyan's spiritual autobiography every stage of his conversion is seen as a result of divine manipulation. Bunyan assures us that God had 'designed me for better things' than the principles of the Ranters; God, he explains, 'would not suffer me . . . to undo and destroy my soul' by doubting his faith. And what he doubts is 'whether I was elected?' Bunyan pondered the scriptures, and recorded that

I evidently saw, that unless the great God, of his infinite
grace and bounty, had voluntarily chosen me to be a
vessel of mercy, though I should desire, and long and
labour until my heart did break, no good would come of
it. Therefore, this would still stick with me, How can
you tell if you are elected? And what if you should not?
How then?

Bunyan's worry was founded on the firm belief that 'the elect
only attained eternal life' (*Grace Abounding*, i. 11–13).

The doctrine of election was thus crucial both to Bunyan's
theology and to his own experience of salvation, and yet it
does not affect the Christian of *The Pilgrim's Progress*. Only
the related doctrine of reprobation enters *The Pilgrim's Progress*, and that by way of explanation. Belief in reprobation,
the decree of God condemning the greater part of mankind to
eternal damnation, is implied in Faithful's remark about
Pliable's spiritual condition: 'who can hinder that which will
be?' Christian is not distressed by this view, and instantly
decides to abandon Pliable to his fate: 'Well, neighbour
Faithful, said Christian, let us leave him, and talk of things
that more immediately concern ourselves' (p. 103). The fate
of Ignorance (whom Christian pities) is also explained in
terms that recall the doctrine of reprobation, for Christian
quotes the Bible to the effect that '*He hath blinded their eyes,
lest they should see*', and Hopeful notes that 'one may see, *it is
not every one that cries, Lord, Lord*' (pp. 190, 192). The doctrine
of reprobation explains the fate of Pliable and Ignorance. But
neither election nor reprobation touches Christian's own
experience. Bunyan is determined in *The Pilgrim's Progress* to
present the experience of a Christian, and this emphasis
precludes the serious treatment of doctrines that relate to the
mind of God rather than the mind of Christian.

The Pilgrim's Progress is a religious work rather than a
theological work; the overtly theological passages in the
book tend to be incidental to Christian's journey, even
though that journey is allegorically soterial. None the less,
one can recognize Bunyan's Protestant bias clearly enough.
Christian's emphasis on his book, for example, is characteristically Protestant. To illustrate the point we need only think

of Chillingworth's dictum: 'the Bible, I say, the Bible only is the religion of Protestants'. The lack of emphasis on the dropping of the burden at the cross is also revealing, in that it shows Bunyan's sympathies were firmly with the Puritan and sectarian churches rather than with the Anglicans. Whereas an Anglican or Catholic would have dwelt on the cross at considerable length, sectarian writers like Bunyan instinctively avoided the fleshy incidents of the Nativity and the Crucifixion. For Christian the cross is not a place for meditation but a place of release. The cross is not the object of his soterial journey; rather it is an early stage in that journey. The absence of any extended reflection on the Passion reminds one of Milton, who found himself unable to finish a poem on that subject, and who chose when writing a poem about the regaining of paradise to discuss the temptations in the desert rather than the redemptive sufferings of Christ.

Although Bunyan's debt to Puritan theology is considerable, one can see a characteristic sectarian feature in his distrust of theoretical discussions of theology. The only good systematic theologian in *The Pilgrim's Progress* is Talkative, who is condemned. We may again note a parallel with Milton, who was not without his sectarian sympathies. Both writers wrote theological treatises, but both none the less distrusted theory; and just as Talkative is condemned for subscribing to a wholly theoretical theology, so in *Paradise Lost* the fallen angels in hell are depicted as active theologians who

> sat on a hill retired,
> In thoughts more elevate, and reasoned high,
> Of providence, foreknowledge, will and fate,
> Fixed fate, free will, foreknowledge absolute,
> And found no end, in wandering mazes lost.
> (*Paradise Lost*, ii. 557–61)

Many Puritan theologians wrote systems of theology based on logic, usually the reformed logic of Peter Ramus. Some, such as Dudley Fenner and Milton, even wrote logic books in order to present the reasoning that lay behind their theological conclusions. At the lunatic extreme we may observe the phenomenon of John Eliot translating Ramus

into Algonquin so that his 'praying Indians' could understand the Bible. Bunyan the sectary stands in opposition to
this respect for reason; although he was capable of 'picking
the bones of [an adversary's] syllogisms', he proclaimed in *A
Case of Conscience Resolved* that 'for my part, I am not
ashamed to confess, that I neither know the mode nor figure
of a syllogism, nor scarce which is major or minor' (ii.
661–2). This same sentiment finds its way obliquely into *The
Pilgrim's Progress* in the figure of Money-Love, who can chop
logic with any Puritan theologian. Bunyan never escapes
completely from the temptation to systematize—when Faithful says that 'a work of grace in the soul discovereth itself,
either to him that hath it, or to standers-by' (p. 118) his
words are those of systematic theology—but he nevertheless
attempts to make his theology purely Biblical.

This tendency to distrust theoretical theology is exacerbated in *The Pilgrim's Progress* by virtue of the fact that it is
an imaginative work. The most startling rejection of the
theology of the intellect in favour of a theology of experience
occurs at Doubting Castle when Christian suddenly finds the
Key of Promise in his bosom (p. 156). Christian's intellect
has failed, and he must look into his heart; Bunyan's point is
made at the cost of a disruption in the narrative, but that
disruption reflects an authentic interior, or psychological,
process. More often the narrative triumphs to the extent that,
as I suggested earlier, we cannot translate the narrative of the
soterial journey back into the precise language of Bunyan's
theology. Another case in point is the roll which Christian is
given at the cross. We are not told the meaning of the roll
when Christian receives it, but learn simply that the Shining
One 'gave him a roll with a seal upon it, which he bid him look
on as he ran, and that he should give it in at the Celestial
Gate' (p. 70). Christian repeats this information a few pages
later, adding only that the reading of the roll was meant to
comfort him. Are we to think of the Holy Spirit as Comfor-
ter? We are not told. When Christian reaches the Arbour on
the Hill Difficulty he pulls the roll out of his bosom and reads
it for his comfort. He falls asleep, and in his sleep his roll falls
out of his hand. On waking he continues his walk up the hill,
and he eventually realizes that he has forgotten his roll. He

prays forgiveness of God for having slept, and rushes back down the hill to retrieve the roll. At this point we are told that 'this roll was the assurance of his life, and acceptance at the desired haven' (p. 77). When Christian and Hopeful eventually reach the Celestial City they submit their rolls: 'then the pilgrims gave in unto them each man his certificate, which they had received in the beginning'. The King reads the certificates, and admits the men (p. 203). Finally, Ignorance crosses the river and seeks admission. He is asked for his certificate, fumbles in his bosom for it, and on failing to produce it is bound hand and foot and hurled into Hell (pp. 204–5). This summary of the appearances of the roll shows that it does not merely serve as an allegorical representation of some doctrinal truth. Indeed, although we are told at one point that the roll represents assurance, one clearly does not submit one's assurance at the Heavenly Gate. And poor Ignorance, who brims with confidence, is not given a false roll to represent false assurance, but is not given any roll at all. The narrative function of the roll has superseded its allegorical function. It is Bunyan's invention, and takes on a life of its own. Ten years later he returned to the same metaphor in *A Discourse of . . . The House of God:*

> But bring thou with thee a certificate,
> To show thou seest thyself most desolate;
> Writ by the master, with repentance seal'd,
> To shew also that here thou woulds't be heal'd,
> By those fair leaves of that most blessed tree,
> By which alone poor sinners healed be.

If one enters without a certificate, one will '*find / To entertain thee here are none inclin'd*' (ii. 580). The lines which Bunyan has italicized remind us of the fate of Ignorance, even though in the poem Bunyan is describing entry into the church rather than entry into heaven. The metaphor is sufficiently free from a specific meaning to allow it to function in several related ways.

When the discovery of Milton's systematic theology was announced in 1824, readers of his poem suddenly realized that his theology was not what they thought it was. Similarly, we should be ill-advised to search for Bunyan's theology in *The Pilgrim's Progress*. Many of the doctrines to which Bunyan subscribed are mentioned incidentally in the course of the book, but none is essential to Christian's progress. The fiction of *The Pilgrim's Progress* creates its own truths through the imaginative efforts of Bunyan. In part this distinction between the doctrines affirmed in Bunyan's theological writings and the truths implicit in his account of Christian's journey may be understood in terms of the differing points of view in the formal theology and the imaginative work. In Bunyan's theological writings he attempts to articulate divine truth; in *The Pilgrim's Progress* he eliminates the truths that are set in the mind of God, such as the doctrine of election, and presents a theology accommodated to the experience and limited perspective of man. The effect is similar to that created in *Samson Agonistes*, for Milton removes God from that poem and thus makes Samson's struggle more acute, more painful. And so Christian.

NOTES

1. G. B. Harrison (ed.), *The Church Book of Bunyan Meeting 1650–1821* (London and New York, 1928), folio 24.

2. On the elusiveness of the term 'Puritan' see the first chapter of Christopher Hill's *Society and Puritanism in Pre-Revolutionary England* (London, 1964); also *Church Book*, folio 1, which alludes to 'the non-conformity men, such as in those dayes did beare the name of Puritanes'.

3. G. Offor (ed.), *The Works of John Bunyan*, 3 vols (1862), i. 13. Page references to works other than *The Pilgrim's Progress* are to this edition.

4. Cf. Bunyan's *Differences in Judgments about Water Baptism, No Bar to Communion* (ii. 616–47), which was written in response to a Baptist pamphlet which had taken issue with his *Confession*.

5. In *A Book for Boys and Girls* Bunyan uses the term 'sacrament' rather than 'ordinance', and his short poem emphasizes his refusal to see these ceremonies as means of grace while allowing that they afford some benefit:

> Two sacraments I do believe there be,
> Baptism and the Supper of the Lord;
> Both mysteries divine, which do to me,
> By God's appointment, benefit afford.
> But shall they be my God, or shall I have
> Of them so foul and impious a thought,
> To think that from the curse they can me save?
> Bread, wine, nor water, me no ransom bought.
> (iii. 752)

6. T. Tuke (ed.), *The Workes of . . . William Perkins* (Cambridge, 1616), ii. 656A.

7. See C. A. Patrides, *Milton and the Christian Tradition* (Oxford, 1966), pp. 9–10 and R. M. Frye, *God, Man and Satan* (Princeton, 1960), *passim*.

8. George Chapman, Preface to *Whole Works of Homer*, in J. E. Spingarn (ed.), *Critical Essays of the Seventeenth Century* (London, 1908), i. 67–8; Stephen Hawes, *The Pastyme of Pleasure* (1509), chap. 8, st. 2 (1555 edn, reprinted in *Percy Society* xviii (1846), p. 29).

9. William Alexander, *Anacrisis*, in Spingarn, ed. cit., i. 182.

10. Tophet is one of the many names for hell. See Bunyan's *Come and Welcome, Works*, i. 272.

11. For an excellent account of the central doctrines of Bunyan's theology see Richard L. Greaves, *John Bunyan* (Courtenay Studies in Reformation Theology no. 2, Abingdon, Berks., 1969).

Rival Fables:
The Pilgrim's Progress and Dryden's *The Hind and the Panther*

BERNARD BEATTY

The Pilgrim's Progress and *The Hind and the Panther* are more or less contemporary religious fables by major authors. We would expect them to have been compared frequently and readily. That this has not happened is not altogether surprising, however. There is still some uneasiness at accepting either work simply as literature. They have attracted very different readers. Even when read by the same reader, they have been regarded as different species. Readers have been supported in this by scholars whose natural bias is always to establish a discrete context for any work which they are placing.

It comes therefore as a shock when, in the midst of a discussion which moves naturally between Dryden, Homer, Virgil, Chaucer, and Keats, Earl Miner suddenly asserts:

> 'Good life be now my task,' he resolves in *The Hind and the Panther*, but throughout his career he had in effect asked the question in *The Pilgrim's Progress* and in Cowley's 'Dangers of an Honest Man in Much Company': not perhaps 'whither shall we fly,' but 'what shall we do?' It is indeed a question that exercised his century, and if Bunyan's road was shown him by the inner light, or if Cowley's led to an ambiguously happy retirement, Dryden's was the highway of Christian humanism.'[1]

We are surprised, I think, when we are asked here to consider Bunyan's and Dryden's work as their response to the same question. That it is a question that 'exercised' the seventeenth century may reassure us a little. It is evidently not *our* question. Nevertheless, if it is a single question and if it receives, as it apparently does, different answers, then it looks as if both works can be held together in the mind. If we do this, they become rival fables.

To maintain such a sense of rivalry between the two works is difficult. It is easier to see them as answers to different questions than to keep in view some common ground for both. Moreover, apparently common concerns are apt to slip and slide into something else.

For example, although both Bunyan and Dryden describe a life changed beyond recognition because it is now based on faith, 'faith' means different things for each of them. Dryden, to continue Professor Miner's quotation from *The Hind and the Panther*, writes:

> Good life be now my task: my doubts are done;
> (What more could fright my faith than Three in One?)
> (Part I, ll. 78–9)[2]

Such faith is *fides dogmatica*. It is a submission of the understanding to the will which enables the former to accept undemonstrable propositions such as the doctrines of the Trinity and transubstantiation. This submission of the understanding annihilates doubt ('my doubts are done'). Bunyan's faith is *fides fiducialis*. It is a personal conviction that he is saved. As presented in *The Pilgrim's Progress*, it appears to form part of the character of experience. As such, it will be subject to the fluctuations of experience. Indeed, Bunyan's Christian could well cry out, 'My doubt is just begun'.

What seems then to be a shared concern of both writers turns into the safe stereotypes of seventeenth-century Catholicism and Protestantism. Such stereotypes are not of course to be rejected out of hand. *The Hind and the Panther* and *The Pilgrim's Progress* do reinforce certain stereotypes and it would be absurd to minimize their importance. For instance, 'interpret' is a key word in *The Pilgrim's Progress*. Scripture, experience and the book itself are all given to us to interpret. But we must interpret them correctly:

> Now reader, I have told my dream to thee,
> See if thou canst interpret it to me,

> Or to thyself or neighbour: but take heed
> Of misinterpreting.
>> (Conclusion to Part I, p. 207)

Interpreting is an anxious individual business in which the possibility of error is strongly emphasized. One thing is certain, there can be no relief from this burden by any reference to public tradition:

> *Christian.* But will it not be counted a trespass against the Lord of the City whither we are bound, thus to violate his revealed will?
> *Formalist and Hypocrisy.* They told him, that as for that, he needed not to trouble his head thereabout, for what they did they had custom for; and could produce, if need were, testimony that would witness it for more than a thousand years.   (p. 72)

In *The Hind and the Panther*, on the other hand, 'interpret' in Bunyan's sense is subjected to withering sarcasm:

> The jolly *Luther*, reading him, began
> T' interpret Scriptures by his *Alcoran*.
>> (i. 380–1)

In the place of myriad private interpretations,

> As long as words a diff'rent sense will bear,
> And each may be his own Interpreter . . .
>> (i. 462–3)

Dryden prefers 'the Church-interpreter' (ii. 358). The Church, as interpreter, will and should be guided by public tradition:

> What weight of antient witness can prevail,
> If private reason hold the publick scale?
>> (i. 62–3)

These differences are real and not unexpected. But they are not as central as they might appear and confirm all too readily a predictable rivalry quite different from that to which we are momentarily alerted by Professor Miner's implicit assertion that both answer the same question.

Let us allow ourselves another failed attempt to establish a living rivalry between the two works before attempting to alter the terms of the inquiry. If we consider the rôle of danger in both fables, we appear to be on firmer ground. Danger is a common feature of the historical situation of their authors. Their work rises directly out of their sense of danger and seeks to project and transform it. Part I of *The Pilgrim's Progress* is the record of a series of dangers which the pilgrim overcomes or to which he succumbs. In this, Bunyan is drawing formally on Romance and folk-tale precedents, and doctrinally on St Paul who describes the dangers which he has been through and constantly warns his readers against danger of all kinds. Dryden's scenario seems comparable. The Hind is a frail animal menaced by wild beasts. Despite the protection of the Lion (James II), which is a beast friendly to defenceless females for Dryden as for Spenser and Blake (but not Bunyan), the Hind is presented as fundamentally timorous when it approaches the common drinking pool used by all the beasts. The situation is not too remote from that of Christian and Faithful approaching Vanity Fair:

> Among the rest, the *Hind* with fearful face
> Beheld from far the common wat'ring place,
> Nor durst approach; till with an awfull roar
> The sovereign Lyon bad her fear no more.
>
> (i. 528–31)

Elsewhere in the poem we are reminded of the past and present dangers which menace the Hind. Yet the similarity with *The Pilgrim's Progress* is again more apparent than real, for Dryden makes it clear at the beginning of his poem that 'She feared no danger for she felt no sin' (i. 4). The Hind has faith but she is also the object of faith. As such, though apparently vulnerable, she is in fact secure:

> . . . [she] was often forc'd to fly,
> And doom'd to death, though fated not to dy.
>
> (i. 7–8)

The Hind is part of history in a sense that Bunyan's pilgrim is not, but on the other hand the Hind does not herself undergo the processes of time as Christian does. It is as though the Hind embodies simultaneously Christian the pilgrim and Christian the heavenly citizen.

Perhaps we can continue the argument if we resort to Dryden's own distinction between the unerring Church and its frightened, erring members (i. 9–12). Particularly important here are the two fables with which the poem ends. Can we not compare the fears and dangers suffered by Catholics in the fables of the swallows and the pigeons with the danger-filled progress of Christian? Such a comparison seems plausible on purely formal grounds too. Both works, after all, deploy narrative and conversational modes. The balance between these modes is much more naturally calculated in *The Pilgrim's Progress* than its rival. *The Hind and the Panther*, like its medieval precedent *The Owl and the Nightingale*, is essentially a debate poem. Yet the description of the various beasts at the beginning of the poem leads us to expect a certain amount of narrative. This is confirmed by the evident relation of the debate to current history rather than to perennial argument. The reader of *The Pilgrim's Progress*, like the pilgrim himself, is often perplexed and loses his way. But Bunyan establishes from the outset, clear formal directives to his reader. We soon become accustomed to moving naturally between places, journeys, encounters, conversations, and argument. This is just what we do not do in *The Hind and the Panther*. Everyone finds the transitions from debate to narrative awkward in the poem, though this awkwardness has itself been defended very ably by William Myers.[3] Only in the two expertly managed fables which conclude Dryden's poem then is the reader in a comparable formal position to that in which he reads *The Pilgrim's Progress*.[4] These fables are clearly concerned moreover with the fearful predicament of the members of the 'Church Militant' (or indeed 'pilgrim') rather than the serenity of the 'Church Triumphant'. It ought therefore to be possible, in form and content, to compare these fables very closely with *The Pilgrim's Progress*. Consider, for instance, the sense of fear which is communicated so strongly by both. Let me briefly document this.

In *The Pilgrim's Progress*, the function of the House of the

Interpreter is so to condition Christian's mind by certain powerful images that he will retain their force in the different circumstances of his life and thus be able to interpret these circumstances correctly. When he has gone some way on his journey, he arrives at the Palace Beautiful and recalls those images from the House of the Interpreter which have remained with him most:

> *Piety*. But did you not come by the House of the Interpreter?
> *Christian*. Yes, and did see such things there, the remembrance of which will stick by me as long as I live; specially three things; to wit, how Christ, in despite of Satan, maintains his work of grace in the heart; how the man had sinned himself quite out of hopes of God's mercy; and also the dream of him that thought in his sleep the Day of Judgement was come.   (p. 81)

It is entirely appropriate that two out of the three things remembered directly induce fear, for Christian's is a pilgrimage of fear. Mr Sagacity describes it without exaggeration in Part II:

> *Sagacity*. Hear of him! Aye, and I also heard of the molestations, troubles, wars, captivities, cries, groans, frights and fears that he met with, and had in his journey.   (p. 220)

One further text indicates the rather peculiar character of this fear:

> *Hopeful*. I do believe as you say that fear tends much to men's good, and to make them right at their beginnings to go on pilgrimage.
> *Christian*. Without all doubt it doth, if it be right: for so says the Word, *The fear of the Lord is the beginning of wisdom*.
> *Hopeful*. How will you describe right fear?
> *Christian*. True, or right fear, is discovered by three things. . .   (p. 191)

Christian then proceeds, characteristically, to apply scholastic distinctions to psychological material. It must be surely a pervasive and a peculiar kind of fear which makes you frightened as to whether or not you are feeling the right kind of fear.

I am not raising superior Enlightenment eyebrows at this association of fear and religious experience. On the contrary, my hesitation is directly related to religious (and therefore moral) objections to the quality and quantity of Bunyan's fear. It certainly seems at times that Bunyan is more attracted by the intensity which Christian's fear-filled life offers than by its truth. Most readers notice the thinness of Bunyan's heavenly city in which our desires should find rest and fulfilment. If we contrast *The Pilgrim's Progress* and *The Divine Comedy*, we may well say that Dante puts fear in its place and that a fear-ratio of one part to three is better than Bunyan's reverse ratio. The works differ of course in scale, scope, and intention much more than *The Pilgrim's Progress* and *The Hind and the Panther* but the comparison of Bunyan's dream and that of Dante is instructive. Samuel Johnson observed, 'It is remarkable, that it [*The Pilgrim's Progress*] begins very much like the poem of Dante'.[5] Johnson was himself something of a connoisseur of religious fear and his observation is a helpful one. It is to my purpose, however, to stress that the two works are very much unlike one another in their endings. Dante is successful not only in making his readers assent to the existence and desirability of his Paradiso but also in convincing them that it is both unimaginably different from and better than present reality and yet that it is possible for individual human identities to remain themselves when glorified. Bunyan's heaven does not earn this kind of assent. Indeed his heavenly city is, it seems to me, exposed to the profoundly half-true scorn directed by Nietzsche at the Christian heaven.[6] Bunyan's heavenly citizens appear to do very little other than walk about with crowns, savour their nice equipages, and look forward, as Nietzsche proposes, to their King's punishment of his and their enemies. It is difficult to see what they are or could be in themselves. Similar difficulties attach to Milton's heaven and this suggests the religious (but also I would argue the human) drawbacks of a central attachment to the notion of 'experience' with which seventeenth-century Puritanism in particular and later consciousness in general are entangled.

There is, inevitably, gain as well as loss here. *The Pilgrim's Progress*, astonishingly popular as it has been throughout the secularizing centuries from the seventeenth century to the present, whilst gaining access to religious minds by its language and ostensible purpose, has fed emerging modes of consciousness and value which overthrow the typology it assumes. It has promoted the moral Copernican revolution in which human experience has become the central concern of human experience. Whatever our political or religious allegiance, this is bound to excite and to gain some kind of inmost assent. We cannot imagine Christian continuing as a recognizable individual in the heavenly city because too much secret value attaches to the intensity of his fear-filled consciousness for us to accept him as having any possible existence (even less a superior one) when he is finally set free from fear. It is clear that his 'authenticity' is guaranteed by his fear. Is Christian, now that he has reached the end of his pilgrimage, to live in Heaven with the insouciance of Ignorance or Mr Worldly-Wiseman?

A sense of fear caused by constantly disguised dangers of all kinds creates and sustains the superior personality of Christian from his opening conviction of sin in the first paragraph of the book—'and as he read, he wept and trembled'—until his final immersion in the River of Death where 'all the words that he spake still tended to discover that he had horror of mind and hearty fears that he should die in that River' (p. 198). All this is as it should be, for Bunyan, as we know from *The Life and Death of Mr Badman*, had a strong suspicion of easy deaths. Fear is proper to Christianity but something rather strange is going on when it becomes impossible to imagine an individuated consciousness which lacks it. The most startling result of this, if I am right, is Bunyan's specific inability to imagine and experience the risen Christ.

Many readers notice the surprising absence of Christ from *The Pilgrim's Progress* and suggest various explanations. Could the underlying cause of this omission be the same inability to credit or imagine a real person whose depths are untroubled by fear? This, to me, seems to be the implication of Bunyan's use of tenses. Consider for example the tenses in another part of the dialogue in the Palace Beautiful:

> *Prudence.* And what is it that makes you so desirous to go to Mount Sion?
> *Christian.* Why, there I hope to see him alive, that did hang dead on the cross.   (p. 83)

> And all their talk at the table was about the Lord of the Hill; as namely about what he had, and wherefore he did what he did, and why he had builded that House; and by what they said I perceived that he had been a great warrior, and had fought with and slain him that had the power of death.   (p. 85)

> And besides, there were some of them of the household that said they had seen, and spoke with him since he did die on the Cross.   (p. 86)

Bunyan, here and elsewhere, seems to have great difficulty in using the present tense of Christ. I am sure that he would deny this. Hopeful, for example, suggests, 'Ask him if ever he had Christ revealed to him from Heaven' (p. 189). Clearly, it is not assumed that Ignorance will get the answer to this question right. Equally, it is implied that Christian and Hopeful have had direct revelations of Christ. However, Ignorance's reply has some force:

> I believe that what both you, and all the rest of you say about that matter, is but the fruit of distracted brains.   (p. 189)

Certainly, the reader encounters Christ in *The Pilgrim's Progress* either as a past historical figure or as an aspiration or as a possible interpretation of the turmoil of present experience—which indeed may be 'the fruit of distracted brains'.

The Jesus of history, perceived as a present and transfigured Saviour, is not there in Bunyan's fiction. I am not reporting the absence of some esoteric theological requirement. It is, after all, the customary Christ of Christians—for example of George Herbert's Dialogue

'Sweetest Saviour, if my soul'—who is absent. To repeat, I am suggesting that, for Bunyan, fear and the sense of self are so closely linked that he cannot envisage a glorified Christ or a glorified Christian as an identifiable person.[7] This necessarily undermines the intended religious, and I would say moral, force of the work and explains the sense of puzzlement which many readers feel at its conclusion. Even there of course, Bunyan, by a brilliant stroke, manages our attention with his customary originality by a fear-filled final paragraph. The originality consists in the alarming shift of perspective:

> Then they took him up, and carried him through the air to the door that I saw in the side of the hill, and put him in there. Then I saw that there was a way to Hell, even from the Gates of Heaven, as well as from the City of Destruction. So I awoke, and behold it was a dream.   (pp. 204–5)

The two fables which conclude *The Hind and the Panther* are also much concerned with fear. They make explicit the latent violence contained in the earlier references to savage beasts and recent history. The Panther, for example, in the very act of peaceably accepting the Hind's hospitality is revealed as potentially ferocious:

> But civily drew in her sharpen'd jaws,
> Not violating hospitable laws,
> And pacify'd her tail, and lick'd her frothy jaws.
>   (ii. 718–20)

These, and other hints, prepare us for the violence of the concluding fables even though actual history, in the shape of James II's Declaration of Indulgence, made Dryden rework the final fable to a comparatively tame conclusion.

Once again, however, 'fear' for Dryden seems to represent something quite different from Bunyan's conception. *The Pilgrim's Progress* is present as a dream. Like a dream, it is a fiction full of analogies to the fearful processes of life. The fears of the self are revealed more nakedly in dreams. We read *The Pilgrim's Progress* in the customary way that novels are read, which despite critical effort to the contrary, is usually the same as that in which we experience dreams, namely as 'real' whilst they are happening and fictions when we have finished them. *The Hind and the Panther*, on the other hand, remains continually a fiction in the acting of reading it and yet also, like a cartoon or an argument, is part of the historical reality to which it alludes. A dream cannot be part of history, though it is experienced as a history. For example, it occasions the same fears as personal life. Dryden's fiction, however, is not like this. It is like one of Scott's historical novels, a fiction rooted in and essentially concerned with fact.[8] More so than Scott. For Dryden is writing about contemporary history and therefore cannot supply an already known ending to the plot he relates. History must do that for him. Consequently, the very real fear which is present in *The Hind and the Panther* is located in history rather than generated by the work itself. There is no conspiracy of consciousness between reader and story-teller as there is in *The Pilgrim's Progress*. It is the casual way in which violence is assumed to be part of religious politics in the seventeenth century which frightens Dryden and his reader. For instance, to revert for a moment to the main body of the poem, consider the vicious twist given by the Panther to the Hind's reference to Jacob's ladder in Part II. The Hind invokes the ladder as a symbol of the inherited tradition of the Church proceeding ultimately from Divine reality. The Panther singles out the word 'ladder' and presents a grotesquely different picture of recent Church history:

> Sternly the salvage did her answer mark,
> Her glowing eye-balls glitt'ring in the dark,
> And said but this, since lucre was your trade,
> Succeeding times such dreadfull gaps have made,
> 'Tis dangerous climbing: to your sons and you
> I leave the ladder, and its omen too.
>
> (ii. 222–7)

The sudden shift from Jacob's dream ladder and an idea of tradition to a picture of the derided climb of some unfortunate accused by Titus Oates up the ladder at Tyburn is chilling enough, and the almost playful menace sustaining this picture, and willing to sustain it into the future, disturbs us still more deeply.

The Panther's fable of the Swallows is just such an extension of past terrors into an imagined but wholly plausible future:

> Excepting *Martyn*'s race, for they and he
> Had gain'd the shelter of a hollow tree,
> But soon discover'd by a sturdy clown,
> He headed all the rabble of a town,
> And finish'd 'em with bats, or polled 'em down.
> *Martyn* himself was caught a-live, and try'd
> For treas'nous crimes, because the laws provide
> No *Martyn* there in winter shall abide.
> High on an Oak which never leaf shall bear,
> He breath'd his last, expos'd to open air,
> And there his corps, unblessed, are hanging still,
> To show the change of winds with his prophetick bill.
>
> (iii. 627–38)

The readiest parallel to this account of the Jesuit, Edward Petre's imagined death on a real gallows (the 'oak which never leaf shall bear' is presumably another grim reference to Tyburn) is Faithful's death in the town of Vanity. Faithful's torture and death is given in the kind of representative detail which accommodates it immediately to the pattern of the martyr. Nothing is left of Faithful's body in the end ('they burned him to ashes') but the 'real' Faithful is taken up 'through the clouds'. From Dryden's point of view, recent persecution of English Catholics was also yielding martyrs. Some of those put to death during 'the Popish Plot' trials have indeed been canonized recently on the basis of their martyrdom. What Dryden pictures for us in the lines I've quoted, however, is not a death like Faithful's but one modelled on the extinction of vermin. The bodies do not disappear but hideously persist. There is no possibility of 'a chariot and a couple of horses' standing ready to take Martin anywhere. Of course, this is how the Panther wants to present it but it is, in a way, how Dryden sees it too. This occasions the difficulty readers often find in interpreting these fables. Certainly there is nothing so gruesomely realistic in *The Pilgrim's Progress* as this wholly imagined vision of the future gibbeting of a living historical person. The true 'realism' of *The Pilgrim's Progress* is in quite a different dimension and it is not helpful to single out, as many English critics have done, the relationship of Bunyan's work to seventeenth-century English life and history as though it were of central importance.

We begin to see more precisely essential differences between the two works. For both authors, the processes of history cannot be trusted. They are blank, violent, and hostile to faith. On the other hand, for both authors temporal sequence is the 'bearer' though not the 'generator' of meaning. I borrow this useful distinction gratefully from Stanley Fish's 'Progress in *The Pilgrim's Progress*'.[9] Dryden's faith, embodied in the Hind, acknowledges the fearful mess of history, but believes that the Church cannot fail to witness unequivocally to transcendent reality in, through and despite of that fearful mess. Fear is something external to faith.[10] Bunyan's faith, on the contrary, originates in and is both nourished and matured by an interior fear. Christian for example asks this question of those without faith:

> Have they at no time, think you, convictions of sin, and so consequently fears that their state is danger-
> ous?   (p. 190)

Christian, unlike Ignorance, is capable of progress only in so far as he experiences and re-experiences what Wordsworth was to call 'blank misgivings'. Fear and danger are the only available guarantors of meaning.

The realization of fear operates in an altogether different dimension in Dryden's work. The immediate purpose of *The Hind and the Panther* was to persuade moderate Anglican opinion that they had nothing to fear from James II or Catholicism. 'Persuade' is not the best word. Dryden's whole strategy in choosing the Hind to represent the Catholic Church and the Panther to represent the Anglican is to make fear of English Catholicism seem ludicrous. It is the Catholics who are and have reason to be frightened. His secondary aim doubtless was to recommend the frail yet transcendent figure of the Hind to the minds and hearts of his readers. In both aims, but more especially the first, he failed. And the two most recent biographies of James II, which convicingly document the desperate reasonableness of Dryden's argument, still assume an unconvinced audience.[11] Bunyan, curiously, appears to share Dryden's opinion as to the present impotence of Popery (see pp. 99–100). His larger purpose remains that of arousing religious fears in his readers rather than diminishing political fears. He refused to accept the Declaration of Indulgence that James II offered and Dryden, reluctantly, celebrated. The 1688 Revolution, fostered by that alliance of Dissent, the City, Latitudinarians, and the House of Orange which *The Hind and the Panther* had specifically predicted as the downfall of a national government supported by the country but centred in the Court (i.e. Toryism), simultaneously made *The Pilgrim's Progress* acceptable as an English religious masterpiece and *The Hind and the Panther* appear the eccentric propaganda of a bigot. Such are the ways of history and they cannot be ignored by critics. It is an accident of English history as much as of critical history that the rivalry of the two works should be felt so little.

We have failed yet again to establish a living rivalry between the two works in the course of this extended consideration of the role of danger and fear in them. Concepts and situations which appear comparable acquire puzzlingly different definitions upon examination. We will need, as I hazarded earlier, to alter the terms of our inquiry. Instead of beginning from apparently similar concerns, can we trace some underlying connections in apparently opposed emphases?

Let us reconsider that crucial word 'interpret' from *The Pilgrim's Progress* and, instead of asking what Dryden thinks about the word itself (which will take us into familiar territory), ask whether Dryden's poem discloses any emphasis that could be equivalent to Bunyan's?

What of the following?

> If then our faith we for our guide admit,
> Vain is the farther search of humane wit,
> As when the building gains a surer stay,
> We take th' unusefull scaffolding away:

Reason by sense no more can understand,
The game is play'd into another hand . . .
To take up half on trust, and half to try,
Name it not faith, but bungling biggottry.
(i. 122–7, 141–2)

These extracts come from a longer argument which insists, and surely this is Bunyan's implication too,[12] that experience constantly misleads us, that a fundamental attachment to common sense with a judicious glossing of Christian vocabulary won't do, and that faith is the only sure interpreter of reality. Here at last there does seem to be a close correspondence between the two. The only snag is that Dryden's argument is concerned with transubstantiation. This is not surprising, for Dryden refers to it frequently in *The Hind and the Panther.* It, presumably, loomed large in his conversion and was certainly a common topic of religious propaganda. More especially, like Bunyan's particular faith, belief in it had political consequences. The Test Acts were specifically designed to endanger and debar from public office those who professed belief in transubstantiation. From Dryden's point of view, transubstantiation was indeed a test of faith in an opposite sense. Belief in the real presence of Christ's Body and Blood seems to have been for him equivalent to accepting, for the first time, supernatural faith as the only true interpreter of quotidian reality. (It is in direct contrast with the common-sense limits to faith urged by him in the conclusion to *Religio Laici*.)[13] Such a faith, constantly renewed and sustained by the will, cannot of its nature disguise the fact that appearances are against it and that it is therefore open to derision from without and from within. Dryden himself had publicly sneered at transubstantiation in *Absalom and Achitophel* (see lines 118–21).

Bunyan refers very little to the Eucharist and did not, of course, believe in transubstantiation, which doubtless he would have thought an unscriptural irrelevance to the life of faith. Yet his own relation of faith to experience may be considered a diffused form of transubstantiation. The force and character of the two beliefs are comparable and, in important respects, surprisingly close. Both depend upon taking words literally.

And if he can, why all this frantick pain
To construe what his clearest words contain,
And make a riddle what He made so plain?
(*The Hind and the Panther*, i. 138–40)

Then he gave him a parchment roll, and there was written within, *Fly from the wrath to come.*

The man therefore read it, and looking upon Evangelist very carefully, said, 'Whither must I fly?'
(*The Pilgrim's Progress*, p. 41)

There is an obvious literary difference in these two extracts. Bunyan is dramatizing a metaphor. Dryden is arguing a point. But the sense of stubborn attachment to a truth, both fantastic and extremely simple, is identical. The effect of these beliefs is the same too. It makes Bunyan and Dryden politically dangerous and socially unacceptable since they remain committed to the reality which they and their contemporaries inhabit but can no longer subscribe to a 'commonsense' interpretation of it. Both therefore must use their wits to present a rival commonsense which they know in advance will be taken as eccentric.

There is sufficient common ground here for us to recapture that earlier fleeting sense that *The Pilgrim's Progress* and *The Hind and the Panther* may address the same question. Further prospects begin to emerge. One of the problems in comparing the two works to which I have not yet alluded is that Dryden is concerned with conciliating a middle ground, Bunyan is concerned with alienating it. Thus, whilst both works depend upon dialogue, in *The Pilgrim's Progress* only one point of view is allowed to be true. Dryden (and his Hind), however, are anxious to honour and compliment the Church of England. Dryden's position is here the opposite of Bunyan's. The latter appears to be most hostile to points of view very similar to his own (for example, those of Talkative or Ignorance) because they represent the biggest danger to his salvation. Dryden, on the contrary, treats the Anglican Church with marked respect because it is the closest in teaching to Catholicism. Probe this difference, though, and we find another similarity. For one thing, Dryden's intention and his practice do not altogether coincide. It is true that there are several moving passages in the poem where the Hind pays tender compliment to the Panther, but the poet is not always able to muzzle his mordant wit. It is difficult to imagine Anglicans being actually conciliated by reading Dryden's dazzlingly provocative lines. He cannot sufficiently suppress the grimness of his new apprehension or the excitement and triumph of his new conviction to gain their assent. Politically, Dryden sees the necessity for a rapprochement between kindred religious groups. Like Bunyan, he genuinely believed in toleration. But the effect of their faith, with its distrust of common interpretations of experience, necessarily leads them to celebrate the difficult progress of Hind and Christian, Church and Soul, through the mad, violent and self-assured landscapes of 'commonsense'.

It is not, finally, this common progress that I want to examine—it would sustain further but not indefinite examination—but rather the common landscape. *The Pilgrim's Progress* has been sufficiently praised for its representation of seventeenth-century English life. The 'realism' of Bunyan's work is, however, deeper than this and it is illumined by the analogous claim now advanced for Dryden's work:

> Until recently it would have been thought nonsense to claim that *The Hind and the Panther* was 'realistic'. Superficially it is a ludicrous exercise in allegory.[14]

William Myers, to whose work I am heavily indebted, goes on to demonstrate that it is anything but nonsense. It would be easy enough to demonstrate differences in this 'realism' common to both works. I would rather point to the similar role it plays in both and refer this back to the fundamental similarity of their relationship to commonsense 'reality' despite the obvious discrepancies of doctrine and sensibility between them. In other words, I would emphasize that the worldliness common to both works proceeds (as it usually does in literature, as in Dante, Chaucer, Jonson, Byron, Tolstoy)[15] from a religious commitment profoundly suspicious of the mere show of things. This may seem too paradoxical to be true and the larger claim is not one that should be substantiated here. In Dryden's case it seems clear, however, that the deliberate truthfulness of his account of contemporary history in *The Hind and the Panther*, which contrasts with a series of evident adjustments in *Annus Mirabilis*, *The Medal*, and *Absalom and Achitophel*, proceeds from a new incapacity to believe in the meaningfulness of human history, and a corresponding belief in the secretly sustained life of the Church. The fidelity of Bunyan's observations of everyday occurrence—especially acute when the experience is being painfully misinterpreted—surely comes from the same source.

I have argued then that *The Hind and the Panther* and *The Pilgrim's Progress* can only be read properly if they are seen, for all their evident differences of idiom and audience, as containing real answers to the same questions and therefore as potential rivals. Such questions too, however antique in form, do not belong simply to the past but trouble any reader. The works, moreover, cannot be approached as literature unless we take these questions seriously. The attempt to discover such common concerns foundered when apparently similar topics such as 'fear' and 'danger' were examined closely. On the other hand, apparently opposed beliefs turned out to underlie comparable attitudes to everyday reality and comparable literary procedures. It is not at all impossible, I suggest, to read both works with a fairly precise sense of where they bear on the same questions.

There are many clearly relevant matters that remain to be investigated. Above all the 'fable' character of both works deserves more extended analysis than this brief essay really admits. I would in no way wish to retract my emphasis on the grimness of Dryden's poem and the integral element of fear in Bunyan's fiction, but there is a real playfulness in both which, paradoxically, authenticates these darker drives. This common playfulness would bear closer questioning. Nevertheless we may well need a firmer hold on the common ground which sustains this and other elements in these 'rival fables' before such comparison can be confidently attempted.

NOTES

1. Earl Miner, *Dryden's Poetry* (Bloomington, 1967), p. 308.
2. J. Kinsley (ed.), *The Poems and Fables of John Dryden* (Oxford, 1962). All references to Dryden's poems are to this edition.
3. W. Myers, *Dryden* (London, 1973), p. 117 et seq.
4. This conclusion of a debate poem by two fables is, I hazard, indebted to the practice of Spenser in his eclogues.
5. R. W. Chapman (ed.), *Boswell's Life of Johnson* (Oxford, 1953), p. 529.
6. Throughout his writings but especially in *The Anti-Christ* and *The Genealogy of Morals*.
7. Emmanual (that is, Christ) in *The Holy War* is an effective parabolic figure but no more.
8. It is no accident that Scott edited and deeply admired Dryden's verse.
9. Stanley Fish, *Self-Consuming Artifacts* (Berkeley and London, 1972), p. 237.
10. There are lines in Dryden's verse which do not fit this statement but its general force is, I believe, true.
11. Maurice Ashley, *James II* (London, 1977); John Miller, *James II: A Study in Kingship* (Hove: Wayland, 1978).
12. Stanley Fish demonstrates this, to me, convincingly in 'Progress in *The Pilgrim's Progress*', op. cit., *passim*.
13. See *Religio haici*, ll. 427–50.
14. W. Myers, op. cit., pp. 116–17.
15. Byron's presence in this list may appear capricious. It is not so, but justification of it must await another occasion.

Index

states of minimal feeling, 33–4;
theology and doctrine
  subordinated to, 24–5;
Miner, Earl, 263
Mistrust, 36, 122, 145, 166
Money-love, Mr, 53, 175, 259
Morality, village of, 10, 100, 163
Moses, 94
Mount Calvary, 94
Mount Marvel, 108, 241
Mount Sinai, 94, 98, 144, 163–4
Mr Badman:
  as a companion piece, 7;
  correlated with Part II, 3;
  death in, 270:
  slang of, 237;
  social realism of, 3, 55
Much-afraid, 56, 57, 198, 242
Myers, William, 267, 279
Mystery Plays, 227–8

Nash, Thomas, 121
Newman, J. H., 244
Nietzsche, F. W., 269
No-good, Mr, 121

Obstinate, 82, 89, 122
Offor, G., 67n6, 120
Orwell, George, 132, 134
Owen, John, 106
Oust, G. R., 127, 131n8

Page, Norman, 79, 90n2
Passion, 102
Patchell, Mary, 211–2, 213, 217
Patience, 4, 102
Penn, William, 120
Perkins, William, 15, 235
personal history:
  importance of, in self-stability, 25,
  31–2;
  treated as inspirational logos, 32,
  45n7, 151
Peter, John, 131n7

Petre, Edward, 274
Pickthank, 120–1
Piety, 35, 36, 74
place:
  as a passage in a text, 108;
  as power and property, 97,
  99–101;
  as stage in an argument, 107;
  Austen's treatment of, 101;
  Bunyan's sense of, 91–109;
  dangers in applying topographical
  criteria, 105–6;
  despatializing of locations and
  movement, 106–7;
  gentleman-poets' view of, 101–2;
  in *Grace Abounding*, 108;
  inner landscapes, 97, 100;
  literalization of semantic
  associations, 107–8;
  loci and *imagines*, 107;
  Sherman's treatment of, 91–2,
  101;
  spiritualizing the landscape, 101–2;
  theory of linking social, physical
  and mnemonic senses of, 108;
  topographical inconsistences,
  95–6;
  topographical realism and
  carnality, 98;
  walking, 92, 106–7, 110n15
Pliable, 82, 122, 139, 144, 166, 257
Ponden, Nathaniel, 155
Pope, Alexander, 235
practicality, 15–16
preaching:
  and motives for successive parts,
  7, 9;
  experience between Parts I and II,
  64;
  technique, 54–5;
  tradition of pre-Reformation
  pulpit, 127
Presumption, 4, 130, 144, 200, 221
progress:
  acceptance of precariousness,
  36–7;
  anti-progressive view, 24, 34, 40,
  183–4, 192, 202n8, 207, 219;